CRASHBACK

THE POWER CLASH BETWEEN
THE U.S. AND CHINA IN THE PACIFIC

MICHAEL FABEY

SCRIBNER
New York   London   Toronto   Sydney   New Delhi

Scribner
An Imprint of Simon & Schuster, Inc.
1230 Avenue of the Americas
New York, NY 10020

First Scribner hardcover edition October 2017

SCRIBNER and design are registered trademarks of The Gale Group, Inc.,
used under license by Simon & Schuster, Inc., the publisher of this work.

For information about special discounts for bulk purchases,
please contact Simon & Schuster Special Sales at 1-866-506-1949
or business@simonandschuster.com.

The Simon & Schuster Speakers Bureau can bring authors to
your live event. For more information or to book an event, contact the
Simon & Schuster Speakers Bureau at 1-866-248-3049 or visit
our website at www.simonspeakers.com.

Interior design by Kyle Kabel

Manufactured in the United States of America

1 3 5 7 9 10 8 6 4 2

Library of Congress Cataloging-in-Publication Data is available.

ISBN 978-1-5011-1204-1
ISBN 978-1-5011-1206-5 (ebook)

To Barb, Megan, and Jason.
Each of you is my compass, my anchor, and my North Star.

Contents

Preface

It is never easy to write a book that tries to capture immediate history. Most of the "research" for this effort is based on direct observation and on-the-scene interviews with those directly involved in, or witnesses of, many of the events detailed in the pages, during my reporting as the naval editor of *Aviation Week*. I was provided unparalleled access to officers, sailors, pilots, ground crews, ships, aircraft, and exercises for not only the American navy, but its allies, partners, and even adversaries. In some cases, as noted, I have found other reports that supplement with a fact or quote, but in all cases, even with those reports, I have followed up with my own interviews of authors or other sources not only to verify what happened but also to note any changes or clear up any discrepancies. In many cases, it has been necessary to keep those sources anonymous because of the risk to their careers or personal freedom. In all cases, I have endeavored to combine the sourcing for the most accurate picture of events I could provide.

Timeline

1979—U.S. and China establish diplomatic relations. U.S. recognizes "One China" policy but continues economic and defense ties with Taiwan.

1994—China seizes Mischief Reef, just 135 miles off the Philippine coast, and builds bunkers on the reef. China says they are shelters for fishermen in distress.

1995-96—In an attempt to influence the presidential election in Taiwan, China "tests" missiles and conducts naval exercises, effectively closing the Taiwan Strait to shipping. In response President Bill Clinton sends two U.S. Navy aircraft carrier strike groups to the strait, forcing the Chinese to back down. Chinese leadership launches a crash program to enlarge and modernize China's navy.

1999—U.S. military spending falls to 3.4 percent of GDP, the lowest since World War II.

2000—Chinese GDP quintuples in just two decades, soaring from $218 billion in 1978 to $1.2 trillion in 2000. At the new millennium's beginning, military spending is increasing about 10 percent each year.

2001—A Chinese fighter pilot tries to intimidate the crew of a navy EP-3E Aries II reconnaissance plane as it flies over the South China Sea, but the pilot ventures too close and is killed in the collision. The damaged Aries is forced to land on Hainan Island, where the twenty-four crewmembers are held for eleven days. Terrorist attacks in New York City and Washington, D.C., divert the U.S. military's focus toward Afghanistan and the Middle East.

2007—China launches an antisatellite missile and destroys an old weather satellite. It's the beginning of a long-term plan to develop ground-based and space-based antisatellite technology.

2011—The Obama administration unveils an economic, diplomatic, and military "pivot" away from the Middle East and toward the Asia-Pacific region.

2012—Chinese maritime paramilitary forces and fishing boats force Filipino forces off disputed Scarborough Shoal to take sole control of the reef in the South China Sea.

2015—Admiral Harry Harris, commander of the U.S. forces in the Pacific, says China is building a "Great Wall of Sand" in the South China Sea, rapidly building artificial islands that will serve as forward bases and be used to enforce territorial exclusivity.

2016—Admiral Harris sends USS *John C. Stennis* carrier strike group on two-month patrol in the South China Sea to assert freedom of navigation. Defense Secretary Ash Carter visits the ship and says U.S. presence in the region will continue.

2017—The Trump administration signals that it is rethinking the One China policy. China responds by sending a carrier group through the Taiwan Strait. America's "warm war" with China in the Western Pacific continues.

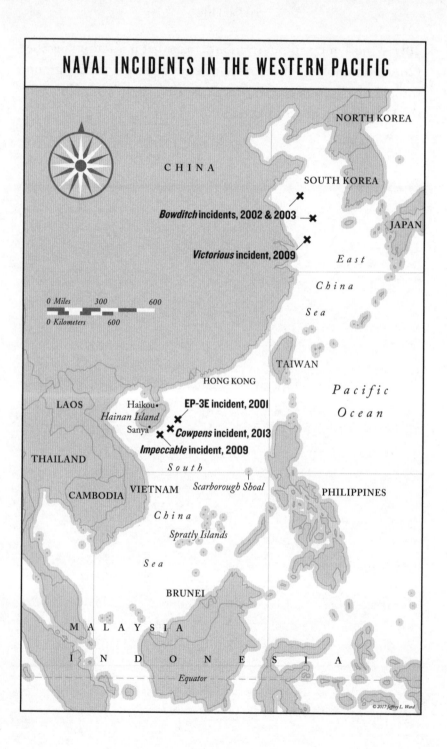

NAVAL INCIDENTS IN THE WESTERN PACIFIC

NORTH KOREA

CHINA

SOUTH KOREA

Bowditch incidents, 2002 & 2003

JAPAN

Victorious incident, 2009

East

China

0 Miles   300   600

Sea

0 Kilometers   600

Pacific

TAIWAN

Ocean

HONG KONG

LAOS   Haikou•
Hainan Island   EP-3E incident, 2001

Sanya   **Cowpens** incident, 2013

THAILAND   **Impeccable** incident, 2009

South

China   Scarborough Shoal

CAMBODIA   VIETNAM   PHILIPPINES

China

Spratly Islands

Sea

BRUNEI

M A L A Y S I A

I N D O N E S I A

Equator

© 2017 Jeffrey L. Ward

Prologue

The United States and China are at war in the Western Pacific. That probably comes as a surprise to most readers, and so it bears repeating. The United States and the People's Republic of China are at war in the Western Pacific. As you read this, tens of thousands of American sailors, soldiers, airmen, and marines are out there fighting that war, putting their lives in peril—either on, under, or over the sea.

Obviously it's not a hot war. American and Chinese military forces aren't shooting missiles or torpedoes or naval artillery at each other—although in an instant of miscalculation or misjudgment, that could easily happen. And it's not a U.S.–Soviet Union style cold war, either. Chinese leaders aren't banging their shoes on tables and vowing to bury us; American leaders are not calling the People's Republic an "evil empire." On the contrary, at the highest levels of Chinese and American diplomatic and military relations there is publicly a lot of smiling and bowing and hand-shaking and promises of mutual cooperation.

But while the war may be neither hot nor cold, China and the United States—and particularly the United States Navy—are engaged in a warm war in the Western Pacific. It's a war over tiny specks of land and vast reaches of sea and sky, a warm war of dangerous confrontations and small escalations, a war over military hegemony and the diplomatic and economic influence that naturally follows that hegemony. It's a war that pits a diminished U.S. Navy, which sailed the Pacific virtually unchallenged for decades, against a burgeoning Chinese navy that is evolving with astonishing speed from a coastal defense force to a "blue-water" fleet capable of projecting power throughout the region. It's a warm war in which China is trying to gain ownership and military control of some of the world's most economically vital waters.

And it is a war that the United States has been losing.

Of course, the concepts of "losing" or "winning" are different than in a traditional conflict. For the United States to win does not imply the destruction or subjugation of China and the signing of surrender documents on the steps of the Great Hall of the People in Tiananmen Square. Even if the United States could achieve such an outcome—which it can't—why would it want to? China's four-decade transformation from an isolated, impoverished Third World nation to a thriving market- and trade-based economic power has overall been good for the world, and for the United States. It has helped lift hundreds of millions of people out of poverty, not only in China but throughout the Asia-Pacific region, and it has stimulated trade around the globe. It's why Americans can buy a laptop computer for two hundred bucks. An actual war between the United States and China, even a limited one, would be a human and economic catastrophe for both sides. America does not win by seeing China fall.

Instead, to win this warm war requires only that the United States force China to peacefully operate within the very system that made China's economic rise possible in the first place. In other words, America must require China to respect and maintain the status quo. That may not sound like a particularly inspiring rallying cry—"Forward, forward, to maintain the status quo!"—but for the United States and the world it is the best possible outcome. The status quo in this case means the observation of international rules by all nations, China included; the peaceful resolution of disputes through international law and not through bullying and intimidation; and, most important, the maintaining of safe, free, and unrestricted passage over the Western Pacific and its subordinate seas for ships of all nations. Ever since World War II, the United States Navy has successfully stabilized and protected that safe and free passage in the Western Pacific and around the world. If it continues to do so, if it can deter China from its goal of imposing a new order on the high seas, then America wins. If it can't or won't do that, then America—and the world—will lose.

For the United States to lose this nontraditional conflict with China does not require its ships to be sunk, its aircraft to be shot down, its young men and women to be killed in combat. The United States can lose without a shot being fired, simply by reducing or withdrawing its military and especially its naval power from the Western Pacific region. That withdrawal could be prompted by economic considerations, popular isolationism, or even fear of conflict on the part of the nation's military and political leaders. In short, America could lose simply by not trying to win.

And for too long that's exactly what American political leaders and some American military leaders have been doing—not trying to win. In the past, they've failed to even acknowledge that the warm war with China exists, preferring instead to view China as a potential military partner rather than a military competitor. They've refused to accept that China's current leadership doesn't respond to Western concepts of moral persuasion, that the leadership responds only to displays of strength—economic, diplomatic, and military. It's been a policy of accommodation—some might call it appeasement—with a Chinese leadership that has taken full advantage of American complacency to expand its aggressive military reach in the Western Pacific region to the detriment of its neighbors. Only relatively recently has the American defense establishment begun to recognize that America's economic and national security depends on having the will to win the warm war with China.

So how did that happen? And how in the face of an increasingly assertive and militarily powerful China can the United States continue to keep the seas open and free? Those are the questions this book tries to answer.

This is not a policy book written for defense establishment insiders. It is not an examination of dueling think-tank position papers or congressional research reports. Instead, it is written from the perspective of people who have actually stood on the pitching decks of American warships and flown dangerous reconnaissance missions in American aircraft, people who have seen the warm war with China firsthand. Those people are mostly sailors and aviators in the U.S. Navy. Although the air force, the army, and the marines (which are part of the Navy Department) all play vital roles in defense of America's interests in the Western Pacific, it is the men and women of the U.S. Navy who most often find themselves in direct confrontations with the Chinese military on the sea and in the air—and so this is primarily their story.

Readers will quickly notice that this book is written from a decidedly American point of view. Simply put, we Americans are the guys in the white hats, and the Chinese political and military leadership are the guys in the black hats—or at least the dark gray hats. The reason for that is simple: For all of its faults and past mistakes, the United States overall is a liberal, peace-seeking, pro-democracy, pro–human rights, pro–freedom of trade player on the world stage. And so far the Chinese Communist Party leadership—not the Chinese people, but the leadership—has been none of those things. Despite its liberalized economic policies of recent decades, the Chinese government remains authoritarian, oligarchical, repressive to its own people, and disdainful of the rights of other, smaller nations. The Chinese point of view will be given its just due here, partly through the eyes of Chinese sailors who serve their country as bravely and loyally as American sailors serve theirs. But no one should expect a sense of moral or ethical equivalence between America and the current Chinese leadership—because there isn't one.

And finally, this book is about a recent and relatively brief period in the history of America's relationship with China. But while it may be brief, it may also be crucial, setting the stage for decades, perhaps even centuries, of history to come.

No one can predict with certainty what the future of America's relationship with China will be. But wherever America and China stand in ten or twenty or thirty years, this story may help explain how they got there.

CHAPTER I

The Mission

It's a calm, almost serene day in December as the USS *Cowpens* sails alone through the dangerous blue-green waters of the South China Sea. With the American flag snapping at the masthead, the *Cowpens* and its four hundred officers and crew are tense, primed, ready—and they are closing fast on their target.

The target on this day is an aircraft carrier, a carrier that's flying the flag of the People's Republic of China. And for the *Cowpens* crew, this is no drill.

The *Cowpens* is a guided-missile cruiser, one of the Ticonderoga class of U.S. warships, and as such it exudes both beauty and power. Almost six hundred feet long, low-slung and sleek, the ship slices through the sea at up to thirty-seven miles per hour—a speed that feels far more intense and urgent than it would on land. Standing on its deck, with the surge of its eighty-thousand-horsepower propulsion plant humming through the hull, with white water cascading past the bow and with that red, white, and blue flag streaming proudly in the wind—it's like riding a nine-thousand-ton living thing. For an American surface warfare sailor, such a ship at sea is a beautiful sight.

But the beauty is secondary. The *Cowpens*'s primary purpose is destruction.

For that there are the missiles. Packed into loading racks below its main deck or locked onto deck launchers are more than a hundred missiles designed for a host of violent missions, both offensive and defensive. There are antiaircraft missiles, anti-ship missiles, antimissile missiles. There are million-dollar-apiece Tomahawk cruise missiles that can destroy land targets a thousand miles distant, and surface-skimming Harpoons that can put a quarter ton of high explosive into an enemy ship that's over the horizon. An ideal cruiser weapons load includes ASROC missile/torpedoes that can hunt down and sink a lurking enemy submarine, and twenty-two-foot-long SAMs (surface-to-air missiles) that can blow an enemy plane out of the sky more than fifty miles away.

There's more. For closer work—for example, supporting an amphibious assault on a disputed island—mounted fore and aft are two five-inch guns capable of lobbing seventy-pound explosive shells fifteen miles. For still closer work—say, mixing it up with an enemy high-speed catamaran gunboat that's closing fast—there are a couple of 25mm Bushmaster chain guns and a couple of .50-caliber machine guns. And if things get really hot in combat, if an enemy missile somehow manages to evade all the defensive firepower and is screaming toward the *Cowpens* at Mach 2, there's a 20mm Phalanx gun that can spit out bullets at the rate of seventy-five rounds *per second* and put up a missile-busting wall of lead.

It is an astonishing amount of firepower. In fact, the Ticonderoga-class cruisers are designed to be the most powerful surface warships ever to put to sea, under any flag, in any century. They and their weaponry are meant to impress, to intimidate, to inspire awe—and if necessary, to deliver shock in paralyzing quantities. That's why the USS *Cowpens* is here on this day in the South China Sea.

That's the theory, anyway. But aboard this ship, not all is quite as it seems.

Alternating between the sunlit bridge and the dim, green-glowing confines of the ship's Combat Information Center (CIC) is the man entrusted with the *Cowpens's* massive collection of lethal weaponry, and with the lives and well-being of the crewmembers who operate it. Captain Greg Gombert is tall (six-foot-six) and lean, with blue eyes and a shock of brown hair, dressed in the navy's new working uniform of one-piece blue coveralls. Intense, driven, supremely self-confident, he pushes his ship and his crew—and himself—hard. The product of a strict midwestern Catholic upbringing, steeped in the concepts of duty and hard work, at age forty-four Gombert is a man who has never failed at anything—and he doesn't intend to fail in this mission.

In a low, even voice Gombert says a few words to his officer of the deck (OOD), a young lieutenant, and a second later those words blare over the ship's loudspeakers.

Set modified Condition Zebra. Set modified Condition Zebra.

The order sends sailors racing through the ship, closing and dogging watertight hatches and shutting off valves. Damage control and firefighting squads stand by; sonar and radar and electronic warfare operators stare at their display screens with renewed intensity. Senior chiefs check and recheck every system. Condition Zebra is the navy's second-highest level of combat readiness, just below General Quarters. GQ is when you're under threat of imminent attack; Zebra is when you might soon be.

The process takes only a few minutes. Watching from the bridge, listening as the various department heads' readiness reports come in, Gombert isn't completely satisfied. He knows the crew is doing its best. But there just hasn't been time. . . .

With two decades of service behind him, Gombert is a rising star in the navy, this despite the fact that he's not a "ring knocker"—that is, he began his career as a navy ROTC midshipman at Notre Dame, not at the Naval Academy in Annapolis. Still, he has an enviable record, with all the necessary ticket-punches required for rising to even higher command: multiple sea tours on frigates and destroyers, including a much-praised tour as captain of a new destroyer, the USS *Gridley*, and all of that mixed in with a master's degree and four years of obligatory desk duty in the Pentagon. He's been the commanding officer of the *Cowpens* for just six months.

A command like this should be a pinnacle in any navy surface warfare officer's career. After all, while there are fifty-five thousand active duty officers in the U.S. Navy, at any given moment fewer than three hundred of them are entrusted with command of a navy ship. It is a singular honor, although you wouldn't know it from the pay scales. Depending on rank and years of service, a navy ship commanding officer earns a base pay of between $80,000 and $120,000 a year—about what the manager of a Walmart superstore makes. But nobody is in the navy for the money.

And of those fewer than three hundred ship commanders, only twenty-two, Gombert included, are in command of a guided-missile cruiser like the *Cowpens*. All the old World War II–style battleships are long gone now, turned into razor blades or floating museums; cruisers are the navy's new battlewagons. And in an already elite subset of navy officers who command warships, cruiser captains are special.

True, submarine commanders are an elite group as well. But a sub's job is to hide, to lurk unseen and quietly gather intelligence or wait for orders to launch its missiles; you don't use subs to display power, to show the flag. It's true also that aircraft carriers are bigger, and their captains more high-profile. But carriers never operate alone. While at sea they are always surrounded by other warships in a carrier strike group—which means that while a carrier captain commands his ship, he always has an admiral standing over his shoulder who commands the strike group. Carrier captains are on a pretty short leash.

Cruiser captains are different. Although cruisers often operate as part of carrier strike groups, they are also capable of performing "lone wolf" missions, racing from hot spot to hot spot alone, independent, with thousands of miles of ocean between them and the navy brass and the navy bureaucracy; they're the front line, the point of the spear. To command such a ship on such a mission is what young and ambitious navy surface warfare officers dream about. It's what Greg Gombert dreamed about.

And yet, on this day—specifically, December 5, 2013—as he and his ship steam toward their rendezvous with the Chinese navy aircraft carrier in the South China Sea, Captain Greg Gombert is a man beset with a daunting array of problems.

Of course, for anyone who presumes to command a U.S. Navy ship of war, problems—or as navy officers call them, "challenges"—are the daily fare. Equipment breaks down, computer systems malfunction, human beings fail. And the captain owns all of it—every stripped nut and bolt, every burned-out microchip, every eighteen-year-old sailor fresh out of boot camp who doesn't do his job. As far as the navy is concerned, anything that goes wrong aboard a U.S. Navy ship is not just the captain's responsibility; it's the captain's *fault*.

Does an inattentive junior officer of the deck somehow manage to run the ship aground on an uncharted sandbar while the captain is sound asleep in his cabin? It's the captain's fault. While the captain is deep in the bowels of the ship for an engine room inspection, does an inexperienced radar operator or bridge lookout fail to spot that tiny fishing boat directly in the ship's path? It's the captain's fault for failing to maintain the ship and the crew in a proper state of readiness and training. And if serious damage to life or property results—well, the only thing that ship's commanding officer will ever command again is a desk.

It's a harsh and unforgiving system, and one that every

commanding officer of a U.S. Navy ship has to accept. He or she knows any problem, no matter how seemingly small, can wind up ruining a career.

But aboard the *Cowpens*, Captain Gombert's problems—challenges—far exceed the normal.

There's the crew, for one thing. The 340 enlisted sailors aboard are a mix of early twentysomethings with a few years' navy experience and fresh-faced teens just six months past their high-school proms. Yes, they're eager, and earnest, and they try hard enough. But they've only been aboard the *Cowpens* for ten months at the most, with the majority of that time spent in port, not at sea. Even those who have served on other Ticonderoga-class cruisers haven't had time to learn all the quirks and idiosyncrasies of this particular ship; they just don't yet have a feel for it.

The same thing goes for the twenty-seven chief petty officers, the noncommissioned officers who are the backbone of any military organization. They're solid, and experienced; some of them have been knocking around the Western Pacific—they call it "the WestPac"—on destroyers and cruisers for the past decade. But they don't have experience on the *Cowpens*. It's like they're living and working in a new and unfamiliar city.

The thirty-two junior commissioned officers aboard the ship also have their limitations. Gombert has already effectively relieved—fired—the ship's executive officer, the second-in-command, categorizing him as a "significant leadership team weakness." It's an unusual move for a captain to make, especially in the middle of a sea deployment; it's also an indication of how tough a commander Gombert can be. So for now the ship is sailing without an XO, increasing the burden on the captain. As for the other junior officers, men and women in their midtwenties and early thirties, in Gombert's view many of them seem tentative, unsure of themselves, hesitant to take on new and greater responsibilities.

In the sometimes old-fashioned way he has of phrasing things, Gombert has described them as "nervous Nellies."

And then there is the ship itself. It's a crisis waiting to happen.

Like other Ticonderoga-class cruisers, the *Cowpens* (hull number CG-63) is named after a battle, specifically the pivotal American victory over a British army near the small town of Cowpens, South Carolina, in 1781. (The ship's nickname is the "Mighty Moo," and continuing with the bovine theme, the crew collectively is known as the "Thundering Herd.") Commissioned in 1991, the ship has seen more than two decades of service, much of it hard service. Until six months earlier the *Cowpens* had been slated to be put into "reduced commission," that is, to be "preserved," nearly mothballed, until the navy decided whether to overhaul or decommission the ship. But then the U.S. government revealed its so-called Pacific pivot, an economic, diplomatic, and military shift of emphasis away from the Middle East back toward Asia and the Western Pacific. The navy decided that it needed the *Cowpens* to project power and show the flag in the region, so after a hasty and mostly cosmetic $7 million refit in San Diego, in September the Cowpens and its new crew headed west.

And on the outside the ship *looks* good. Its decks and towering superstructure gleam, the crew looks sharp in their dark blue uniforms and baseball caps, the ship can still speed across the ocean with a bone in its teeth and the flag flying. But inside it's a different story. The internal mechanical systems are old, the ship needs miles of new electric wiring and fiber-optic cables. Worse, the *Cowpens* is equipped with an antiquated version of the Aegis Combat System, the complicated array of interconnected radars, sonars, computer systems, and missile launchers used to identify, track, and destroy targets. The *Cowpens*'s new crew is accustomed to working with a newer, more capable version of the Aegis system— so for them, operating the *Cowpens*'s outdated system is like going from Windows 10 to Windows 2.5. They haven't yet learned to handle it effectively.

Given enough time, can the *Cowpens*'s crew and its outdated combat system still fire the ship's missiles? Sure. Can the ship defend itself against one or two incoming enemy anti-ship missiles? Almost certainly. But could the *Cowpens* effectively identify, track, and destroy *dozens* of enemy missiles suddenly coming in at the same time from ship- and land-based missile batteries—an enemy attack tactic that is indelicately known among navy officers as a "gangbang"? The answer is, no way. If this mission somehow goes south and the *Cowpens* gets gangbanged by enemy missiles, the ship is in serious trouble. Captain Gombert knows that. And the navy knows it, too.

And there's something else about the *Cowpens*. Publicly, most navy officers would dismiss it as mere superstition, but there's a feeling among many sailors that the *Cowpens* is an unlucky ship. In fact, as far as its commanding officers' careers go, some believe the ship is actually cursed.

The year before, in 2012, the *Cowpens*'s then commanding officer was summarily relieved for having an improper physical relationship with another navy officer's wife. The navy officially calls that "conduct unbecoming an officer"; unofficially, navy officers call it a "zipper malfunction." And two years before that, another *Cowpens* commanding officer, Captain Holly Graf, the first woman ever to command a U.S. Navy cruiser, was also summarily relieved, for physically and verbally abusing her subordinates. Officers and crewmembers told dark tales of being pushed and shoved by the captain, of being subjected to shrieking F-bomb tirades, of being made to stand in a corner like misbehaving children. News reports about "Horrible Holly" and the "Sea Witch" cast a pall over the *Cowpens* name; chatter on unofficial navy blog sites portrayed the *Cowpens* as a star-crossed ship, a career killer.

But as he guides the *Cowpens* through the South China Sea, Gombert isn't thinking about bad luck and curses—although, given what will happen to him later, maybe he should be. Instead, his mind is focused on the current mission.

It is a mission riddled with uncertainties, and fraught with physical and professional peril.

On its face it seems simple enough. For the first time, a Chinese navy aircraft carrier, the *Liaoning*, is about to sally from its port on Hainan Island to conduct carrier task force training operations in international waters in the South China Sea. The U.S. Pacific Fleet in Hawaii and the Seventh Fleet brass based in Japan want the *Cowpens* to shadow the Chinese carrier and its escort ships, to gather intelligence, to see how the carrier operates and how it conducts air operations, to document what its capabilities are.

Cowpens can do that, easy. Its electronics may be old, but they can still vacuum up the *Liaoning*'s electromagnetic emissions and tap into its wireless communications systems. The *Cowpens* also has two Seahawk helicopters that can take off from the ship's landing deck and hover near the Chinese carrier task force, taking film and photographs and generally eyeballing the situation.

Navies around the world routinely conduct such operations against other nations' ships, although the name for them varies. The basic rule is: When we do it, it's intelligence-gathering; when the other guy does it, it's spying. But when done in international waters, it's all perfectly legal under international law and long-accepted maritime practice.

But the *Cowpens*'s mission isn't just to gather intelligence—spy—on the Chinese carrier. There's a political purpose as well. The *Liaoning*'s foray into the South China Sea is yet another escalation in the Chinese navy's growing presence in the region—a presence that is scaring the hell out of America's Pacific friends and allies. The Philippines, Indonesia, Australia, Japan, South

Korea, Thailand, Taiwan, Malaysia, even the Socialist Republic of Vietnam—they all look with trepidation at the Chinese navy's growing power, not only in the South China Sea but throughout the far Western Pacific. And they all want to know what the U.S. is going to do about it. So the *Cowpens*'s secondary mission is to show the American flag, to reassure the allies and other nations in the region. The *Cowpens* is going to get in close to the Chinese carrier and let everybody know that the sheriff—the U.S. Navy—is still in town.

Again, for the *Cowpens* all that seems completely doable. But in this particular case, there are a couple of potentially serious complications.

For one thing, the *Liaoning* isn't just *a* Chinese navy aircraft carrier; it's the *only* Chinese navy aircraft carrier, the first aircraft carrier ever in the history of the People's Republic and the People's Liberation Army Navy. And as such it is an object of enormous national pride, an announcement that China is finally about to step onto the world stage as a naval power. Already in the past decade the Chinese navy has become the world's second-largest naval force in terms of warship tonnage, behind only the U.S.— and except for aircraft carriers, in the Western Pacific it is now arguably the U.S. Navy's equal in maritime military power. With its new carrier program, it's embarking on a long-range plan to become the dominant naval force in the region.

So to the Chinese government, the *Liaoning* isn't just a ship; it's a symbol.

And it's not just the government that feels that way. It's probably fair to say that not more than a relative handful of Americans could name a single U.S. aircraft carrier, much less name its commanding officer. But a billion people in China have heard about the *Liaoning*, and its dashing, urbane commander, Senior Captain Zhang Zheng. (It doesn't hurt that his wife is a popular morning talk-show host on Shanghai television.) After Chinese TV showed video of the carrier's flight deck crews directing jet takeoffs and landings—waving their arms, dropping to one knee—"Carrier Style" dance moves actually supplanted "Gangnam Style" as the hottest thing on Chinese teen social media.

The point is that to the Chinese people the *Liaoning* is a national treasure, and its commander the military equivalent of a rock star. Any real or perceived insult to that national treasure—for example, a U.S. Navy warship getting up in its grille on the high seas—will not be taken graciously.

And there's still another complication for the *Cowpens* and its mission. In an attempt to shield their carrier and its escorts from prying Western eyes, the Chinese government has declared a forty-five-kilometer "safety zone" around the *Liaoning* while it's at sea. According to the Chinese, no ship or aircraft, military or civilian, can enter that safety zone without permission from the *Liaoning*'s commander—permission that the commander is not about to give to a U.S. Navy ship of war.

Well, it's outrageous.

Yes, a U.S. carrier strike group conducting at-sea operations will also enforce a safety zone around its ships; you don't want a commercial fishing boat laying down a seine net in front of an oncoming aircraft carrier. So U.S. commanders will suggest— politely—that other vessels lay off for a few miles around the strike group.

But the Chinese are trying to take the safety zone concept to a whole new level. Forty-five kilometers? That's about *twenty-eight miles*. That's over-the-horizon stuff. In effect China is trying to declare its sovereignty on, over, and below a moving area of more than two thousand square miles of international waters. It violates every principle of international maritime law and the freedom of the seas. Not even haughty Britannia, when it ruled the waves, ever tried a stunt like that in peacetime. If this is allowed to stand, what's to keep the Chinese navy from claiming a similar two-thousand-square-mile sovereignty zone in the Sea of Japan or the Taiwan Strait—or twelve miles off the Golden Gate Bridge, for that matter?

In fact, the *Liaoning*'s safety zone is just the latest in a long series of hostile moves by China to deny to other nations access to the commercially vital South China Sea, the U.S. included. They're trying to turn the South China Sea into a Chinese lake. By sending the *Cowpens* into the South China Sea to challenge the *Liaoning*, the U.S. Navy is showing the Chinese America will have none of that.

That's the navy's public posture, anyway. But behind the scenes, at the U.S. Pacific Command headquarters in Hawaii and at the Pentagon, the navy top brass aren't so certain. After all, nobody on the American side is sure what the Chinese reaction will be when they see a U.S. Navy warship bearing down on them from over the horizon, safety zone be damned. Yes, they want China to ramp it back, to respect the rules of free navigation of the seas. And yes, they want to reassure the nervous Western Pacific allies that the U.S. still has their backs against China. But how far should the U.S. go to demonstrate that commitment?

At the highest echelons of the navy and the American civilian defense establishment there is a sharp, bitter, and ongoing fight over that question. The fight is so bitter, in fact, that the opposing sides have derisive names for each other. Those who want to take a low-key, nonconfrontational approach to China are dismissed as "Panda Huggers." Those who want to respond aggressively, with muscular shows of U.S. naval force, are sarcastically known as "Dragon Slayers." As the *Cowpens* steams into the South China Sea, that internal navy struggle has yet to be resolved.

And as a result, Captain Gombert's orders are a masterpiece

of ambiguity; they are part Panda Hugger, part Dragon Slayer. Gombert has been told to ignore the declared twenty-eight-mile safety zone and intercept the *Liaoning*, while at the same time he is to maintain a "de-escalatory posture." He is to get close to the carrier—within three miles—but not too close, meaning not less than one mile. If there is any radio communication with the Chinese commander, he is to be firm and resolute but also "cordial and respectful"; he's to be careful not to piss them off.

In short, Captain Gombert's orders are to boldly take his ship and his crew into harm's way—but for God's sake, don't let anything unpleasant happen out there.

And now that's what is confronting Captain Greg Gombert as he takes the *Cowpens* into the South China Sea on this day in December 2013. He has a troubled ship, with a struggling crew, and they are sailing alone into dangerous waters, with uncertain orders, for a rendezvous with a proud and unpredictable adversary.

And the outcome of this mission could help determine whether the Pacific will remain "America's Ocean."

CHAPTER 2

America's Ocean

Pigafetta had it right and wrong about this ocean. He was right about its vast distances and its seemingly boundless reach. But he was dead wrong about its character.

Antonio Pigafetta was a young Venetian scholar and scribe who sailed with Ferdinand Magellan and 269 men on the Spanish circumnavigation of the globe in 1519–22; he was also one of only eighteen men (not including Magellan himself) who survived the trip. It was Pigafetta who left the first eyewitness account of what it was like to sail across this ocean. Other, more ancient sailors may have crossed it before him—Chinese, Polynesians, perhaps some storm-tossed Japanese fishermen—but if so, they left no acknowledged record. Even with steady winds behind them, it took Magellan and his tiny fleet almost four months to sail from the tip of South America to Guam, months of starvation and scurvy and death. This is what Pigafetta wrote of the journey:

"We remained three months and twenty days without taking on board provisions, and we ate only old biscuit turned to powder, all full of worms and stinking . . . and of rats, some of us could not get enough. . . . We made a good four thousand leagues across this [ocean]. . . . And if our Lord and the Virgin Mother had not aided us . . . we would have died in this very great sea."

And Magellan and Pigafetta only saw a tiny portion of "this very great sea." This ocean covers no less than 64 million square miles, far more if you count its primary subsidiary seas—the South China Sea, the East China Sea, the Yellow Sea, the Sea of Japan. Even without the subsidiaries, this ocean alone exceeds the land area of all of Earth's continents combined. A westbound voyage along the equator from South America to this ocean system's terminus at the Strait of Malacca would cover twelve thousand miles, half the Earth's circumference; a southbound voyage from its Arctic border to the Antarctic would cover almost the same. Even though there are more than twenty-five thousand islands scattered across this ocean, Magellan managed to spot only two of them—both uninhabited atolls that he and his weary men couldn't even land on. That's how vast this ocean is. It's big enough to hide twenty-five thousand islands.

Magellan called those two uninhabited islands *las Islas Infortunatos*—the Unfortunate Islands—which may have been apt. But his name for this ocean was far less so. After he had left the Atlantic and made a difficult and dangerous traverse of the strait that bears his name, Magellan had favorably compared this ocean to the turbulent Atlantic—and thus he named it *el Mar Pacifico*, the Peaceful Sea. And Pigafetta agreed with him.

"Well was it named the Pacific," he wrote, "for during [the entire crossing] we met no storms."

But they were lucky. Because in many ways, the Pacific is the angriest and least peaceful ocean on Earth.

Take the cyclonic tropical storms, known as hurricanes east of the International Dateline and typhoons west of it. In an average year there may be ten to fifteen hurricanes in the Atlantic and Caribbean and Eastern Pacific, but there will be double that number of typhoons in the Western Pacific. And Pacific cyclonic storms generally are stronger in intensity; cyclonic storms feed off warm water, of which the Pacific has plenty. In terms of sustained wind speed, the most violent tropical cyclone ever recorded was a 2015 Eastern Pacific hurricane, Patricia, which at its peak saw a wind speed of 215 miles per hour. In 2013 another Pacific cyclonic storm record-breaker, Typhoon Haiyan, hit the Philippines with 195-mile-per-hour winds and a storm surge up to twenty feet high, drowning more than six thousand people. Over the millennia, this peaceful ocean has killed humans by the millions.

Ships, too, die in those storms. The list of modern ships lost to wind and waves is far too long to recount, but a few examples can make the point. In 1944 a typhoon with 100 mph winds and up to seventy-foot-high waves hit a U.S. Navy fleet east of the Philippines and three destroyers capsized, drowning 790 American sailors. In 1980 the British ore carrier *Derbyshire*, a thousand feet long and displacing ninety thousand tons, as big as an aircraft carrier, was lost with all forty-four souls aboard after being caught in Typhoon Orchid two hundred miles off Okinawa. In 2013 a six-hundred-foot-long Chinese bulk cargo ship sank off Hong Kong in fifty-foot waves whipped up by Typhoon Utor. The point is simple: The ship hasn't been built that has nothing to fear from Pacific typhoons.

There are other dangers lurking in and under these so-called pacific waters: uncharted or mis-charted reefs and seamounts, ocean floor earthquakes or landslides that cause tsunamis, undersea volcanos. Again, just a few examples. In 1987 the 245-feet-long U.S. Navy research ship *Melville* was shaken and pelted with exploding gas bubbles and rocks from an underwater volcano eruption a thousand miles southwest of Tahiti. In 2005 the nuclear-powered attack submarine USS *San Francisco* was cruising at a depth of five hundred feet when it ran into an uncharted undersea mountain off the coast of Guam, killing one American sailor and injuring almost a hundred more. In 2011 at least two dozen cargo ships and fishing vessels were damaged or tossed ashore by a tsunami that struck northeastern Japan; one unmanned 164-foot-long fishing boat—known as the "Ghost Ship"—drifted for thousands of miles until it was sunk by gunfire a year later off the coast of Alaska.

And those are just the natural dangers. The Pacific also boils with past, present, and future man-made calamities.

Nearly three dozen nations small and large have coastlines in the Asia-Pacific, with a combined population of about 3.5 billion people—about half of all the people on Earth. Nearly a third of the world's maritime trade annually transits the South China Sea alone, including about $1.2 trillion in shipborne trade bound for the United States. Every year some ninety-four thousand oil tankers, container ships, bulk carriers, and other commercial vessels pass through the narrow, five-hundred-mile-long Malacca Strait that is the gateway from the Indian Ocean to the South China Sea and the Western Pacific. Eastbound from the Indian Ocean and into the South and East China Seas come Middle Eastern oil and African raw materials and European cars and Indian farm machinery; westbound along the same route go computers and smartphones and coffee and cheap T-shirts. Were anything to disrupt or cut off that seaborne traffic, entire economies could wither and die.

And so to help protect that trade and their own security, nations build navies.

True, navies are shockingly expensive to build and operate. Just one small modern frigate costs at least $300 million to build and about $20 million a year to operate, while even a single small aircraft carrier could set a country back several billion dollars in construction costs—which is why only a handful of countries in the world have them. But despite the massive expense, in the second decade of the twenty-first century, most of the major countries of the Western Pacific and environs are trying to build up and modernize their navies and their sea-striking military capabilities.

Grab a map—or better yet, a globe—and take a quick selective tour of the region and its naval forces.

Start with Russia and its naval port of Vladivostok on the Sea of Japan. Once a significant nineteenth-century Pacific imperial power, its great fleets were humiliatingly sunk—and thousands of its sailors drowned—by an emerging Japanese navy at the beginning of the twentieth century. During the Cold War the USSR rebuilt its Pacific Fleet, but after the fall of the Soviet Union most of the fleet was left to rust at the docks. Today Russia's Pacific surface fleet remains small, consisting primarily of a few cruisers, a half dozen destroyers, and several frigates and corvettes. But the Russian Pacific Fleet has some two dozen submarines, including some new, fourth-generation nuclear-powered ballistic-missile subs—and like all things Russian under the Vladimir Putin regime, that growing fleet will bear watching.

Now head south along the coast to North Korea, the people's hermit kingdom run by the seemingly mad scion Kim Jong-un, whose nuclear weapons development program terrifies almost everyone within potential missile range, which now includes the western portions of the United States. Small, often famished, with a population of just 25 million people, North Korea has a military force of more than a million personnel, which makes it one of the world's largest. (One of every twenty-five people in the country is on active military service; in the U.S. the figure is about one in three hundred.) Its naval forces consist mostly of coastal submarines and small frigates and scores of tiny gunboats and attack boats, but those naval forces can still be lethal; in 2010, for example, a North Korean sub apparently fired a torpedo at a South Korean corvette, killing forty-six South Korean sailors, which was only the latest in a string of such incidents over the decades. North Korea also has an extensive network of land-based missile batteries that can extend its reach out to sea.

Assuming you make it out of North Korea—not all foreign visitors do—walk carefully across the two-and-a-half-mile-wide Demilitarized Zone and into another world: South Korea. Urbanized, economically dynamic, politically democratic, with a population of 50 million and a per capita GDP forty times higher than its bellicose brother to the north, South Korea has reinvented itself in the six decades since the end of the Korean War—a war that left a million South Korean civilians dead, wounded, or missing, along with thirty-three thousand American soldiers killed. Because of North Korea, South Korea also maintains a large standing army—some five hundred thousand men, backed up by twenty-eight thousand U.S. military personnel. South Korea's navy is one of the largest in the region, with 160 commissioned ships—including submarines, amphibious warfare ships, destroyers, and smaller-than-a-destroyer frigates; future plans call for the addition of Aegis-equipped destroyers and upgraded missile defense systems.

From South Korea head west across the Sea of Japan, and there you'll find a navy that isn't called a navy—but still manages to be one of the best navies in the world. Because its post-WWII constitution prohibits it from using war or even the threat of war as an instrument of national policy, Japan instead has a maritime self-defense force. The force includes about fifty principal surface combatants—including guided-missile destroyers and frigates equipped with Aegis electronic tracking and targeting systems—as well as ten technologically advanced diesel-electric submarines, several large amphibious landing ships, and more than a hundred other vessels. Japan also has a land-based naval aviation force that flies F-15 Eagles, F-4 Phantom IIs, V-22 Ospreys, and electronic-intelligence-gathering E-2 Hawkeyes and P-3 Orions. By some estimates the JMSDF is the world's fifth-strongest surface and air naval force—or rather, maritime self-defense force. A mu-

tual defense treaty ally of the U.S., Japan also is home to tens
of thousands of U.S. Navy, Marine Corps, Air Force, and Army
personnel, the majority of them based on the southern Japanese
island of Okinawa.

From Japan fly southwest more than a thousand miles across
the East China Sea to Taiwan, aka the Republic of China—and
sometimes called "Asia's Berlin." Democratic and economically
prosperous, with one of the highest per capita GDPs in Asia, the
breakaway Chinese island has since 1949 lived under constant threat
that tomorrow or next year or next decade the People's Republic
of China will decide to take it back by force or blockade it into
submission—and without outside help for Taiwan from the U.S.,
mainland China could almost certainly do so. Taiwan's naval fleet
of destroyers and frigates and fast-attack boats is complemented
by just two aging submarines, but the Taiwanese government has
announced an ambitious $14 billion program to modernize its
naval forces. We'll see if that's allowed to happen.

Two hundred miles due south of Taiwan is the Philippines,
America's first Western Pacific possession and the scene of some
of the most savage land and naval battles with Japan in World War
II, a conflict that Filipinos have not forgotten—or in some ways
forgiven, either. Large in population (100 million, twelfth-largest
in the world) but poor and underdeveloped, Filipinos have had a
checkered history with their former protector. After fighting the
Japanese alongside Americans in World War II, in the early 1990s
the Philippine government kicked the U.S. out of its huge naval
and air bases at Subic Bay and Clark Field—and then almost immediately regretted it, since that left the nation of seven thousand
islands with virtually no sea protection. The Philippines remains
a U.S. mutual defense treaty partner, and receives equipment and
training from U.S. forces. But the Philippine naval forces remain
weak—a dozen frigates and corvettes, some coastal defense and

patrol vessels; of submarines it has zero. The Philippine government talks about building a better naval force—new submarines and better radars, ocean sensors, new frigates, modern jet fighters and surveillance aircraft and missile systems—but in the often chaotic Philippine political and financial system it's hard to get things done. The Philippines is not by any measure a significant naval force, but it would like to be.

Two thousand miles south of the Philippines, though, there is a naval power, at least regionally. Australia is a continent-sized country with a small-country population—just 25 million, about half the population of geographically small South Korea. But that population invests heavily in its navy. The Royal Australian Navy fleet is relatively small numerically, with just over fifty commissioned ships. But the Australian fleet includes frigates with upgraded radar and missiles, and in the coming years it plans to spend heavily on new-generation submarines and surface ships and amphibious assault ships. Australia's naval power stems from quality, not quantity. The northern coastal city of Darwin also hosts a rotating force of U.S. Marines, expected to number about twenty-five hundred in the next few years, and U.S. Navy amphibious assault ships. It's strategically located close to the South China Sea.

Northwest of Australia is the former Dutch colony of Indonesia, the fourth most populous nation on earth (250 million). Largely Muslim, with simmering ethnic and political rivalries, it's also rife with corruption that extends into the military and has hampered its planned naval expansion. Still, like almost everybody else in the region, it's trying. It has a couple of updated submarines and a few modern small corvettes and coastal defense vessels.

Sitting above Indonesia is Malaysia, a relatively new and booming industrialized market-economy nation once ruled by the British, now a majority Muslim indirect democracy with a significant Chinese and Indian minority. Small in population (29 million) and bifurcated by geography—half the country is on the Malay Peninsula, the other half across the South China Sea on the island of Borneo—Malaysia traditionally has been more concerned with internal security on the ground than with its navy. But like most Pacific nations whose economies are booming, now that it has money Malaysia wants a modernized navy. The Malaysian navy now has a couple of modern diesel-electric subs—which cost about $450 million each—and it has replaced much of its old frigate and corvette fleet with newer models. It has also ordered a half dozen brand-new "stealth frigates" to add to the fleet, and it has a couple amphibious warfare ships capable of blue-water operations; the amphibs have been participating in international antipiracy operations off the coast of Somalia for several years. Malaysia's most important strategic factor is that it covers most of the eastern shore of the vital Strait of Malacca. (The Indonesian island of Sumatra occupies the western shore.)

And then there's Singapore, the tiny (280 square miles, population 5 million) island city-state at the narrow, just-six-miles-wide end of the Strait of Malacca. Once a British bastion, later a part of newly independent Malaysia, just four decades ago Singapore was a pestilential Third World hellhole. Now it's a nation of superlatives, ranked highest in Asia (and in some cases the world) on health care, life expectancy, education, business efficiency; it's ranked lowest in corruption, infant mortality, and even adult obesity. In 1965 the Singaporean navy had exactly two ships, both made out of wood. But now that it can afford it, Singapore has created one of the most technologically capable navies in the region, including two modernized super-quiet subs and new frigates with advanced missile capabilities. Singapore is also an important forward operating base for the U.S. Navy's new littoral combat ships and a rotational base for P-8 Poseidon reconnaissance aircraft. Like Malaysia's, the Singaporean navy has participated in blue-water international antipiracy operations off the Somali coast, and also conducted antipiracy efforts closer to home in the Strait of Malacca.

Almost sixteen hundred miles northwest of that vital strait, across the Bay of Bengal, is India. Not technically a Western Pacific nation, it is a major player in the region that is sometimes called the "Indo-Asia-Pacific." In population the second-largest nation on earth, it has a navy to match, with two aircraft carriers (it's one of only a handful of nations with carriers), dozens of destroyers and frigates, fourteen submarines (including a ballistic-missile sub capable of launching nuclear missiles), hundreds of naval aircraft, and a host of other vessels. The Indian navy makes almost everyone's list of the world's top ten most powerful navies—and with a planned deployment of six new nuclear-powered ballistic-missile subs, it soon will be even more powerful. The Indian navy is also one of the few navies of the world with relatively recent combat-at-sea experience. During the 1971 war with Pakistan, the Indian navy sank a number of Pakistani ships, including a submarine, and played a vital role in Pakistan's ultimate defeat.

Your tour is almost over. Sail back across the Bay of Bengal and you'll hit Thailand, whose beaches, cultural sites, and Bangkok sex trade have made it Southeast Asia's number one tourist destination. Relatively small in population (68 million), in per capita GDP it ranks fourth highest in Southeast Asia. It has one of the best-funded militaries in the region—perhaps not surprising when you consider that since 2014 it's been ruled by a military junta, a development that has cooled the long-friendly relations with the U.S. (Thailand has been a treaty partner of the U.S. since way back in 1837.) The Royal Thai Navy has one small (just six hundred feet long) 1990s aircraft carrier, although it is used primarily for helicopters, not fighters. But its surface fleet includes updated guided-missile frigates and corvettes and some new landing platform dock ships. The government had planned to buy three new diesel-electric subs, and although that plan was put on hold, the intention remains.

From Thailand travel east across landlocked Laos to Vietnam, which for a generation of Americans was not so much a country as it was a war. To Vietnam, though, the war with the U.S. is not much more than a footnote in a thousand-year history of conflicts; almost two-thirds of Vietnam's 92 million people weren't even born when the last American helicopter left Saigon. With its socialist-communist-capitalist economy heavily dependent on international trade, and with eight hundred miles of coastline on the South China Sea, Vietnam is an important strategic player in the region. Its surface fleet is mostly older frigates and smaller corvettes, but it recently added six updated Kilo-class diesel-electric subs to its fleet. More significant are its land-based anti-ship missile batteries and its long-range SU-30 multipurpose fighter aircraft that can project power far out to sea. Vietnam's military relations with the U.S. are cautious but increasingly close; the Vietnamese and U.S. navies routinely conduct joint "naval engagements"—a less formal phrase than "naval exercises"—and U.S. Navy ships make port calls there.

South Korea, Japan, Taiwan, Australia, Thailand, Vietnam—throughout the Western Pacific, nations are trying to get into the modern navy game in a way they never have before. And then there's China, whose naval expansion is one of the focal points of this book—and one of the primary reasons that those other nations in the region are building up their own navies.

Of course, with a couple of exceptions none of those navies could even dream of completely dominating the Western Pacific, much less the entire Pacific from the Americas to the Strait of Malacca. The Pacific is simply too big, too vast, with too many players in the game for any one nation or navy to control it completely.

In fact, in all of history only one navy has ever been powerful enough to call this ocean its own.

As the USS *Freedom* makes its way slowly up the channel to Pearl Harbor, sailors begin to assemble in ranks on the deck under the ship's main gun near the bow. Pearl Harbor—usually referred to by sailors simply as "Pearl"—is *Freedom*'s first U.S. port visit after a ten-month forward deployment in the Western Pacific, and the crew is looking forward to shore leave after long and arduous weeks at sea. But at this moment the crewmembers assembled on the deck are solemn. Because right now there is homage to be paid.

Looming ahead on the *Freedom*'s port side, off the east shore of Ford Island, there's a low, sleek, two-hundred-foot-long structure rising above the water. Pure white and gleaming in the sun, with an American flag flying from its center, the structure is both a shrine and a colossal gravestone. It is the USS *Arizona* Memorial, and below it, still visible from the surface, lies the rusting, ghostly corpse of the battleship sunk by Japanese bombs on December 7, 1941, along with the remains of more than eleven hundred American sailors and marines who died aboard her.

It's almost impossible to overstate the impact that the surprise attack on Pearl Harbor had and still has on the U.S. Navy. For more than seven decades, preventing another such surprise attack has informed the military strategies of the navy and the U.S. in general. Even today, while memories of the 9/11 terrorist attacks remain fresh and the living memories of Pearl Harbor have started to fade, the U.S. Navy remembers Pearl Harbor and honors the 2,471 Americans killed that day.

And that's what the crewmembers aboard the *Freedom* are doing. As the ship passes by the memorial, all crewmembers not needed to run the ship stand at parade rest on the deck, heads bowed, honoring the dead from that day and from the years that followed. Mind you, this ceremony aboard the *Freedom* isn't because it's Pearl Harbor Day or some other special event. Every time a U.S. Navy ship passes the *Arizona* Memorial, on any day of the year, the ship's crew conducts a similar ceremony. The navy does not forget.

That's not to say that the history of the U.S. Navy in the Pacific began in 1941. In fact, the navy was a force in the Pacific even before it had territory on its shores. In 1821, long before America acquired California and the Oregon Territory, the navy created a Pacific Squadron to advance U.S. interests and protect American merchant ships and whalers that were sailing the waters from China to Hawaii to South America. That concept of using navy ships to demonstrate American "presence" in far-off seas still guides American policy today.

Of course, mere "presence," just showing the flag, isn't enough by itself; if you just wanted to show the flag, you could do it with a rowboat. To be effective, a navy also has to have power—what modern-day naval strategists call "posture"—that can be projected across vast distances. One of the navy's first demonstrations of American "posture" in the Pacific came in 1831, after Malay pirates on the island of Sumatra attacked an American merchant ship and killed three sailors. President Andrew Jackson dispatched the sail frigate USS *Potomac* to "chastise" the pirates—and chastise them the *Potomac* did, sending a force of sailors and marines ashore at the village of Kuala Batu, killing 150 Malay fighters. That cooled things down for a while, but then in 1838 there was another massacre of an American merchant crew by the Malays, after which the navy sent two frigates to bombard two Malay villages. That, along with British and Dutch antipiracy efforts in the region, helped quell widespread piracy in the Malacca Strait.

Of far more historical import than fighting pirates was the

U.S. Navy's dramatic "opening" of Japan. Back in 1853, America was feeling substantial annoyance at Japan's refusal to trade with Western nations and its harsh treatment of shipwrecked sailors. So that year Commodore Matthew Perry sailed uninvited into Edo (now Tokyo) Bay with his famous "black ships"—three combination sail- and steam-powered warships and one sailing sloop, armed with technologically advanced cannons. After a campaign of threats and intimidation—but no actual fighting—Perry forced the Japanese to sign a treaty and open two ports to American ships. The shock of their weakness in the face of Western sea power launched Japan on a course of modernization, militarism, and territorial expansion that would last until 1945.

Commodore George Dewey and ships of the navy's "Asiatic Squadron" made short work of the antiquated Spanish fleet when they sailed into Manila Bay in 1898, sinking eight Spanish ships, killing scores of Spanish sailors, and suffering only one American dead—of heatstroke—while wresting the Philippines away from Spain. The victory gave America its first large territorial acquisition in the Western Pacific, and it also set off a vicious guerilla war with Filipinos seeking full independence. It was the start of the complicated love-hate relationship between Americans and Filipinos that persists to this day.

The navy didn't have much to do in the Pacific in World War I, but the early twentieth century did see a rise in the navy's "gunboat diplomacy" in China. Since the mid-1800s the navy's Yangtze River Patrol had shown the U.S. flag on China's major rivers, protecting American merchant interests and missionaries from bandits and warlords. Small and lightly armed with only a few machine guns, the navy gunboats penetrated as far as twelve hundred miles inland from the coast—the equivalent of Chinese gunboats entering the Mississippi at New Orleans and steaming all the way past Minneapolis. As depicted in the Steve McQueen

film epic *The Sand Pebbles*, the presence of armed American and
other nations' vessels plying their inland waters deeply offended
Chinese nationalists' sensibilities—and the memory of it hasn't
faded much.

And then came Pearl Harbor.

It's not this book's purpose to recount the epic naval battles fought on and over and under Pacific waters during World
War II—Coral Sea, Midway, Leyte Gulf, Okinawa. It's enough
to note that when the war ended with the Japanese surrender on
the deck of the USS *Missouri* in September 1945, this is where
the U.S. Navy stood in relation to the navies of its enemy and its
allies in the Pacific Theater:

By September 1945 Japan's navy had been annihilated. Twenty-
five aircraft carriers, eleven great battleships, and hundreds of
other ships lay rusting on the bottom of the ocean, along with
the remains of more than four hundred thousand Japanese sailors
and navy aviators—ten times the number of U.S. Navy combat
deaths. The British Royal Navy, at the start of the war the biggest
navy in the world, had concentrated on the Atlantic and played
only a small role in the war against Japan; in 1945 it had about six
hundred major combatant ships—carriers, battleships, cruisers,
destroyers, submarines—but with Britain broke and its empire soon
to crumble, the Royal Navy would never regain its prewar status.
The Australian navy, in 1945 the fourth-largest navy in the world,
with more than three hundred ships, likewise would no longer be
able to send large fleets to sea. The once great Dutch navy, which
had ruled Southeast Asia in the seventeenth century, had been
almost completely destroyed by the Japanese in the early months
of the war, and the semi-collaborationist French navy had been
reduced by half. The Philippines, Indonesia, Malaysia, Vietnam,
Korea—they had no navies at all, and China's navy consisted of
a few riverine gunboats.

Compare that to the U.S. Navy. In 1945 the navy had almost *seven thousand ships*, about fifteen hundred of them major combatant ships. Of all the large navy ships in all the world, 70 percent of them flew the American flag. Starting from about three hundred thousand personnel in 1941, the navy had grown to 3.4 million men and tens of thousands of women. It could go anywhere in the world and do anything the nation's leaders ordered without any serious challenge from anyone. In all of human history there had never been such a navy on a global scale—and chances are there never will be again.

Of course, after the war the navy was dramatically downsized, with hundreds of carriers, battleships, cruisers, destroyers, and other ships being cut up, mothballed, or, in the case of the smaller ships, given or sold to U.S. allies like the Republic of China. But despite the cutbacks, by the beginning of the Cold War in 1947 the navy could still muster more than eight hundred ships of all types, including a dozen aircraft carriers. No other navy in the world could challenge it.

But there was one navy that was willing to try.

The Soviet Union sat out the war with Japan until just before Japan surrendered, so its relatively small navy played no role in the conflict. In the Cold War the Soviets tried to counter U.S. Navy superiority with a huge fleet of submarines, both as anti-ship weapons and later—with the introduction of sub-launched nuclear ballistic missiles—as strategic weapons. Although the Soviets built a few small aircraft carriers, most of their surface fleet was designed to support the submarine fleet and to conduct antisub warfare against U.S. Navy ships.

The Cold War was a more than four-decade-long era of naval confrontation and brinksmanship around the world, the Pacific included. Soviet ballistic-missile subs lurked off the California coast, MiG fighters buzzed navy ships, Soviet "fishing trawlers" packed with electronic eavesdropping gear shadowed navy ships. The trawlers, known as AGIs (auxiliary general intelligence), were a particular pain, parking themselves outside U.S. naval bases and sometimes interfering with U.S. aircraft carrier operations; on occasion U.S. destroyers had to "shoulder" a trawler out of the way of a carrier. Unfortunately for the navy, although the trawlers looked their part, they were manned by professional Soviet naval officers who were not easily discouraged.

Naturally there were incidents—spy planes shot down, Soviet ships and trawlers intentionally bumping into U.S. ships and vice versa, submarines colliding. For example, in 1957 the diesel sub USS *Gudgeon* was cornered by Soviet destroyers while it was snooping outside the Soviet naval base at Vladivostok; after repeated depth-charging the American sub surfaced and was allowed to go on its way. In 1968 the attack sub USS *Scorpion* was lost with all ninety-nine crewmen while it was returning from a patrol in the Atlantic; an onboard battery explosion is believed to have sunk the American sub. In 1970 the nuclear-powered attack sub USS *Tautog* was shadowing a Soviet nuclear missile sub in the Northern Pacific when the Soviet sub made a radical turn—known as a "Crazy Ivan"—and slammed into the *Tautog*'s sail (sometimes mistakenly called a "conning tower" by civilians). The Soviet sub reportedly broke up and sank while the *Tautog* limped back to port; not until decades later did the U.S. learn that the Soviet sub had in fact survived.

The list of fatal or near-fatal Cold War mishaps could go on. But while it may sound strange, many current and former U.S. Navy officers and sailors look back at the Cold War with a sense of—well, nostalgia. Yes, the navy played roles in the Korean and Vietnam wars, with carrier air strikes and shore bombardments and amphibious landings. But those were primarily ground wars, with the navy projecting power from sea to land.

Here's how one former junior officer who served on a destroyer in the 1980s remembers those exciting Cold War days when the navy performed an important global function in the nation's defense at sea:

> It was an exciting time. We were dealing face-to-face with the Soviets, they'd chase us around, we'd reciprocate—it was a testosterone test. You'd get an adrenaline rush on every watch. We'd go to one of their op areas during a fleet exercise, put out sonobuoys, then get into a little whale boat to pick them up. And we actually thought this was a good idea! We're in a little DDG [destroyer], there's one cruiser with us, and meanwhile there are thirty Russian ships out there and they've got MiGs loaded with munitions flying right over our mast. But nobody wanted to back down. We were doing this for our country, and I'm sure they [the Soviets] were doing much the same thing. I look at it now, I mean, talk about stupid, you're on the edge of killing people. It was fortunate we didn't have more bad things happen out there. But all in all, it was a great experience.

A great experience! That may be hard for civilians to understand. But going face-to-face with the Soviet navy gave American sailors a sense of seriousness and immediacy that no training exercise could ever provide. Generations of American sailors spent their entire navy careers knowing just who the enemy was.

And then, almost overnight, it was over. The Soviet Union collapsed in 1991, and the new Russian Federation couldn't afford to send ships to sea, much less build more. The Soviet naval threat was finished—although it's arguable whether that naval threat had been quite as great as it appeared. Like so many other things built in the Soviet Union, from cars to washing machines, Soviet naval construction suffered from quality-control problems. For much of the earlier part of the Cold War, Soviet subs were notoriously noisy, and thus easy to track. As for their surface fleet, that same former young navy officer who thought being surrounded by a fleet of Soviet ships was scary also recalls visiting one of those ships, a cruiser, soon after the Cold War ended. It still bristled with weaponry, but the young American officer also found hatches that wouldn't close and decades-old layers of paint covering rusting steel.

Predictably, the end of the Cold War brought drastic cuts to the U.S. Navy. In 1990 the navy had almost six hundred ships of all types; a little over two decades later it was down by more than half, to under three hundred ships. Of course, raw ship numbers don't necessarily define a navy's power and capabilities; for example, one modern guided-missile destroyer equipped with the latest electronic targeting systems and anti-ship missiles could easily wipe out an entire fleet of early Cold War–era destroyers. But there's no doubt that since the end of the Cold War the navy's ability to project both "presence" and "posture" in the Pacific and around the world has declined.

Still, compared with other countries, the U.S. Navy remains the overwhelmingly most powerful navy in the world. It's also the world's most expensive, with a yearly base budget of about $155.4 billion and a plan to spend about $826.4 billion between 2017 and 2021. Given that price tag, an American taxpayer might legitimately wonder: What kind of a navy is it? As America is not involved in an officially declared shooting war, what exactly does the U.S. Navy do out there in the Pacific Ocean?

If a place dedicated to warfare can ever be called lovely, then Camp H.M. Smith is easily one of the loveliest military bases in the world. A former navy hospital complex in World War II, named after Marine General Holland M. "Howlin' Mad" Smith, it sits on a lush hillside overlooking Pearl Harbor, its low buildings almost blindingly white, its grounds dappled with palm trees swaying in the tropical breeze. It's also the nerve center of the U.S. military in the Pacific region, a "unified combatant command" called Pacific Command or PACOM.

The U.S. military divides up the world into six regional combatant commands that report directly to the U.S. secretary of defense, and through him or her to the president. Northern Command (NORTHCOM) handles North America, Central Command (CENTCOM) covers the Middle East, Europe Command (EUCOM) handles Europe, and so on. (There are also three worldwide combatant commands that oversee special operations, nuclear weapons and space technology, and military transport.) Each combatant command is headed by a four-star admiral or general who exercises operational control over all U.S. military units in that region—navy, marines, army, air force. The idea is that if the different military branches are all working under the same chain of command, they'll cooperate better and not fall into the bitter interservice rivalries that historically characterized the U.S. military; the military refers to this as "jointness," and to some degree it works.

By far the biggest combatant command geographically is Pacific Command, covering more than 100 million square miles and stretching from the U.S. West Coast to the western coast of India and from the South Pole to the North Pole—or, as some say, "from Hollywood to Bollywood and from penguins to polar bears." (Unlike other combatant commands, because of its large naval component Pacific Command has nearly always been headed by an admiral.) Pacific Command comprises about 140,000 sailors, 86,000 marines, 106,000 army soldiers, 46,000 air force personnel, about 2,500 aircraft of all types, and about 200 ships including submarines and support vessels—nearly half of the navy's entire worldwide fleet.

That may sound like a lot of ships—but remember, this is the Pacific. Remember also that at any given moment, only about a third of the navy's combatant ships are fully ready for sea duty. For every ship that's out there, there's one of the same type that's undergoing major maintenance and modifications, and another of the same type that's doing "workups" to train and test the crew and the ship in preparation for sea duty. In other words, when you consider the navy's ship numbers and its ability to maintain both presence and posture in the Pacific, divide by three.

The ships in the Pacific Fleet come in a range of sizes, with a range of missions. There are eleven small (about two hundred feet long) wooden-hulled mine countermeasures ships, and five large (more than eight hundred feet long) amphibious assault ships that can carry a battalion of marines to a hostile shore. There are thirty-five guided-missile destroyers in the fleet, and nearly a dozen cruisers like the USS *Cowpens*. There are about thirty Pacific-based nuclear-powered fast-attack submarines that can kill other subs and ships and launch land-attack cruise missiles, a couple of Ohio-class guided-missile subs that can launch Tomahawks from under water, and about eight Ohio-class subs with nuclear ballistic missiles to provide a deterrent against a first-strike nuclear attack on the U.S. There are also littoral combat ships like the *Freedom* (more on those later), "ocean surveillance ships" (read "spy ships"), and navy-controlled but largely civilian-manned "replenishment ships" to deliver oil and other supplies to ships at sea. But at the core of the navy's ability to project tactical power across the Pacific are the nuclear-powered "super-carriers."

The carriers are the glamour boys, the ships that Hollywood makes movies about; they're also the first thing a U.S. president thinks about when there's trouble in some far corner of the world and the U.S. needs to apply presence and posture in a hurry. Currently there are eleven carriers in the U.S. fleet, of which five are assigned to Pacific-anchored naval bases. But let's pick one—say, the USS *Ronald Reagan*, commissioned in 2003 and home-ported at Yokosuka naval base in Japan, formally known as the U.S. Fleet Activities Yokosuka. (As of 2016 the *Reagan* was the only carrier that was forward-based outside the U.S.; all the others were home-ported in the U.S.)

Obviously the first thing you notice about the *Reagan* is how enormous it is. It's almost eleven hundred feet long—nearly four football fields—with a superstructure that towers twenty stories above the waterline; at ninety thousand tons displacement, it's far bigger than the aircraft carriers of World War II. It's not the biggest ship in the world—there are cruise ships and oil tankers and container ships that are much bigger—but it's big.

Its crew is enormous as well, with about thirty-two hundred officers and crew permanently assigned to the ship, along with another twenty-five hundred aircrew members—pilots, aircraft mechanics, and so on—who are aboard while the carrier is deployed. Because of the sheer size of ship and crew, carriers are often described as being like small cities—and it's true the *Ronald Reagan* has some citylike features.

For example, there's a kind of community center (the "welcome room" for visiting guests) decorated by Nancy Reagan herself, with plush red curtains, plush red chairs, plush red everything; Mrs. Reagan liked red. There are restaurants (mess halls) ranging from the upscale Rancho del Cielo mess hall for high-ranking officers and visiting VIPs down to more cafeteria-like messes for enlisted ranks; there are also Starbucks-style coffee shops and an Internet café with a sign that says "Loose Tweets Sink Ships!" There's a hospital (sick bay) and dental office staffed with navy MDs and DDSs, a church (chapel) with stained glass windows and a staff of chaplains and "religious facilitators" of various faiths.

There's a library, a fitness center, a TV station and radio station, a small jail (brig). Aboard the ship there are paralegals (known as "legalmen") and accountants (finance officers) and cops (masters at arms). There's even a ship's psychologist.

So sure, a carrier like the *Ronald Reagan* has some resemblance to a city. On the other hand, what small city with a population of almost six thousand souls has an average age of just nineteen? What small city is 85 percent male and 15 percent female—and has "non-fraternization" rules that strictly forbid that 85 percent and that 15 percent from so much as holding hands in the movie theater? In what small city does the vast majority of the population share tiny staterooms or sleep in bunks or "racks" stacked three high, sixty racks to a berthing room, with communal toilets and showers? And what small city's municipal airport is crammed with ninety or so airplanes and other aircraft laden with bombs and missiles?

No, a carrier like the *Ronald Reagan* isn't a small city; it's a giant warship—emphasis on the "war." Referring to its displacement weight, some navy officers and shipbuilder executives sardonically describe the *Reagan* as "ninety thousand tons of diplomacy"—and while that's partly true, the diplomacy a ship like the *Reagan* carries out is hard diplomacy, not soft.

In fact, it's because of its war-making mission that the *Reagan* and all U.S. Navy ships require such large crews. The biggest civilian container ships in the world, ships that are even bigger than the *Reagan*, require only a dozen or so crewmembers to man them at sea, with automated systems doing most of the work. That's because a civilian cargo ship's only mission is to get from point A to point B without sinking. A carrier like the *Reagan* has to get from point A to point B without sinking, too, but it also has to be prepared to wage war along the way—and that requires manpower.

Unlike the old battleships, the *Reagan* and other carriers do not bristle with offensive weaponry—big naval guns, Tomahawk guided missiles, and so on. The *Reagan's* sole offensive weapon is its aircraft—F/A-18 Hornet and Super Hornet fighters, EA-18G Growler electronic warfare aircraft, Seahawk helicopters.

Although the *Reagan* carries a few last-ditch self-defense weapons—some Sea Sparrow missiles, a bullet-spitting close-in defense gun, a few machine guns—without its aircraft the *Reagan* and every other carrier would basically be an oversized gunboat. It is designed to project airpower hundreds of miles away, not to protect itself from attack. For that you have the "small boys."

As noted earlier, no aircraft carrier goes anywhere alone. Instead it's the center of a "carrier strike group." Although strike group compositions vary, usually there'll be one or two guided-missile cruisers like the USS *Cowpens* and two or three smaller Arleigh Burke–class guided-missile destroyers surrounding the carrier at sea. The destroyers' and cruisers' missions can be offensive—launching cruise missiles—or defensive—protecting the carrier from incoming missiles or finding and destroying enemy subs. The carrier strike group may also include one or two Los Angeles–class attack subs that can launch cruise missiles or sniff out lurking enemy subs. As a nuclear-powered ship, the carrier could circle the Earth for decades without refueling, but it still needs fuel for the planes, and the small boys need fuel for their engines, which can burn a thousand gallons or more per hour. (The navy spends about $4 billion just on fuel every year.) So to round out the strike group there may also be a "fast combat support ship" that's crammed with millions of gallons of diesel and jet fuel and tons of food and munitions.

It's almost impossible to convey the complexity—and intensity—of a navy aircraft carrier strike group operating at sea. Radar systems, navigation systems, sonar systems, electronic warfare systems, weapons systems, fuel systems, firefighting and damage control systems—the ships bristle with them, many of them redundant, serving as backups to backups to backups in case of malfunction or combat casualty. And twenty-four hours a day, seven days a week, for weeks at a time, thousands of mostly young men and women are either operating those systems or checking them or fixing them—or practicing what to do in case something goes wrong.

Every sailor on every ship in the strike group has his or her specific job, most of them requiring extensive training. On a cruiser, a damage controlman pulls on a fire-resistant suit, hood, and helmet, and goes racing with her team toward a simulated fire during a drill, or heads to the helicopter flight deck to stand by in case of a crash. Deep inside the hull of a destroyer, a sonar technician (surface) stares at a display screen and listens on headphones, trying to separate the sounds of waves breaking and the *glup-glup-glup* of fishing boats from the faint whirrs and clicks of a submarine. On deck a boatswain's mate (pronounced "bosun's mate") goes through the checklist of all the equipment his or her team will have to maintain or repair that day—boat davits, anchor chains, refueling lines, and on and on. On a carrier, an aircrew survival equipmentman checks parachutes, life vests, rubber rafts—everything a pilot needs if he or she winds up in the water—while a culinary specialist (they don't call them cooks anymore) helps prepare the eighteen thousand meals that are served on a carrier every single day.

The number of specialized tasks is almost endless. On a cruiser, a ship's serviceman makes sure the ship's store is stocked and the vending machines are full and the washing machines in the laundry room are working. In the engine room, where temperatures can sometimes hit 115 degrees, a gas turbine systems technician sweats over engines that produce more than 150,000 horsepower. In the hangar deck of a carrier, an aviation machinist's mate who earns a base pay of about $27,000 a year takes apart a million-dollar jet engine. And on and on. Although shifts vary with the job, almost all day every day, sailors are either working, studying for qualification tests to advance in grade, getting ready for the frequent inspections, or just cleaning the ship; at sea, eighteen-hour days aren't at all unusual.

Despite the long hours, if you ask a group of young sailors about their navy jobs, you'll hear words like "exciting," "intense," "fun." (Maybe that's predictable; in the all-volunteer military, malcontents and total slackers usually don't last long.) That damage controlman? She insists her job is the most important one on the ship. That sonar tech (surface)? He brags to his friends about getting to "see"—that is, hear—submarines. That gas turbine systems technician in the 115-degree engine room of a cruiser? He talks about the power of those engines like they were his own personal motorcycle.

Young sailors also talk about the close friendships, the camaraderie of shipmates. Occasionally, when schedules allow, there are volleyball games in a hangar deck or "steel beach picnics" on a fantail, featuring barbeque and soft drinks. Navy ships have officially been "dry" for more than a century, but if a ship has been continuously at sea for more than forty-five days it may qualify for a "beer day" celebration—at which each crewmember gets exactly two beers.

And of course sailors talk about the "port calls," the shore visits to exotic locales that are one of the prime selling points for every navy recruiter—although port calls in the new navy aren't quite what they were in the old navy. The occasional "beer day" notwithstanding, the navy strongly discourages excessive alcohol use ashore, especially in foreign ports—partly for the sailors' own good and partly to avoid unpleasant international incidents. That's why when a ship makes a port call at Hong Kong or Singapore or Subic Bay, the ship's sailors are encouraged to sign up for such healthy organized endeavors as mountain bike rides, museum tours, visits to local schools and cultural attractions, and so on. Most sailors take advantage of those opportunities; others take a more traditional route and head straight for the bars and other less cultured cultural attractions.

As you might expect when so many people are working around so much equipment and machinery at sea, being aboard a navy ship can be dangerous, even in peacetime. Carriers are particularly susceptible.

The worst peacetime carrier accident in navy history happened in 1981, when an EA-6B Prowler electronic warfare plane trying to land on the USS *Nimitz* missed all of the arresting cables designed to stop the aircraft. The Prowler then collided with other planes on deck and exploded into flames; fourteen men were killed and forty-seven others injured. (After autopsies of six of the dead sailors showed signs of marijuana use, the Reagan administration implemented a military-wide policy of "zero tolerance" and routine mandatory drug testing. In practice the policy means that if you have a history of serious drug use you can't get into the navy, and if you pee dirty in a drug test you'll probably get kicked out of it.)

Mass casualties like the one on the *Nimitz* are rare. But on any carrier, a moment's inattention is an accident waiting to happen. Sailors miss a signal and get knocked down by a plane, or they stray too close to a jet blast deflector or engine intake; there's a video that captures a carrier crewman being sucked headfirst into a jet engine, and although he survives, his "cranial" (helmet) is sucked right off his head and destroys the engine. And you don't have to be on the flight deck to get hurt on a carrier. In 2010 a chief electrician's mate aboard the *Reagan* was electrocuted while doing maintenance work; five years before that a machinist's mate was scalded to death while working on a valve in the *Reagan*'s steam plant. The list could go on.

Faulty maintenance is another accident waiting to happen. For example, in March 2016 an E-2C Hawkeye landing on the USS *Eisenhower* caught the arresting cable, but as the cable stretched it snapped like a broken guitar string, sending it whipping back across the flight deck and leaving eight sailors with injuries ranging from bruises to broken bones to a fractured skull; the navy blamed poor maintenance of the arresting gear.

For carrier pilots the dangers are obvious. The navy has a designation known as "Class A Aviation Mishaps," meaning accidents that involve fatalities or serious damage to planes or ships. In one recent twenty-month period the navy reported fourteen hundred mishaps, with more than $4 billion in damages. Worse, in that same period, thirty-one navy and marine personnel were killed, among them a twenty-six-year-old Hornet pilot whose aircraft collided with another plane shortly after launching off the USS *Carl Vinson*; the only thing that was ever found was his flight helmet.

It can be dangerous on the small boys as well. In 2007, two sailors were scalded to death and eight others injured when a steam pipe burst aboard the submarine tender USS *Frank Cable*. In another, earlier accident, aboard the frigate USS *Thach*, a chief petty officer was killed when a helicopter rotor dipped and hit him in the head. In 2013 two navy fliers were killed aboard the destroyer USS *William P. Lawrence* when a wave washed their MH-60S Seahawk helicopter over the side. Less lethally, hatches get shut on feet, hands get caught in machinery, sailors fall out of their racks in heavy weather and hit their heads—a ship at sea offers plenty of opportunities to get hurt.

Sailors sometimes fall overboard—although sometimes it's not clear whether they fell or jumped. For example, in 2016 a female sailor aboard the dock landing ship USS *Carter Hall* went missing and was never found; a pair of boots with a note inside was found near the fantail rail. (As of this writing, the case is still under investigation.) Sometimes even well-honed rescue procedures can't save a sailor accidentally tossed overboard. In 2010 a sailor working near the rail of the cruiser USS *Shiloh* off the coast of Japan fell into the water, and although fellow sailors immediately threw him a life ring and had a rescue boat out in just minutes, he was never found. The same thing happened to a sailor who was chasing a football on the deck of a navy amphibious assault ship returning home from the war in Iraq; he fell over the side and was never seen again.

Modern navigation and meteorological systems allow navy ships to avoid the worst parts of typhoons, but sometimes there's no way to avoid heavy seas. It's not so bad on the carriers—they're like cruise ships—but for the small boys it can be daunting. Imagine trying to climb a flight of stairs (what the navy calls ladders) when the ship is climbing up waves and plunging into troughs and those stairs are rolling from side to side over a forty-five-degree arc; just getting from point A to point B can be exhausting, and if you aren't careful, dangerous. Sometimes it gets so bad that the CO will secure (close to foot traffic) the weather decks and order everyone not standing watch to stay in his or her bunk—which is why some sailors love bad storms. They get to catch up on their sleep.

Entire ships can have accidents as well—accidents that can be both expensive and embarrassing. For example, in 2009 the cruiser *Port Royal* ran aground on a reef as it left Pearl Harbor, causing $40 million in damage; the beached cruiser stayed there for four days in full view of passengers on flights coming into Honolulu International Airport. In 2013 the mine countermeasures ship USS *Guardian* ran aground on a reef in the Sulu Sea off the Philippines, causing extensive environmental damage; there were no serious injuries but the ship was a total loss. In both cases the commanding officers were relieved, their careers ruined.

For obvious reasons, submarines guided by sound and not by sight while underwater are particularly susceptible to collisions—such as the fatal collision with a seamount by the USS *San Francisco* in 2005. In 2009 the attack sub USS *Hartford* collided with the amphibious assault ship USS *New Orleans* in the Strait of Hormuz, causing more than $100 million in damage; the navy blamed inattentive crewmembers on the sub. In 2012 the attack sub USS *Montpelier* was hit by the cruiser USS *San Jacinto* when the sub popped up front of the cruiser during an antisubmarine warfare exercise; damages were estimated at $70 million. And in the worst sub collision in recent history, in 2001 the attack sub USS *Greeneville* was hosting a group of civilians on a day cruise off Hawaii when the captain ordered a demonstration of an "emergency ballast blow," a maneuver that causes a sub to shoot to the surface like a breaching whale. Unfortunately the sub came up directly under a Japanese fishery training boat, killing nine people aboard, including four Japanese high-school students. Seven months later, under another CO, the *Greeneville* ran aground when entering port in Saipan, and five months after that, under still another CO, the *Greeneville* collided with another navy ship.

Don't get the wrong idea. It's not as if U.S. Navy ships are banging into each other like bumper cars out there; given the millions of miles that navy ships collectively travel every year, collisions are rare. But with even a moment's inattention, they can happen.

And what do all those navy ships actually do when they're traveling those collective millions of miles? Well, consider the itineraries of some Pacific-based navy surface ships during one six-month period. (The navy usually doesn't supply detailed itineraries for its subs, especially the "boomers," the nuclear missile–carrying subs. The most they'll say about any given "boomer" is that on such and such a day it returned to its home port after a "strategic deterrence patrol.")

Start with a six-month itinerary for the USS *Ronald Reagan*. After four months of maintenance work it sails out of Yokosuka for four days of sea trials, then departs with the rest of its strike group for "summer patrol," steaming eight hundred miles to Okinawa to conduct "dual carrier flight operations" with the USS *John C. Stennis* carrier strike group. It then sails another thousand miles to the Philippines, transits the Strait of Luzon westbound into the South China Sea, after which it steams another two thousand miles back to Yokosuka following a total of seven weeks at sea. Three weeks later it has to do an "emergency sortie" out to sea to avoid an approaching typhoon—carriers are safer running away from a typhoon than riding one out at the dock. Two weeks after that it departs for its "fall patrol," sailing fifteen hundred miles to participate in a two-week-long joint exercise off the Mariana Islands with marine and air force units—a mission that includes a "sinking exercise" (known of course as a "SINKEX") in which carrier planes and helicopters fire live missiles at a decommissioned and thoroughly cleaned and detoxified U.S. Navy frigate, sending it to the bottom in water thirty thousand feet deep. After that the crew finally gets a five-day liberty in Guam.

To pick another ship, how about the guided-missile destroyer USS *Decatur*? During that same six-month period it departs its home port in San Diego as part of a three-destroyer "surface action group" and sails twenty-six hundred miles to Hawaii. Two days later it sets out for the four-thousand-mile trip to Yokosuka, after which it sails into the Sea of Japan for joint exercises with destroyers from the Korean navy. After that it stops for a couple days at the American naval base at Sasebo, on the southern Japanese island of Kyushu, then it steams south a thousand miles through the Taiwan Strait, then another nine hundred miles to the Luzon Strait, then another eighteen hundred miles or so back to Sasebo. Four days later the *Decatur* and its crew are at sea again, steaming about twenty-five hundred miles for a three-day port call at Changi Naval Base in Singapore, after which the ship sails all the way back to Sasebo to participate in a week of antisubmarine warfare exercises with the Japanese navy.

Or consider the aforementioned submarine tender USS *Frank Cable* during that same six-month period. The long (850 feet), slow (top speed 25 mph), and lightly armed (20mm cannons and several high-caliber machine guns) supply ship leaves its home port at Apra Harbor in Guam and steams about fourteen hundred miles to the Philippines, where it makes a couple of port calls. After that it sails more than four thousand miles through the Sunda Strait and halfway across the Indian Ocean to the navy support facility on the tiny island of Diego Garcia. After that it sails two thousand miles north to the Indian state of Goa on the subcontinent's west coast. After a six-day visit it sails another thirteen hundred miles across the Arabian Sea and through the Strait of Hormuz to the United Arab Emirates, where it provides supplies and support services to a U.S. Navy attack submarine. Two weeks later it starts back to Guam, with stops in Sri Lanka and the Philippines, and finally, accompanied by the destroyer USS *John S. McCain*, it makes a port call at the old American navy base (and later Soviet navy base) at Cam Ranh Bay in Vietnam; they are the first U.S. warships to visit that base since the end of the Vietnam War.

And remember, those schedules cited above represent just three navy ships, over the course of just six months. At any given moment there are tens of thousands of young American sailors and scores of navy ships out there in the Pacific, steaming hundreds of thousands of miles here and there, showing the flag at port calls, displaying "presence" and "posture." It's what the navy has done in the Pacific for more than two decades, ever since the end of the Cold War.

And yet, during those more than two decades, and for all those millions of miles traveled, and for all the hundreds of billions of dollars spent, the navy has not faced a serious enemy at sea in the Western Pacific.

True, the navy does conduct antiterrorism operations and training and support in the Philippines and elsewhere. It also provides relief from natural enemies such as typhoons. For example, after Typhoon Haiyan hit the Philippines, killing six thousand people, the navy dispatched a carrier strike group (including the USS *Cowpens*) and a thousand marines to provide relief supplies, medical treatment, and search and rescue.

But again, over the course of a generation, all those ships and all those sailors in the Western Pacific haven't faced a serious traditional enemy or even a potentially serious one at sea.

That is, until now. Now China and its naval and military forces are challenging the U.S. Navy on what was once America's ocean. And although admirals and think-tank analysts in Washington, D.C., may disagree about what that challenge means, and whether the Chinese navy is really an enemy or even a potential enemy, the situation seems pretty clear to the guys on the ground—or rather, on the water. Here's how one command master chief, a guy with more than twenty years in the navy, a dozen of them spent knocking around in frigates and destroyers and cruisers, describes the view from the deck of an American warship in the Western Pacific in the second decade of the twenty-first century:

"Every time you go out of Yokosuka, you have to remember that you're in the enemy's waters," the chief says. "You have to think like that, you have to breathe like that. You have to understand that at any given time, anything can happen. The Chinese are a lot more aggressive than they were ten or fifteen years ago. Their ships are getting a lot closer to ours, they're listening more, trying to understand us, taking our technology, learning from our technology. They're building more ships, their aircraft are getting more sophisticated, their subs are going further and further out [from their bases]. They're going to keep pushing us, see how far they can go, and it's going to escalate.

"The only question is, who's going to blink first?"

CHAPTER 3

Lieutenant Wu's New Navy

Lieutenant Wu Chao Huang is standing on the swaying deck of the Chinese missile destroyer *Haikou*, giving a briefing to two American journalists. Hands clasped behind his back, legs easily braced against the pitch and roll, Lieutenant Wu is young, good-looking, self-assured, and immaculate in a blue-green camouflage uniform with three gold stars on the collar. In almost perfect English, Wu is describing the impressive complexities and capabilities of the *Haikou* when his face suddenly darkens.

Nearby, on the aft end of the upper deck, three young sailors are attaching a red-and-yellow signal flag to a halyard. They, too, look sharp, in their cammies and matching baseball caps, but one of them looks a little different than the others. He has the sleeves of his uniform rolled up—and this is what has attracted Lieutenant Wu's attention.

Wu turns away from the foreign visitors and barks an order. The sailor in question reacts as if to an electric shock. He presents himself at attention in front of Wu, who leans forward and points to the sailor's bare forearms and then to his own crisply rolled down sleeves. Wu starts to speak in Chinese, not loudly but in a stern command voice. The American journalists can't pick it up, but it's clear that Lieutenant Wu is delivering unto the hapless young sailor a thorough and comprehensive ass-chewing.

Sailor, you are out of uniform! he seems to be saying. *It's unmilitary! It's a disgrace to the navy—and in front of foreigners, yet! Get yourself squared away—NOW!*

Chastened, the sailor quickly rolls down his sleeves, buttons them, and pats the wrinkles smooth. Wu turns back to the visitors, his face again composed and self-assured. Problem detected, problem corrected—and that young sailor won't make the same mistake again.

The trio of sailors hauls the red-and-yellow signal flag hand-over-hand to the top of the mainmast, where it snaps in the wind next to the red and gold-starred flag of the People's Republic. Lieutenant Wu points to the masthead and proudly tells the foreign visitors, "The flag means we are the leader."

He means that in more ways than one.

On this day in July 2014 the *Haikou* is the lead ship in a three-ship Chinese navy task force that's participating in the biannual Rim of the Pacific (RimPac) naval exercise in Hawaii and San Diego. (More on the RimPac exercise later.)

This is the first time the Chinese navy has participated in the naval exercise; it's also the first time ever that American journalists have been allowed aboard a People's Liberation Army Navy warship at sea. And it's clear that in the destroyer *Haikou*, and in Lieutenant Wu Chao Huang, the Chinese navy is putting its best on display.

On this day the *Haikou* is steaming under way about a hundred miles off the Hawaiian coast, with the frigate *Yueyang* and the replenishment ship *Qiandaohu* following behind, all in smart formation. (Another Chinese navy vessel, a medical ship named *Peace Ark*, also is at RimPac but isn't part of today's exercise.) The Chinese task force is conducting joint antiterrorism and antipiracy drills and air operations with the American cruiser USS *Port Royal*. As the Chinese and American ships turn and maneuver in unison, armed assault teams on rigid-hull inflatable boats zip from ship to ship, practicing their at-sea boarding skills. U.S. Navy Seahawks and a smaller Chinese navy Z-9 helicopter hover overhead.

Even while sailing near an American cruiser, the *Haikou* is an impressive ship. Commissioned in 2005 as one of the Luyang II–class of new-generation Chinese guided-missile destroyers, at just over five hundred feet the *Haikou* is almost as long as an American cruiser, and almost as fast. Its decks are spotless, the superstructure scraped free of any trace of rust, every ladder handrail polished. It is a showcase ship, a ship that is often selected for high-profile missions involving cooperation with foreign navies. (For example, in 2008 the *Haikou* was the flagship of a three-vessel Chinese task force dispatched to a joint international antipiracy effort in the Gulf of Aden—which, as we'll see, was the Chinese navy's first overseas operational deployment in almost *six hundred years*.)

And as a showcase ship, the *Haikou* also has a showcase crew.

No longer are Chinese navy ships mostly manned by two-year conscripts, draftees who just as they achieved a barely adequate level of training were released back to civilian life and replaced with a new crop of raw recruits. These days most enlisted personnel are long-term volunteers. The new system gives the Chinese navy a bigger pool of experienced young sailors to draw on for the junior and upper petty officer ranks. In the past, the Chinese navy ship crews consisted of officers and lowly sailors, without the middle ranks of tough, knowledgeable noncoms that form the sinew of any military organization. That is now changing—and the future result will be a better-trained, better-motivated, and more professional naval force.

The sailor with the rolled-up sleeves notwithstanding, aboard the *Haikou* that new professionalism is evident. Its virtually handpicked crewmembers carry out their duties with a snap and military bearing that should impress any U.S. Navy officer. The sailors' off-duty deportment is impeccable as well. In the enlisted men's mess, which resembles a small hospital cafeteria, the young sailors are polite and respectful, with only occasional boyish giggles over the presence of two American journalists. During shore leave the Chinese sailors are closely supervised; the Chinese navy brass wants no incidents, and there are none.

The *Haikou*'s junior officer contingent is also handpicked—Lieutenant Wu among them.

Wu is twenty-eight, a graduate of the Dalian Naval Academy, China's Annapolis—a military university that like Annapolis is extremely hard to get into. Like most young, career-minded surface warfare officers in any navy, Wu hopes to someday command a ship like the *Haikou*—or bigger. For now, though, he is the *Haikou*'s intelligence and electronic warfare officer. Although he doesn't say so, Wu also appears to be the *Haikou*'s "political officer"—the "commissar"—the man entrusted to serve as the back-channel eyes and ears of the Party. Officers of equal or even superior rank seem to defer to him.

"When I was a child, I wanted to join the navy," Wu tells the visiting journalists. "It was my dream. I just liked the warships. I liked the uniforms. I wanted to be a true man!"

Navy service may have been Wu's boyhood dream, but for him and other junior navy officers it's also a demanding and Spartan life. Junior officers like Wu earn the equivalent of about U.S. $800 a month, less than a similarly educated civilian professional in Beijing makes, and far less than one of their U.S. Navy counterparts. Time at sea is long, expectations high, discipline strict. Throughout the ship, signs remind officers and crew to "Maintain a strong and correct political position," and "Endeavor to build a strong, modern revolutionary force." In the junior officers' spotlessly clean and rigidly ordered four-bunk staterooms, each bunk displays a mug shot photo of a young officer along with a phrase in Chinese that translates as: "I was born, I must be useful" or "Be humble, work aggressively."

Those are the sort of group-over-the-individual exhortations common in countries whose names have the word "People's" in them. But Lieutenant Wu and other junior officers aboard the *Haikou* are not the mindless automatons of the old Western anti-Communist propaganda. Far from it.

Because of the Chinese government's one-child-only urban population control edict, and the Chinese cultural preference for sons, many of these young men are part of a male generation known in China as the "Little Emperors." As single children, single sons, they have grown up as the absolute center of their parents' and grandparents' universe, the bearer of all their hopes and aspirations—and with expectations to match. It doesn't take a child psychologist to figure out what effect the so-called Little Emperor Syndrome can have on the young male ego. Humble these young men are not. Almost to a man the young officers of the *Haikou* carry themselves with a determination that borders on swagger, and self-confidence that edges over into cockiness. Think Maverick and Iceman in *Top Gun*. They are an extraordinarily proud group of young men—proud of themselves, of their ship, of their navy, and of their country. And they are certain about their country's destiny.

It's a destiny clearly spelled out in the wildly popular and widely influential 2010 book *The China Dream: Great Power Thinking and Strategic Posture in the Post-American Era*. It was written by a retired People's Liberation Army colonel named Liu Mingfu, one of China's most respected military writers and international strategists—and even if they haven't all read it, the young officers of the *Haikou* are all certainly familiar with its theme.

In the book, Colonel Liu posits that America's historically brief time of worldwide hegemony is passing, and that it is China's manifest destiny to take America's place as the leader among the world's nations—starting in the Western Pacific. America will resist, the colonel says, the U.S. and China will initially fight a "warm war"—he uses that very phrase—for military and geopolitical hegemony in the region. There will be confrontations, shows of force, periodic crises. But in the end, the colonel says, China will prevail. And one reason it will prevail is this: Although it wants peace, China is not afraid of war. And America is.

The China Dream is not just a book; it's an attitude, one that Chinese president Xi Jinping has repeatedly invoked in public speeches. In fact, at the *Haikou*'s welcoming area there's a sign in Chinese that says "The Dream Begins Here." And the young officers aboard the *Haikou* embrace that dream.

It's not that they're hostile to America or Americans; they don't have the "capitalist running dog" vision of America their grandfathers had. But as far as they are concerned, America is the past, and China is the future. And at an informal gathering with the visiting journalists in the officers' wardroom, speaking in passable English, they aren't afraid to say so.

Yes, the young officers say, when they were boys in the late 1990s and early 2000s they looked to America for inspiration—the music, the movies, the economic opportunity. It seemed so golden! But now look at the new China, how far it has come in so short a time. Look at the skyscrapers, the industry, the shopping malls filled with every conceivable luxury and latest high-tech wonder. Look at the Chinese economy, the second-biggest economy in the world—and soon the biggest! Look at the new Chinese navy. In the number of combatant, patrol, and support ships it is now the biggest navy in the world, with more than 450 ships, including the new *Liaoning* aircraft carrier—and although it trails the

U.S. Navy in gross tonnage and certainly in aircraft carriers, the young officers suggest that China's second-place naval status in the Western Pacific won't last for long.

No, they say, of course they don't want war with America. They want peace! But if it comes right down to it—well, man for man and ship for ship, the U.S. Navy better look out.

It's an attitude that informs every conversation as Lieutenant Wu later leads the visiting American journalists on a tour of the *Haikou*'s various weapons systems.

That 100mm gun on the *Haikou*'s main deck, a *Star Wars*–looking cannon that can hurl four-inch-diameter rounds at ships and incoming missiles or aircraft? According to Lieutenant Wu it equals—or even surpasses—anything the U.S. can offer in anti-ship and antimissile naval artillery. Those unseen missiles resting in vertical launch pods, the lids of which line the *Haikou*'s deck like rows of giant manhole covers? Without being too specific about it, Wu suggests that the *Haikou*'s vertical launching system is superior to the American systems, and that the ship's missiles can go farther, faster, with more destructive power than anything the U.S. Navy has deployed. The *Haikou*'s complex array of target tracking radars and fire control systems? Again, without being too specific—and no pictures of the equipment, please—Wu explains that it is at least the equal of the American navy's Aegis Combat System.

"What the U.S. Navy has, we have," Lieutenant Wu says. And his expression suggests that what the Chinese navy has is probably better.

Is all of that true? Or is it simply boastful propaganda? U.S. analysts agree that the *Haikou*'s air defense and anti-ship missiles may have a greater range than similar missiles aboard U.S. warships. And its array of surface-skimming "ship killer" missiles may be updated and more deadly supersonic versions of the older subsonic types. But can the *Haikou*'s complex tracking and control systems adequately deploy those weapons? Can the Chinese navy's increasingly professional but still relatively inexperienced crews handle that advanced technology in combat at sea? Those are open questions.

But whether Lieutenant Wu's boasts about the *Haikou*'s capabilities are accurate or not isn't the point. And whether China is actually destined to become the next region-dominating naval superpower isn't the point, either.

The point is that Lieutenant Wu and other officers throughout the Chinese navy *believe* those things to be true. They believe the Chinese navy will surpass the U.S. Navy in technology and warfighting capabilities within the next decade or so. They believe that China will soon end the United States' decades-long naval hegemony in the Western Pacific.

It's been said that for any nation to actually believe its own propaganda is a dangerous thing—an observation that might also apply to a nation's future generation of senior military commanders.

And by that standard, Lieutenant Wu's new Chinese navy may be a dangerous adversary indeed.

"The Chinese navy." For centuries the very phrase was considered by Western navies to be an oxymoron, a contradiction in terms, a sailor's joke. For Westerners, the Chinese navy set the standard for everything a navy shouldn't be. Generations of tough old navy master chiefs would respond to any instance of incompetence, sloth, or unseamanlike behavior on the part of their sailors with a shouted "What the hell do you think this is, the goddam Chinese navy?"

The attitude has been so deeply and so long ingrained that remnants of it still exist today, even in the face of contradictory

facts. For example, during the RimPac exercise an American reporter happens to mention to the captain of a non-U.S. Western
warship that he has recently been aboard a Chinese destroyer—at
which point the captain rolls his eyes and says dismissively, "Oh,
the *Chinese* navy."

U.S. Navy officers are more circumspect. Officially, on the
record, they will acknowledge China's strides in creating a modern
naval force. But unofficially, in background, many junior and midlevel navy officers take a more condescending view. Yes, they'll say,
China can build modern ships, and maybe develop sophisticated
high-tech weapons systems. But hey, let's face it, as sailors, as
warfighters, they'll *never* be as good as us.

(That's not quite the same as the American army general who in
the fall of 1950, after first encountering Chinese People's Liberation
Army troops near the Yalu River in Korea, exhorted his soldiers
to "not let a bunch of Chinese laundrymen stop you"—and then
watched a few weeks later as those "laundrymen" sent his bloodied
troops reeling back across the 38th Parallel. Still, underestimating
the enemy has been a frequent miscalculation in American military
history. American navy officers today would be wise not to make
the same mistake with the new Chinese navy.)

Of course, traditionally there has been a strong element of
racism in Western attitudes toward China and its naval capability—although it's worth noting that after Japan entered the
modern world in the late nineteenth century, it, too, looked down
on its Asian neighbor's naval forces with contempt.

But racism doesn't explain it all. There is history involved.
Certainly there were individual instances of courage and initiative
in the history of the Chinese naval forces. But the fact is that as
a cohesive and effective fighting force, for most of the past six
centuries the Chinese navy was about as significant as the naval
forces of landlocked Paraguay.

But it was not always so.

In the Chinese port city of Taicang in Jiangsu Province, on the south bank of the Yangtze River, an enormous bronze statue of a man dressed in traditional Chinese robes looks out toward the distant sea. Some fifty feet tall and weighing fifty tons, the statue is the centerpiece of a 120-hectare park built to memorialize China's greatest naval figure—the fifteenth-century Admiral Zheng He. In addition to the statue, the park features a massive exhibition hall and a two-hundred-foot-long replica of one of Zheng He's ships.

In sheer size, Admiral Zheng He's park dwarfs any Western monument to a naval hero; compared with Zheng He's statue, the figure of Lord Nelson perched atop the spire in London's Trafalgar Square looks like a hood ornament. But what's most interesting about the Zheng He statue and memorial park is that they aren't some monument to a contemporary great national hero. Instead, the statue and the park were built in 2008, almost six centuries after Admiral Zheng He sailed his last sea. In fact, the Zheng He memorial park in Taicang is only one of a number of imposing monuments built in recent years to honor the great navigator.

It's almost impossible to imagine twenty-first-century Americans spending millions of dollars to put up a fifty-foot-tall bronze statue in honor of Bull Halsey or John Paul Jones or Christopher Columbus; in Columbus's case, many twenty-first-century Americans would be more likely to tear such a statue down. The fact that the Chinese have invested so heavily in these modern tributes to an ancient admiral says a lot about what China once was—and what it wants to be again.

Zheng He was a member of the Chinese Muslim Hui people who at age eleven was captured and emasculated by Imperial Chinese troops, then pressed into service in the emperor's vast corps of eunuchs. Rising through the ranks as a soldier and diplomat, in 1403 Zheng He began a series of voyages as commander of one of the Ming emperor's so-called treasure fleets. His mission: to sail across the Southern and Western Seas and extract homage to the emperor from the "barbarian nations."

The size and nature of Zheng He's treasure fleets stagger the imagination. On his first voyage to the Indian Ocean, Zheng He reportedly commanded twenty-seven thousand sailors and troops aboard a fleet of some 250—passenger ships, fighting ships, supply ships, troop ships, ships for cavalry horses. The flagship of this vast armada was said to be a nine-masted, junk-rigged monster that was six hundred feet long, could carry up to a thousand passengers and crew, and was equipped with such modern features as watertight compartments and seawater desalination systems.

Even allowing for exaggeration—a six-hundred-foot wooden ship strains nautical engineering credulity—it must have been something to see. Certainly Zheng He's ships made Columbus's ninety-foot-long *Santa Maria* or Vasco da Gama's eighty-eight-foot *São Gabriel* look like rowboats. At that moment, China's navy was the most powerful maritime force in the history of the world, its treasure fleets the fifteenth-century equivalent of U.S. aircraft carrier strike groups.

Over the next three decades Zheng He made seven long voyages, to Southeast Asia, India, Ceylon, Africa, the Strait of Hormuz. (Some writers have suggested, with scant to nonexistent evidence, that elements of Zheng He's fleets even made it to the Americas.) Along the way he gained obeisance to the Chinese Son of Heaven from dozens of foreign kings and potentates. He also brought back to China barbarian envoys, concubines for the emperor's harem, and a variety of exotic gifts: lions, leopards, zebras, ostriches, and most sensationally, giraffes.

It's now a popular historical guessing game to wonder what

would have happened if China had continued its overseas naval explorations. Would China have dominated nineteenth-century Europe, and not the other way around? Would North Americans today be speaking Mandarin?

Maybe. But it didn't happen that way. Instead, China's role as the world's foremost sea power vanished in a historical instant. In 1433, during his seventh voyage, Zheng He died at sea. In China a new emperor took the throne, an emperor who wasn't interested in barbarians or expensive voyages of exploration. Further voyages were banned, the records of past voyages destroyed, the treasure fleets left rotting at the wharves—and China turned inward for the next almost six centuries.

Until relatively recently, the story of Admiral Zheng He and the treasure fleets was largely forgotten in the People's Republic; the glorification of pre-Revolutionary heroes was not generally sanctioned. But with China's expansion as a naval power, today every Chinese schoolchild knows about the great admiral. (Zheng He was also the subject of a hugely popular 2009 dramatic mini-series on China Central TV, the government-controlled national network.) In today's China, Zheng He is both a national hero and a psychological inspiration: The Chinese public thinks, "We were a great naval and global power once; we can be again."

Zheng He's voyages are also a talking point. The Chinese government likes to officially portray them as peaceful affairs, just as they officially portray China's current naval expansion as peaceful in nature. As one Chinese government official put it, "During the overall course of the seven voyages to the Western Ocean, Zheng He did not occupy a single piece of land, establish any fortress or seize any wealth from other countries. In the commercial and trade activities, he adopted the practice of giving more than he received, and thus he was welcomed and lauded by the people of the various countries along his routes."

Well, not exactly. It's true that Zheng He's fleets were so fearsome that most foreign leaders quickly buckled after seeing them, but the eunuch admiral didn't hesitate to use deadly force when necessary. For example, when the ruler of Ceylon wouldn't kowtow to China, Zheng's troops slaughtered thousands of Ceylonese—an incident that still burns in the memory of some modern-day Sri Lankans. Historically, the Chinese have been prone to cloak their aggressive actions with claims of seeking only Confucian-style harmony.

It's not accurate to say that China had no naval military history after the passing of the treasure fleets. There were periodic battles with pirates in the South China Sea and elsewhere, and Chinese emperors occasionally raised fleets for seaborne assaults against rebellious provinces or independent neighboring lands. But for four centuries, while Western nations and their navies built up world-spanning empires, China lacked any unified standing navy.

As a result, China was woefully unprepared for its first significant military clash with the West—the so-called Opium Wars of the mid-nineteenth century, when British warships bombarded Chinese cities after China tried to impose restrictions on British traders and ban the importation of Southwest Asian opium. Morally it was a sorry spectacle, akin to the Medellín cocaine cartel sending a fleet up New York City's East River to protect crack dealers in the Bronx. But as a naval action, it was a rousing British success, pitting Western iron steamships against sail- and oar-powered wooden Chinese junks. The Brits blew them out of the water.

The Opium Wars and the "unequal treaties" that followed were the beginning of what is known—and still painfully remembered—in China today as the "Century of Humiliation" at the hands of the West. England, Russia, France, the U.S., Germany, even Japan—all carved out interests in China without regard to

Chinese law or public opinion. It's impossible to overstate how much that humiliation, now long forgotten by most Westerners, still shapes Chinese popular and strategic thought, infusing them with both paranoia and the entitlement of victimhood.

Even back then, Chinese strategists realized that while through sheer force of numbers China could stand against the West on land, it could not fully protect itself without a viable navy. During the last half of the nineteenth century the Qing Dynasty tried to modernize its naval forces, as Japan was doing, buying battleships, cruisers, and other modern vessels from England, France, Germany. But China's sailors were poorly trained conscripts with low social status, its navy officers too often corrupt and incompetent, its ships not properly maintained. In subsequent nineteenth-century naval wars with France and Japan, the Chinese fleets were routinely sent to the bottom while hardly putting a scratch on the opposing forces.

It was a situation that persisted through World War II. At its best the Republic of China's navy consisted of a few old destroyers and riverine gunboats; it played no significant role in the war against Japan. Afterward, the Nationalists were equipped with some captured Japanese destroyers and outdated American navy ships. But again the navy played little role in the civil war against Mao Zedong's Communist forces, other than to help ferry Chiang Kai-shek and a million Nationalist followers to Taiwan following their defeat by the Communists in 1949.

As for the People's Republic, the very name of its waterborne force reflected its subservient role to the nation's land forces: The People's Liberation Army Navy, or PLAN. Its commanders and senior officers were not navy admirals but rather army generals; not until the late 1980s would the Chinese navy be commanded by a career navy man. At the start the navy's equipment consisted of a few old captured Nationalist destroyers and torpedo boats.

In the 1950s the navy acquired some Soviet Union destroyers and cruisers, along with thousands of Soviet navy advisors; later it began to develop a fleet of diesel-powered attack submarines and missile boats, and to lay the foundations for a fleet of nuclear-powered submarines.

But until only recently the Chinese navy was first and foremost a riverine and coastal defense force, a so-called brown-water navy, able to operate in conjunction with limited-range land-based aircraft and missile batteries but unable to project power much beyond sight of China's shores. In the event of hostilities Chinese navy doctrine called for a "guerilla war at sea." Simply put, the doctrine envisioned waves of small vessels—gunboats, torpedo boats, small missile boats—engaging larger enemy vessels in almost suicidal mass attacks just offshore.

But guerilla wars at sea could not solve the new China's basic strategic problem.

After the Chinese civil war, the People's Republic's two-million-man-plus ground forces were more than sufficient to face down the West, and also the Soviet Union after the Chinese-Russian split in the early 1960s. And as a closed and largely agrarian economy, the People's Republic didn't really need a powerful navy to protect sea trade routes. But when China began its historic shift to a market economy in the late 1970s, protection of sea trade routes became increasingly vital. Ironically, in the complicated three-dimensional chess game that is geopolitics, China actually depended on the *U.S.* Navy to protect it from any aggressive, trade-disrupting moves by the Soviets.

But the equation changed with the dissolution of the Soviet Union in 1991. Now China faced only one potential threat to its increasingly foreign trade–based economy—the United States. And at the time the U.S. Navy outclassed the Chinese navy as thoroughly and completely as the British navy had in the Opium

Wars. It was a disparity that was strikingly—and humiliatingly—made clear to the Chinese in what became known as the Taiwan Strait Crisis of 1995–96.

The crisis of the mid-1990s was only the latest in a series of hot and cold conflicts between China and Taiwan. Alarmed by what China saw as a move toward permanent independence on Taiwan's part, in 1995 the People's Liberation Army began a series of ballistic-missile "tests," lobbing land-fired missiles perilously close to Taiwan's western coast, just a hundred miles across the Strait of Taiwan. The missiles and live-fire naval exercises virtually shut down the strait to commercial shipping and airline traffic, effectively setting up a blockade of Taiwan's western ports.

In response, the U.S. flooded the area with overwhelming naval power. The Clinton administration sent two carrier battle groups through and near the strait—carriers, guided-missile cruisers, destroyers, submarines—and demanded that China cease and desist. It was as if the U.S. Navy were *daring* the Chinese to keep firing those missiles. The U.S. secretary of defense, William Perry, rubbed it in by publicly boasting that while China "is a great military power, the premier—the strongest—military power in the Western Pacific is the United States."

Perry's boast was a simple statement of fact: Since the collapse of the Soviet Union the U.S. was undeniably the most powerful military force in the Western Pacific. Against the U.S. Navy and other American military forces, China wouldn't have stood a chance.

And so in the end, the People's Republic backed down. The missile tests stopped, the strait reopened. There were various diplomatic maneuverings, discussions behind the scenes, conciliatory public statements by the U.S. government, and so on. But everyone knew the truth. Military power, not diplomacy, had decided the issue.

For China, it was humiliating, an almost unbearable loss of face.

Here they were, a great continental military power, an emerging economic world force. And yet a Western nation had insultingly parked a threatening and overwhelmingly powerful naval force virtually within sight of their shores—and there was nothing they could do about it. It was as if the Century of Humiliation had never ended.

There was no public announcement by the Chinese government, no acknowledgment that it had suffered a defeat in the Taiwan Strait. But at the top levels of Chinese strategic thinking, there was a growing consensus that China had to quickly modernize its military forces—and especially its navy.

In fact, even before the Taiwan Crisis some elements of the Chinese military had been pushing for expanding China's naval power—chief among them a septuagenarian People's Liberation Army general named Liu Huaqing. A soldier since the age of fourteen, a veteran of the Long March, Liu was appointed head of the Chinese navy in the early 1980s, and later was vice chairman of the Central Military Commission, which controls all of China's military forces under the auspices of the Communist Party. Although his actual naval experience was limited, Liu had two qualities necessary to eventually earn the title of the "Father of the Chinese Navy." First, he was reportedly close to Chinese Communist leader Deng Xiaoping, and was able to insist that the navy get an increasingly greater share of China's burgeoning military budget to pay for new ships, new weapons, and technological research.

And second, Liu had vision. Liu outlined a strategy that abandoned the coastal defense idea and called for a strategy of projecting Chinese naval power far out to sea—way far out. Liu postulated three stages of Chinese naval development. First, by 2000 the Chinese navy had to be able to project power out to what is known as the "First Island Chain" of Japan—Taiwan and the

Philippines—in the process becoming a naval force to be reckoned with in the Yellow and East and South China Seas. Second, by 2020 the Chinese navy had to be able to project power out to the Second Island Chain, running from the U.S. territory of Guam down to New Guinea. And finally, by 2049, the one hundredth anniversary of the People's Republic, the Chinese navy had to be a global force, complete with aircraft carriers that would supersede even those of the U.S. Navy, confirming China as the world's leader.

The Chinese navy hasn't quite met all of Liu's timetables. But it's coming pretty close.

Senior Captain Zhao Xiaogang, a slim, muscular man in his late forties, dressed in immaculate blue-green cammies, is sitting in the *Haikou*'s wardroom while the ship is under way off Hawaii. Hands clasped together on the gleaming conference table, Captain Zhao is relaxed, friendly, and soft-spoken. He smiles a lot—although the smiles don't always seem to quite make it to his dark, intense eyes.

A graduate of the Dalian Naval Academy and the Naval Command College, Captain Zhao is the commander of the four-ship Chinese navy task force taking part in the 2014 RimPac exercise. And on this day he is giving an interview to an American reporter—the first interview with a Western journalist by a Chinese navy task force commander at sea.

Captain Zhao displays none of the cockiness and swagger of Lieutenant Wu and the *Haikou*'s other junior officers. That may in part be a function of age; Captain Zhao is not a product of the recent Little Emperor generation. It may also be the result of hard experience. After all, the young officers of Lieutenant Wu's navy have never known a time when their navy wasn't vibrant, growing, confident. With thirty years' service in the Chinese navy, Captain Zhao can remember a time when that wasn't so.

When Captain Zhao was a young officer, the Chinese navy fleet of forty-five destroyers and frigates was made up mostly of substandard models of old Soviet designs; more than half of its surface fleet consisted of gunboats and torpedo boats designed to attack enemy vessels close to shore—assuming the weather was good enough for them to put to sea. The navy's submarine fleet was almost exclusively old Whiskey- and Romeo-class diesel-electrics, subs so noisy they would be sitting ducks for modern acoustic detection and targeting systems. The Chinese navy had only one nuclear-powered ballistic-missile sub, and its propulsion system so frequently leaked radiation that crewmembers were routinely put under thirty-day hospital observation after every venture out to sea. Of carriers and carrier-launched aircraft China had zero. Although he doesn't mention it, Captain Zhao surely remembers how his weak navy was faced down by the U.S. Navy in the Taiwan Strait.

But since then, Captain Zhao has seen his navy transformed.

The Chinese navy now has a dozen nuclear-powered ballistic-missile and attack subs, and its fleet of thirty conventional subs are primarily improved, super-quiet electric-diesels—more than a match for the U.S. Western Pacific sub force. The majority of its seventy-five missile destroyers and frigates are modern designs like the *Haikou* that have been commissioned in the past decade or so. Its recently constructed fleet of almost seventy amphibious warfare ships—including four huge "landing ship docks" that are bigger than an American cruiser—has dramatically increased its potential amphibious assault capabilities. The Chinese navy now has one aircraft carrier and sixty carrier-launched aircraft, and is in the process of building two more carriers. Annual Chinese military spending, including the navy budget, has quadrupled since the beginning of the twenty-first century, from $50 billion inflation-adjusted U.S. dollars in 2001 to more than $200 billion in 2013. True, that's far less than the $619 billion in U.S. military spending in 2013, but the U.S. military has worldwide responsibilities while the Chinese military does not. Also, while the Chinese military budget is increasing, the U.S. military budget has been declining about 4 percent a year since the end of the war in Iraq.

(It's worth mentioning that China's merchant fleet has also expanded exponentially. In 1984 China had about six hundred ships engaged in foreign trade; now more than four thousand Chinese-flagged ships are so engaged. By comparison, the U.S. has about eighty merchant ships engaged in international trade—just eighty. Chinese-flagged ships carry 90 percent of China's inbound and outbound international cargo; for the U.S. the figure is a mere 2 percent. The imbalance could be a critical factor in any crisis or conflict between the U.S. and China, allowing China to easily convert a portion of this fleet to military logistical use. State-controlled Chinese companies also own or operate all or part of commercial port facilities around the world, including in Sri Lanka, Djibouti, Pakistan, Bangladesh, and at both ends of the Panama Canal.)

And as General Liu demanded, today's Chinese navy is not a navy exclusively designed or content to hug the shore. In 1997, a two-ship Chinese task force became the first Chinese naval force in history to circumnavigate the globe. Since then the Chinese navy has established a permanent rotating task force in the Gulf of Aden to protect Chinese and other commercial ships from Somali pirates; helped evacuate tens of thousands of Chinese nationals from Libya in 2014; rescued citizens from ten nations during the 2015 civil war in Yemen; helped remove chemical weapons from Syria; dispatched ships for humanitarian missions in the Philippines, Africa, and elsewhere; and conducted joint sea maneuvers with a number of countries around the world.

This is the new Chinese navy—increasingly modern and well

trained, with regional and eventually worldwide reach. But like Admiral Zheng He confronting barbarian potentates in the fifteenth century, Captain Zhao insists that his navy comes in peace.

"Chinese participation [in the RimPac exercise] represents an important measure of the stature of China and the U.S., and the new relations between the major powers," the senior captain says, speaking through an interpreter. "This will enhance relations between our countries and develop friendly and pragmatic cooperation, which should be conducive to promoting peace and stability in the Asia-Pacific region. Through the exercise, briefings, receptions, and ship activities we now have a better understanding of each other. It will enhance mutual trust. This is important for cooperation in the future."

"Friendly cooperation," "mutual trust," "peace and stability." It's the standard diplomatic boilerplate that all countries use, including the U.S. But while their governments don't dare to say so publicly, other countries in the region aren't at all sure that friendly cooperation is uppermost in the Chinese government's mind.

Already China's navy far outstrips the naval capabilities of every country in the Pacific except the U.S.—Japan, the Philippines, Malaysia, Australia, the remnants of the once-powerful Russian Pacific Fleet. About $5 trillion worth of international trade passes through Asian-Pacific waters every year, and if you take the U.S. Navy out of the equation, China has the military capability to restrict that trade at will. Nations involved in territorial disputes with China—especially Japan, the Philippines, Vietnam—could be faced with a grim choice: Give in or suffer economic strangulation.

Having the capability to do that is one thing. But does China have the will to use military force to get its way in the Western Pacific? The answer, demonstrably, is yes. As we'll see, in the first decade and a half of the twenty-first century China has repeatedly flexed its new naval power to intimidate other, smaller nations in the Western Pacific—and it hasn't hesitated to flex that power in the face of the U.S., either.

Of course, from People's Republic president Xi Jinping in Beijing down to Senior Captain Zhao in the wardroom of the *Haikou*, Chinese officials deny any such intent. Any suggestion of hostile or aggressive intentions is treated almost as an insult. How could anyone think such a thing?

"China has always pursued a road of peaceful development and a national defense policy that is defensive in nature," Captain Zhao says. "We stress the development of national defense and economic growth to safeguard our sovereignty and security. Our armed forces and their formidable military strength conform to our national security needs and broad interests. This is similar to all [countries] that develop their armed forces. China's military keeps upgrading weapons and equipment properly, and in a balanced way."

Again, the words are soft, calm, reassuring. But given China's recent history, it would be military and strategic malpractice for the U.S. to believe them.

Senior U.S. Navy officers and defense analysts have a sardonic name for Chinese military and civilian officials who use smiles and dulcet words to assure foreigners of their peaceful intentions. They call such officials "barbarian handlers." But words and smiles aren't the only way that military and defense officials of the People's Republic handle so-called barbarians.

There is an ancient saying in China, one of the famous "Thirty-Six Stratagems" for dealing with an enemy. The stratagem is this: "Conceal a dagger behind a smile."

During the decade and a half of China's rapid naval buildup in the Western Pacific, most senior U.S. policy makers have seen only the smile.

But the U.S. Navy has faced the dagger.

CHAPTER 4

Acts of (Warm) War

It was a little after the second millennium's end when the U.S. Navy first felt an acute sense of the threat that the Chinese would become. Ironically, that threat was felt not on the water but in the air.

It's a little after 9 a.m. on a Sunday, April Fool's Day 2001, and the U.S. Navy EP-3E Aries II aircraft is lumbering through the sky alone over the South China Sea. For the twenty-four crewmembers aboard—eight officers and sixteen enlisted personnel—it's already been a long day, and it's not over yet. They got up in those wee hours of the morning known in the military as "oh-dark-thirty," and after the usual preflight briefings and systems checks they took off from Kadena Air Base in Okinawa for the twenty-four-hundred-mile round-trip flight. Now, after more than a few mugs of strong black coffee and several hours of spying, they're ready to turn around and head back home.

Again, "spying" is a relative term. True, the intelligence and electronic warfare operators and technicians aboard the EP-3E jokingly refer to themselves as "spooks," which is slang for spies. But if you take spying to mean sneaking into an adversary's territory

77

and gathering secrets without him knowing about it—well, that's not what the EP-3E Aries is all about. (Aries does not refer to the astrological sign but is an acronym for "airborne reconnaissance integrated electronic systems"; the plane itself is an advanced version of the venerable P-3 Orion maritime patrol plane.) When the EP-3E is busy spying, everybody—including the spy-ee—can know it's there.

It's big, for one thing, roughly the size of a commercial Boeing 737—about a hundred feet long, with a hundred-foot wingspan and a tail that stands about three stories high. Unarmed and powered by four turboprop engines, it also flies slow and relatively low; mission speed is a mere two hundred or so miles an hour, and normal mission altitude is about twenty-two thousand feet. And if that didn't make it easy enough to spot, the EP-3E exterior fuselage bristles with antennas and electronics pods that give off a pronounced and unmistakable radar return; an enemy's radar operators would have to be asleep facedown on their consoles to miss it. It's not the kind of aircraft you would ever intentionally send into an enemy's airspace, at least not if that enemy possessed anything resembling an air force or a high-altitude surface-to-air missile capability.

So technically, the EP-3E isn't a spy plane; instead, it's a "signals intelligence" or "SIGINT" airplane. Its primary mission in the Western Pacific is to cruise along a foreign shore—say, for example, the coast of China—being careful to stay within international airspace, and use its high-tech electronics equipment to drink in the other guy's electronic signals. Radar emissions, encrypted communications links, radio voice messages between military commanders, electromagnetic emissions from ships and other aircraft—whatever the EP-3E can grab out of the electromagnetic spectrum is processed and analyzed by the cryptologists and electronic warfare specialists sitting at banks of consoles in the back of the plane. The intelligence data is then transmitted back to the area or theater intelligence headquarters, giving U.S. commanders a snapshot of the adversary's capabilities and methods. (It's not just adversaries; the EP-3E flights pick up electronic intelligence on everybody, friends and foes alike.)

True, ground-based listening stations can do some of the same electronic intelligence-gathering the EP-3E does. But an aircraft like the EP-3E (and the U.S. Air Force's RC-135 reconnaissance plane) is able to get in close, where the adversary's signals are stronger and easier to pick up. "Close" can mean anywhere in the international airspace outside the traditional twelve-nautical-mile limit from another country's coastline—although, as we'll see, not everyone agrees with that twelve-mile limit. In practice, however, to avoid any unintentional airspace violations, EP-3E intelligence-gathering missions generally stay considerably farther out than that.

Of course, the countries being spied upon generally don't appreciate the attention—which is actually another advantage that airborne SIGINT missions have over passive ground-based signals intelligence operations. When an adversary spots an EP-3E or other intelligence plane near his airspace, he'll probably light up additional radars, get on the radio with his higher command, maybe arm surface-to-air missiles and scramble some jets to intercept the spy plane—and in the process, he'll create even more electronic intelligence data for the spooks in the back of the EP-3E to pick up. In short, spy missions like the one the EP-3E is flying can actually make intelligence-worthy things happen.

That sort of "tickling" of an adversary to produce useful signals intelligence is known in Pentagon-ese as a "diagnostic irritant." There's no doubt that these intelligence missions irritate China, especially when they're flown over the hotly disputed South China Sea.

And on this day—April 1, 2001—as the EP-3E plods through
the sky about seventy miles off the southeast coast of the Chinese
island of Hainan, the Chinese are irritated as hell.

Sitting in the EP-3E's right cockpit seat is navy pilot and mission
commander Lieutenant Shane Osborn, twenty-six, a husky, former
small-town Nebraska kid and navy ROTC graduate. Osborn
and his crew are assigned to Fleet Air Reconnaissance Squadron
One (VQ-1)—nicknamed the "World Watchers"—home-based
in Whidbey Island, Washington, but currently operating out of
Japan. They and their multiple generations of predecessors have
been flying these kinds of surveillance and reconnaissance flights
for more than half a century now, lurking in the skies off the coasts
of China, the Soviet Union, North Korea, and Vietnam, drinking
in the electronic chatter. And during that half-century, scores of
U.S. airmen have been killed or gone missing while flying missions
in these dangerous skies, even in times of ostensible peace.

Many of those losses were the result of bad weather or mechanical mishap or pilot error. But some of those Americans died
when their planes were ambushed and shot down in international
airspace—including forty-seven members of VQ-1 Squadron. In
1956 a VQ-1 Squadron P4M-1Q Mercator electronic intelligence
plane with sixteen crewmembers was shot down by Chinese MiGs
over the East China Sea; four bodies were recovered and returned
to the U.S., but the fate of the others is still unknown. And in April
1969, North Korean MiGs shot down a VQ-1 Squadron EC-121
reconnaissance plane in international airspace ninety miles off the
Korean coast, killing all thirty-one Americans aboard. Although
Osborn and the vast majority of his crew weren't even born when
those incidents happened, it's a good bet most of them have heard
the stories.

No one aboard the EP-3E really expects to get shot down by
Chinese interceptors. But they also know that it's getting increas-

ingly tense up there. Ever since the Taiwan Strait crisis in 1995–96 China has been steadily building up its military and particularly naval forces, and the U.S. has had a correspondingly growing interest in monitoring their assets and capabilities. Now U.S. Navy and Air Force intelligence-gathering planes like Osborn's EP-3E are flying four or five missions a week off the Chinese coast— missions that are being regularly intercepted by Chinese fighters.

The fact that the U.S. intelligence missions are being intercepted isn't a big deal; the U.S. also sends out interceptors when a potentially hostile aircraft nears its airspace. But there are international rules for these things. The accepted drill is for the intercepting planes to stand off a safe distance, at least five hundred feet or so—close enough for the target plane's pilot to know that the interceptors are there, that they're standing by in case he tries any funny stuff, but not so close as to interfere with the target aircraft's flight. If the Chinese were doing that, if they were following the rules, there wouldn't be a problem.

But in the past several months, the Chinese fighter pilots haven't been following the rules. Instead, they've been getting close—really close. On an earlier mission a week before, two Chinese F-8II fighters had intercepted Osborn's plane and taken up station just fifty feet behind and to the side of it. And during other U.S. recon missions the Chinese pilots have come even closer. Out of almost fifty intercepts by Chinese fighters off the Chinese coast in the previous four months, on six occasions the Chinese pilots have flown within thirty feet of the U.S. planes, and twice they've come within ten feet. Ten feet!

And they aren't just passively hanging off the U.S. planes' wings, either. One of the Chinese pilots' techniques is to fly unseen under the slow-moving American planes and then suddenly swoop up directly in front of them, startling the American pilots and buffeting their planes with jet engine backwash—a move that's known to U.S. pilots as "thumping." It's like giving them the finger.

Of course it's incredibly dangerous—which from the Chinese perspective is exactly the point. The idea is to rattle the Americans, shake them up a little, show them that there's a price to be paid for flying these missions, maybe even deter the Americans from flying them. Even at the risk of their lives they want to show the Americans that they aren't, and China in general isn't, afraid of them. Although the U.S. government has officially protested through diplomatic channels these "reckless and unprofessional" actions by Chinese pilots, the aggressive intercepts have continued. For American aircrews, missions that were once routine have now become almost routinely perilous.

So Lieutenant Osborn and the crew of the EP-3E aren't sure what to expect when they see two Chinese F-8II fighters armed with air-to-air missiles closing fast on them from the direction of Hainan Island. The fighters pass by on the EP-3E's right side and then turn and take up station off the EP-3E's left side, not too close at this point, always staying between the American plane and the island. The EP-3E is on autopilot, flying straight and level at a little over 200 mph.

The F-8IIs, known in the West as Finbacks, are two-engine single-seaters that were designed in the 1960s and upgraded in the mid-nineties. With their small, backswept wings they look a little like the Vietnam-era U.S. F-4 Phantom. With a max speed of Mach 2.2, and a stall speed only a little less than the EP-3E's cruising speed of 200 mph, it's not easy for the fast fighters to stay abreast of the slow-moving EP-3E. The Chinese pilots have to fly flaps-down and a little bit nose-up to create some drag, but not so much as to stall. It's a demanding way of flying, sort of like riding a bike next to someone who's walking; if you don't make constant adjustments you're going to topple over.

Aboard the EP-3E, Osborn and his crew aren't too worried at this point. These two Chinese pilots aren't doing anything really crazy, at least not yet. After about ten minutes, with their mission track completed, Osborn sets the autopilot for a slow, level turn to the northeast, away from Hainan Island and headed for home. Osborn figures the fighters will break off.

But they don't. Instead, one of the fighters—fuselage number 81192—starts moving in closer, then closer still. Members of the flight crew are watching this guy through the porthole windows in the back of the plane, and calling out reports over the onboard communications net. "Hey, he's right off our wing. . . . He's tight, that's the closest I've seen. . . . Oh my God, he's coming closer!" The Chinese fighter is now hanging there ten feet off the EP-3E's left wing, and the pilot makes some sort of a hand motion—maybe a sardonic salute, maybe a wave-off, it's hard to tell.

The Chinese fighter drops back, but then a few moments later he's back off the EP-3E's wing. This time he has his oxygen mask off and crewmembers on the EP-3E can see him mouth something at them. There aren't any lip-readers aboard the EP-3E, so they don't know what the pilot is saying—but the assumption is that it's not complimentary. The EP-3E crew doesn't respond. Standard operating procedure for U.S. aviators during interceptions is to keep the plane flying straight and level, and not respond to any provocation by the jet pilot. That SOP is not always honored; for example, in December 1999 the crew of a closely intercepted EP-3E put on Santa Claus hats and flipped off the fighter pilot. But Osborn runs a tighter ship. There's no radio communication between the planes. They just wait for the guy to go away.

But now, during the Finback's second pass, Osborn is getting concerned. He's guarding the autopilot to make sure the EP-3E doesn't deviate, but he can see that the Chinese pilot is having trouble controlling his aircraft. Again, it's not easy to fly a Finback at 200 mph in the thin air at twenty-two thousand feet, and the Chinese pilot is bucking around out there—an insane situation to put himself in when the margin of midair catastrophe is just a few feet. Finally he drops back again.

Although Osborn and his crew don't recognize him, this isn't the first time this particular Chinese pilot has pulled this sort of crazy stunt. The U.S. Navy knows about this guy; they even know his name.

The Chinese pilot is Lieutenant Commander Wang Wei, age thirty-two, a fourteen-year veteran of the People's Liberation Army Navy who's based at Lingshui airfield on Hainan Island. Even by fighter jock standards, he's a hot dog, a risk-taker, one of those guys who's constantly pushing the envelope. For example, during an earlier intercept of an EP-3E flight a few months before, Wang flew his jet within ten feet of the American plane and held up a piece of paper with his email address written on it, an incident that a U.S. crewmember caught on a camcorder; that's how the U.S. Navy knows his name.

(Wang's airborne antics are reminiscent of the scene in *Top Gun* in which Tom Cruise flies his inverted F-14A Tomcat two feet above a Russian MiG and then flips off the Russian pilot. But if a bootleg copy of *Top Gun* was Wang's inspiration, he should have known the scene was pure fantasy. Maybe the Blue Angels precision flying team could pull off something like that, but no sane U.S. pilot would try it with a potentially hostile aircraft. In fact, when the *Top Gun* producers asked the navy pilots who were flying the planes for the movie to do the plane-over-plane inverted flight maneuver, the navy said no way, too dangerous. The scene was eventually put together with special effects instead.)

It's probably just as well that Osborn and his crew don't know that Wang is flying the Finback; this situation is scary enough as it is. They keep hoping that the F-8II pilot and his wingman, who's been laying back through all this, will drop off and return to base. But no. Wang takes his Finback on a third pass, this time just under the EP-3E's left wing; he may be planning to thump the American plane.

But he doesn't make it. As he's passing under the EP-3E's wing the Finback suddenly lurches up—and the EP-3E's thirteen-foot-long far left propeller chews through the fighter like a chainsaw, cutting the plane in two.

For both planes, it's a catastrophe. The collision shears off the tops of the EP-3E's far left prop blades, and the Finback's nose veers right and knocks off the EP-3E's fiberglass radome nosecone. The front half of the Finback nosedives toward the sea, trailing fire. Osborn thinks he sees a chute, but the Finback's cockpit canopy is crushed and pilot Wang is probably already dead; his body will never be found. Meanwhile flying debris damages the EP-3E's inboard left propeller and peppers the plane with shrapnel. The EP-3E immediately snap rolls to the left, banking at 130 degrees—which means it's almost completely upside down—and starts plunging toward the ocean below at a steep angle. The loss of the nosecone has depressurized the aircraft, and wind is howling through the holes at hundreds of miles an hour. Osborn is using all his strength to hold the yoke vertical and push the right rudder pedal, but the plane is out of control.

And what he's thinking at that moment is—"This guy just fucking killed us."

In the back of the EP-3E it's pandemonium. Everything not secured is flying around—coffee mugs, three-ring technical binders, pens, pencils, pieces of uniforms—and the g-forces are pinning the crewmembers to their seats or to the almost inverted floor. Screams, prayers, and curses are sounding out in almost equal measure. Everyone assumes it's the end. Petty Officer Third Class Jeremy Crandall, from Loves Park, Illinois, is thinking, "Well, I've had a good life." Just twenty years old, Crandall is a cryptology trainee who hasn't even earned his flight wings yet—and now it looks as if he never will.

For thirty seconds the EP-3E plunges upside down toward the sea; for everyone aboard, it's the longest half minute of their lives. Finally, after dropping eight thousand feet, through superhuman effort Osborn manages to get the plane right side up, although the EP-3E loses another six thousand feet before Osborn can get the aircraft under some kind of control. He's flying level, but he's lost some of his avionics, the damaged number one prop is shaking like an out-of-balance washing machine and threatening to tear the wing off, and who knows what other exterior damage the plane has suffered.

There are only three options for the crew of a badly damaged airplane flying over the ocean. They can bail out, they can ditch the plane in the water, or they can try to make it to someplace where they can land on the ground. But for the EP-3E crew, the first two options really aren't options at all.

The only place to bail out of an EP-3E is from the door just aft of the inside left jet engine, but the only way to do that without having the prop blast throw you into the tail is for the pilot to power down that engine. But if Osborn powers down the engine, the plane will start rolling left again. And even if they survive a bailout, where does that leave them? It leaves them scattered across the shark-infested South China Sea, bobbing around in their life vests with no search-and-rescue ships or planes in the immediate area. The crewmembers put on their parachutes in case the plane starts coming apart, but no one wants to bail.

As for ditching, that's not really an option, either, not for this plane. Part of the array of electronic snooping gear on the plane is the "Big Look" radar pod attached to its belly. The Big Look pod is about twelve feet across and shaped like a giant M&M, and when it hits the water it's going to act like a sea anchor, pushing the nose down and the tail up. The EP-3E is probably going to break apart on impact. They'll ditch if they have to, if the plane can't maintain altitude, but nobody wants to try it.

There's really only one option, and it's not a good one. There's no way the damaged plane can make it to a friendly airfield; the airplane could break up any minute. So finally Osborn shifts course twenty degrees.

Osborn and his crew are headed for Lingshui Air Base on Hainan Island. They're going to try to land in China.

Hainan Island hangs like an afterthought off the south coast of China, separated from the mainland by the shallow and narrow Qiongzhou Strait. At thirteen thousand square miles it's a little bigger than Belgium; the land is Florida-style flat in the north but rises up in lush subtropical mountains and valleys as you go toward the southern coast. To the west of the island is the Gulf of Tonkin, the center of many U.S. Navy operations during the Vietnam War, while to the south and east lies the South China Sea.

For centuries Hainan Island was a wild haunt for criminals and outcasts and pirates and early Chinese Communists on the run, a place where Han Chinese immigrants mixed uneasily with the Li people whose ancestors had settled there thousands of years before. As Lieutenant Shane Osborn battles to control his damaged plane, Hainan Island is still something of a political and cultural backwater. A place of rice paddies and jungles, its principal city of Haikou is dominated by a noisy, gritty, blue-collar commercial shipping port.

Still, in 2001 Hainan Island is militarily significant. There are a couple of air bases, including the Lingshui Air Base on the south-eastern coast, as well as the conventional sub facilities at Yulin and a string of powerful radio communications and navigation facilities strung out along the coast. There's enough there to make the Chinese extremely sensitive to the idea of an American military aircraft, even an unarmed and crippled one, entering their territorial airspace—especially after that U.S. aircraft has just been involved in an apparently fatal encounter with one of their pilots. No one on the EP-3E knows how the Chinese military forces will react.

In the past the reaction hasn't been good. In 1965, for example, Hainan-based J-6 fighters shot down a U.S. Air Force F-104 that had strayed over the Chinese island after a mission in Vietnam. The American pilot ejected and was captured, and even though the U.S. and China weren't at war, he was held prisoner by the Chinese until 1973. A year after that another U.S. plane, a Navy KA-3B Skywarrior aerial tanker with a crew of four, was also shot down after straying over the island. The Chinese returned the ashes of one of the crewmembers in 1975, but never fully accounted for the other three.

Obviously, 2001 isn't the mid-1960s. Despite tensions over the spy missions, the Chinese probably aren't eager to kill twenty-four U.S. military personnel aboard a clearly unarmed and damaged plane. (Later, there are reports from Chinese sources that Wang's wingman, pilot Zhao Yu, requested permission to shoot down the American plane but permission was denied.)

But whatever the Chinese intentions are, right now they aren't saying. As Osborn wrestles the plane toward Hainan, he and other crewmembers repeatedly radio Lingshui Air Base over the international emergency frequency, declaring a Mayday and requesting permission to make an emergency landing. The Chinese don't answer. A communications officer aboard the plane also notifies the U.S. chain of command over a secure net about what's happening.

Meanwhile, in the back of the EP-3E, crewmembers are going through the emergency destruction checklist to get rid of classified material aboard the plane. They smash computer discs with a fire ax and stuff classified manuals and binders into jettison boxes, then hurl them out of an open hatch to sink in the sea below. At the same time, the navigator, Lieutenant Regina Kaufmann, twenty-five, a petite but tough five-footer who just a few years before was a lifeguard at Walt Disney World's Typhoon Lagoon, is trying to figure out an approach to the airfield. But there isn't a Hainan Island map or any field approach information aboard the plane; they're going to have to eyeball it.

Finally, after a white-knuckle twenty-minute flight, the EP-3E crosses over the island's white sand beaches and rice paddies and they see it, a long, concrete-block runway with open revetments for Finback jets lined up beside it. Struggling to maintain control, with the aircraft screaming in at 200 mph, Osborn manages to land the plane and bring it to a stop. When he does, cheers and screams of joy and relief break out in the back. But Osborn is having a good news–bad news moment.

He's thinking—"We're alive. But we're also in China."

The plane is quickly surrounded by People's Liberation Army soldiers with AK-47s, most of them teenaged conscripts. All twenty-four crewmembers are taken off the plane, herded onto buses, and taken to a vacant officers' barracks on the base. They aren't exactly prisoners of war—but there's no doubt they are prisoners.

What follows is an eleven-day standoff—and the lowest point in U.S.-China relations since the NATO air campaign against Serbia in 1999, when U.S. planes mistakenly bombed the Chinese embassy in Belgrade, killing three Chinese citizens and sparking violent (and government-sanctioned) demonstrations outside the U.S. Embassy in Beijing and other U.S. consular offices throughout China.

Anti-American factions claimed the U.S. had destroyed the building on purpose to help check rising Chinese power and to test the leadership in Beijing. (The U.S. government quickly apologized for the bombing and later paid China $10 million in reparations.)

No one thinks the Chinese pilot deliberately rammed the EP-3E, or that the Chinese government intended for the crisis to happen. But when it does react, the Chinese government's actions seem more suited to the Cold War than to a nation trying to present itself as a peaceful new player on the world stage. In fact, the Hainan Island incident becomes a case study in People's Republic crisis management—a litany of mock outrage, vicious denunciations, stubborn demands, and outright lies.

According to the Chinese government and the Chinese press—which is essentially the same thing—the collision was the Americans' fault. First, Chinese spokesmen say, the EP-3E—they call it the "culprit aircraft"—illegally violated Chinese airspace by flying over China's "exclusive economic zone" or "EEZ," a two-hundred-mile swath of ocean extending out from the Chinese coast. (More on EEZs later.) Second, after the two F-8II interceptors took up position a safe four hundred meters away—so say the Chinese—the American spy plane "abruptly veered" toward Wang's jet, "making it impossible for Wang to avoid the collision" and causing the Chinese pilot's death. Third, after the EP-3E "rammed" the fighter, the American crew intentionally entered Chinese territorial airspace to land their plane—that much is true—without first asking permission—which is not true. The Chinese government is demanding that the U.S. "apologize to the Chinese [government and people] and shoulder all the responsibility arising from this incident." The clear implication is that they're going to keep Osborn and his crew on ice until that apology comes.

Although the government keeps a lid on violent demonstrations like the ones after the accidental Belgrade bombing, there's no attempt to downplay the incident. Wang's wingman, Zhao

Yu, appears on national TV to repeat the official version of the collision, and state news media also release a letter to President George Bush purportedly written by Wang's widow. The letter says, "In this serious matter with irrefutable facts and the responsibility completely resting on the U.S. side, you are too cowardly to voice an apology. . . . I cannot figure out why you sent the [American plane] to spy along China's coast from such a great distance, and why they rammed my husband's plane."

Of course, the Chinese version of the collision is preposterous. Saying a lumbering EP-3E could "ram" a nimble F-8II jet fighter from four hundred yards away is like saying that a school bus could chase down and ram a Ferrari. The U.S. government also has hard evidence that Wang had a history of dangerous flying—that is, the video of him flashing his email address, video footage that the U.S. government later releases to the news media. The newly inaugurated Bush administration expresses "regret" over the death of the pilot but refuses to apologize.

In the U.S., the situation is somewhat reminiscent of the early days of the 1979–80 Iranian hostage crisis. Yellow ribbons by the thousands festoon oak trees and utility poles at the crew's home base at Whidbey Island and in their hometowns—Show Low, Arizona; Staten Island, New York; Rock Creek, Ohio. There are prayer vigils, angry letters to the editor calling for military action against China, criticism of the U.S. for being too hard or too soft; critics say the holding of the U.S. aircrew is a "national humiliation."

As for Osborn and his crew, their time as prisoners is physically and mentally uncomfortable, but not physically brutal. After a couple days at the air base the Chinese move them to a government-run hotel in the city of Haikou. It's not exactly the Honolulu Hilton—there are crummy beds, bugs, showers with exposed electrical wires nearby—but it's not the infamous "Hanoi Hilton" prison of the Vietnam War, either. The food is lousy, mostly rice and steamed vegetables and pieces of fish, including heads and tails. It's three days before they're allowed to see a representative from the U.S. Embassy.

All of the crewmembers are interrogated as part of the Chinese "investigation" of the collision, Osborn most of all; some of his interrogation sessions last more than five hours. The interrogations are weird, like something out of a 1950s Korean War POW movie, a throwback to the old days of capitalist running dogs and imperialist enemies of the peace-loving peoples of the world. The Chinese interrogators shout, rant, slam fists on the table. They tell the crewmembers they're going to be charged with espionage and intentionally killing the Chinese pilot, that they are air pirates and criminals and "master spies," that they'll never see their families again. On the other hand, if they cooperate and formally apologize—on camera, of course—then in the "spirit of humanitarianism" the benevolent people of the People's Republic will return them to their country.

All of the crewmembers tell the same story—the F-8II ran into them—and none of them agrees to apologize.

But finally the crisis comes to an end. It ends with the so-called "letter of the two sorries."

In Chinese the word for "apologize" means the apologizer not only expresses regret for what happened but takes full responsibility for it; to apologize for something is a formal and stylized process, a kind of verbal bowing or kowtowing that results in a serious loss of face for the apologizer. In American English, on the other hand, the word "sorry" can be taken as an apology—"I'm sorry I wrecked your car"—or as an expression of condolence for something that's not your fault—as in, "I'm sorry your husband passed away."

So after much negotiation, the U.S. ambassador delivers a

letter in English to the Chinese government stating that the U.S. is "very sorry" about the death of the Chinese pilot and "very sorry" that the plane was forced to land without receiving verbal clearance. The use of the English word "sorry" is carefully designed to let both sides put their own interpretation on it. The Chinese government and news media call it an apology; the U.S. calls it simply an expression of sorrow and regret for a lost life, and not an apology at all.

That may sound silly, having U.S.-China relations hinge on a single word. But it illustrates one of the many cultural differences that complicate those relations to this day. Issues that seem insignificant to Americans can be deadly serious to the Chinese. Acutely conscious of their history and their unequal relations with the West, quick to take offense at any perceived slight, stubbornly illogical in the face of the facts, desperate not to lose "face" (a potent and palpable force in Chinese culture) by ever admitting fault—the Chinese have a way of repeatedly driving U.S. military officers and diplomatic officials crazy.

In any event, Osborn and his crew are released and eventually flown back to Whidbey Island, where they're greeted as national heroes. Osborn is later awarded a Distinguished Flying Cross and the other crewmembers receive Air Medals. At the same time, Lieutenant Commander Wang Wei also becomes a national hero in China. The Chinese Central Military Commission issues a decree from Chinese president Jiang Zemin posthumously declaring him an official "Guardian of Territorial Airspace and Waters" and praising his "military struggle against a powerful enemy." Note the word "enemy."

As for the crippled EP-3E, it stays on the runway at Lingshui for two months, being carefully examined by Chinese technicians, until finally it's partly disassembled and flown back to the U.S. aboard a hired Russian civilian transport aircraft.

For the next several months, battalions of China specialists in the U.S. defense establishment try to figure out the reasons behind China's aggressive intercepts and its hard-nosed reaction to the Hainan Island incident. Was it an attempt to tamp down domestic discord by stoking patriotism? A testing of a new U.S. president or an attempt to warn the U.S. off impending possible arms deals with Taiwan? Was it part of an internal struggle between internationalist civilian leaders and hardline military nationalists? No one on the U.S. side really knows the answer.

But despite China's hardline stance, it's clear the Chinese don't want the incident to permanently sour relations with the U.S. China is eager to finally be admitted to the World Trade Organization (it will achieve that goal later in 2001), and it's also campaigning to host the 2008 Olympics. Although U.S. surveillance flights resume after the EP-3E crew's release, China eases off its aggressive responses to them. U.S. aircraft are still being shadowed, but apparently not being thumped.

And then, just five months after the incident over the South China Sea, the whole thing is basically forgotten—at least by everyone not still flying surveillance missions over the South China Sea. Within the space of a few hours in New York City and at the Pentagon and in a field in Pennsylvania, the focal point of U.S. strategy and military might shifts to the land, sky, and seas of Southwest Asia and the Middle East.

Of course, the U.S. and its navy don't disappear from the Western Pacific after 9/11 and during the next decade of wars in Afghanistan and later Iraq. U.S. planes still fly recon missions over the South China Sea, U.S. ships and submarines still conduct WestPac patrols, U.S. Special Forces teams participate in joint antiterrorist operations in the Philippines and elsewhere. Tens of thousands of U.S. sailors and aviators still do their jobs far from home on the vast Pacific Ocean.

But America's attention is riveted elsewhere. And while the U.S. is looking the other way, the Chinese navy comes over the horizon.

Hainan Island today is no longer a backwater. Although the city of Haikou remains gritty and noisy—only bigger, with 2 million people—in just a little over a decade the southern Hainan city of Sanya and its environs have become a major resort destination. Drawn by the relatively clean air (a rare and precious commodity in many populated areas of China) and the white sand beaches, some 30 million tourists now visit Hainan every year, most mainland Chinese but some foreigners from South Korea, Japan, and Russia as well. Hainan has played host to the Swatch Girls Pro surfing competition, the Miss World beauty contest, and other international events. In Sanya luxury golf courses and Western-style hotels—Ritz-Carlton, Hilton, Sheraton—line the shores, while Western-style eateries—Häagen-Dazs, KFC, Starbucks—share the upscale shopping plazas with scandalously overpriced high-end local restaurants.

It all seems very modern and sophisticated, a symbol of the new China. But there's an anomaly to be observed here. Because while Sanya's biggest commercial industry is tourism, today its other primary industry is war—or at least the prospect of it.

Oddly enough for a nation seemingly obsessed with military secrecy, much of Sanya's war-making industry exists within easy sight. In the bay just south of the city is the Yulin Naval Base, home to all of the Chinese Southern Fleet conventional submarines as well as various surface ships—destroyers, frigates, small attack boats. The Yulin base has long been a fixture on the island; it was originally built as a submarine base by Japanese navy occupiers in World War II.

But over the past decade the Chinese navy has dramatically

expanded the Yulin base, with a new sea break at the mouth of the harbor and new docks as well. Farther east, on the other side of a small peninsula in Yalong Bay, and easily visible to tourists sunning themselves on Yalong Beach, the Chinese have built an entirely new addition to the Yulin naval complex. There's now a twenty-two-hundred-foot-long dock that can handle not just one but two aircraft carriers—it's the biggest aircraft carrier dock in the world—and thousands of feet of other docks for surface warfare ships, including the big new Type 071 "amphibious transport dock" ships that in size rival the biggest U.S. Navy amphibs. There's a fifty-foot-wide sea-level tunnel bored into a hill to allow subs to connect with a vast array of underground weapons bunkers and loading facilities, unseen by tourists or spy satellites. There's a submarine "demagnetizing" dock to make subs less susceptible to magnetic detection and mines, and also docks for the Jin-class Type 094 nuclear-powered ballistic-missile subs, of which the Chinese navy has at least four.

Today the Yulin complex is the biggest naval base in all of Asia. And it's these new facilities for aircraft carriers, nuclear-powered "boomers," and even the amphibious transport ships at the naval base that have the U.S. and other countries in the region worried about the future.

For now, China has only one aircraft carrier, the *Liaoning*, and it's primarily a training ship for aircraft carrier operations. But China is in the process of building at least two additional carriers, and probably more. No country needs an aircraft carrier to defend its own shores; smaller ships, land-based planes, and missiles can do that. Instead, carriers are designed to project power far from a country's own coasts—and with a carrier or two permanently based at Hainan Island, China could dominate the South China Sea region and pose a challenge in the Indian Ocean. Although the other countries in the region—Vietnam, the Philippines,

Thailand, Australia—are building up their navies, none (except for India) has an aircraft carrier, or plans to acquire one. Only the U.S. is capable of putting a carrier strike group in the South China Sea—assuming it's willing to do so. The U.S. is willing *now*; the future is unknowable.

Even the seemingly mundane Type 071 amphibious transport ships at the Yulin complex are a potential threat to other countries in the region. Amphibious ships are not coastal defense platforms. The transport ships can carry helicopters, armored vehicles, hovercraft landing boats, and up to eight hundred troops—and obviously, in combat you're not planning to land those troops on your own beach; you're planning to land them on somebody else's beach. The Chinese navy currently doesn't have the logistical and support capability to stage large-scale amphibious landings, but it's working on it; like many countries, it conducts such drills under the auspices of "humanitarian assistance exercises." It's something that every nation in the South China Sea region has to think about.

As for the nuclear-powered ballistic-missile subs at Yulin, they are the ultimate power projectors. If the "boomer" subs on Hainan Island could slip undetected through various choke points and make it to the blue-water Pacific or Indian Oceans, their forty-six-hundred-mile-range JL-2 nuclear missiles could threaten any target in the Western Pacific or on the Indian subcontinent, or even the North American continent—a potent argument in any international crisis. The subs would give China for the first time a credible sea-launched nuclear strike capability—and make at least part of its nuclear arsenal invulnerable to a first strike.

So regionally and beyond, the ships based at Hainan Island are potential gamechangers. Hainan Island has become the focus of China's southern naval strategy, which seeks to dominate the vital shipping lanes of the South China Sea.

In fact, China doesn't want to just dominate the South China Sea—and the East China Sea and the Yellow Sea, for that matter. It wants to *own* them.

It's March 2009, and the USNS *Impeccable* is about seventy-five miles south of Hainan Island, plodding along the surface of the South China Sea at about four miles an hour. It is not minding its own business.

The *Impeccable* is what's known as an "ocean surveillance ship," which is to say, a spy ship. Some 280 feet long, with a twin hull–type construction, the *Impeccable* and four other similar U.S. ocean surveillance ships are operated by the Military Sealift Command, an arm of the navy that controls oil tankers, cargo ships, roll on–roll off ships for vehicles—and "special mission" ships like the *Impeccable*. (USNS stands for United States Naval Ship.) The *Impeccable* is manned by about twenty civilian "mariners" and twenty U.S. Navy personnel, and is completely unarmed. Its mission is not to kill the enemy—that's somebody's else job—but instead to find and identify an enemy's submarines.

To do that, the *Impeccable* uses both active and passive sonar arrays. The passive part is the surveillance towed array sensor system (SURTASS), a mile-long cable studded with hydrophones and electronic sensors that trails behind the ship—sailors call it the Tail—and picks up sounds radiating through the ocean waters: undersea volcanic eruptions or landslides, the clicks and moans of whales looking for love, the sounds of surface ships and especially submarines. Although the *Impeccable* has a maximum speed of about 15 mph, with the cable deployed it can only proceed at the speed of a brisk walk.

The problem with passive sonar from a military point of view is that submarines are a lot quieter than they used to be. When running on battery power, some of the new diesel-electric subs—equipped with sound-absorbing anechoic tiles and other noise reduction features—are far quieter than the nuclear-powered attack and ballistic-missile subs in the U.S. fleet. They're almost impossible to detect with passive sonar.

To address that, the *Impeccable* is also equipped with a low-frequency active (LFA) sonar array, a system that hangs vertically below the ship and can send out electronic sound pulses that will bounce off a submarine's hull and give away its location; it's the sort of *Ping! Ping!* echo-ranging that's familiar to anyone who has seen a World War II submarine movie. (Because of its alleged ill effects on marine mammals—which the navy disputes—the LFA sonar system has been the source of environmental litigation for decades.)

With its passive and active sonar systems the *Impeccable* can not only locate an enemy sub, it can also develop an "acoustic signature" for it. Different classes of submarines emit different sounds—propulsion-plant noises, propeller cavitation sounds, and so on—and individual subs within a given class also give out unique signatures. Based on a submarine's known signature, U.S. assets dedicated to antisubmarine warfare—surface ships, aircraft, other submarines, undersea acoustic sensor surveillance systems—can tell if the sub lurking out there is a Yuan-class sub potentially armed with anti-ship missiles or a Jin-class nuclear-powered sub that is likely armed with ballistic missiles. In war and in peace, the ability to track and identify an opponent's submarines is vital.

The details of the *Impeccable*'s missions are classified. But it's a pretty good bet that on this day, March 5, 2009, it's looking for Chinese submarines.

Of course, just as with the U.S. airborne surveillance flights, the Chinese aren't pleased to see the *Impeccable* operating so near Hainan Island. And they make their displeasure known.

It starts with a People's Liberation Army Navy frigate that shows up and cuts across the *Impeccable*'s path at about a hundred yards; it's sort of like firing a warning shot. Then two hours later a Chinese Y-12 twin-engine turboprop utility plane shows up and makes eleven passes over the ship at about six hundred feet, while the Chinese frigate takes another dash across the slow-moving *Impeccable*'s bow. The *Impeccable* crew ignores these attempts at intimidation. Two days later, another Chinese ship shows up and radios the *Impeccable* that it is operating in sovereign Chinese waters, that it's violating international law, and that it must immediately leave the area "or suffer the consequences."

Sovereign waters? International law? The *Impeccable* is sailing a good seventy-five miles off the nearest Chinese territory—and, as everybody knows, a country's sovereign territory only extends out to the twelve-nautical-mile limit from its coast.

But China takes a different view.

Until fairly recently, the question of who owns the sea was easy to answer, at least in the Western view: No nation owns the sea. For centuries most European maritime powers had generally accepted the premise that any nation's sovereign territory extended no more than three nautical miles from its shoreline—about the range of a cannon shot. Later most countries, including the U.S., extended that territorial limit to twelve nautical miles. In theory, at least, beyond that territorial limit no nation had the right to impede or restrict free passage on the sea in peacetime; to do so was considered an act of war. But in the mid-twentieth century that definition of sovereign waters began to change.

The U.S. started it in 1945 by claiming exclusive rights to develop oil, natural gas, and mineral resources in the U.S. undersea continental shelf, which can extend hundreds of miles out from the coastline. Other nations followed by claiming the right to regulate certain activities, such as commercial fishing, hundreds of miles from their shores. Finally in 1982 the third United Nations Convention on the Law of the Sea (UNCLOS) formalized the concept of "exclusive economic zones," the aforementioned "EEZs."

An EEZ gives a coastal nation exclusive rights to exploit and regulate any natural resources on and under the sea up to two hundred nautical miles from its coastlines. Other nations have the right to sail over those areas of the sea, but they can't fish or drill for oil or conduct other commercial activities in them without permission. The UNCLOS treaty was formally ratified in 1994, and China signed on in 1996. For a variety of reasons the U.S. Senate never approved the treaty. But the U.S. recognizes the treaty's provisions in practice, and has established its own EEZs, not only around the continental U.S. but also around Hawaii and other Pacific islands such as Guam.

The problem is that while it's one thing to pass a law of the sea, it's another thing entirely to get everyone to agree on what that law of the sea means. China takes the position that under the treaty, other nations' commercial ships can sail through China's coastal economic zones, but other nations' military ships and aircraft cannot conduct military operations in the zones—and to the Chinese, "military operations" include electronic signals gathering and reconnaissance. The Chinese even extend that alleged ban on military operations to the airspace above their economic zones.

The U.S. and most other countries reject that interpretation. As long as they're outside the twelve-mile limit, the U.S. says, any country's military ships and aircraft can sail and fly where they want and do what they want under international law. As we've seen, for years the U.S. has been routinely sending aircraft and warships and spy ships like the *Impeccable* into China's EEZ waters, not only in the South China Sea but also in the Yellow Sea and the East China Sea. U.S. sailors aboard those ships have gotten used to having Chinese ships shadow them, but for the most part, ever since the EP-3E incident in 2001 the Chinese haven't been aggressively challenging the American navy incursions into their EEZs. The Chinese have routinely lodged diplomatic protests about the incursions, but with a few exceptions they haven't gotten physical about it.

But now, with the *Impeccable* still plodding through the waters off Hainan Island, the Chinese are getting physical—and dangerous.

The day after being warned to leave the area or "suffer the consequences," the *Impeccable*'s crew finds itself surrounded. Five Chinese-flagged ships are closely arrayed around the American ship—really closely, just a few hundred yards or so away. There's a Chinese navy intelligence collection ship, two armed patrol vessels from the Chinese Fisheries Law Enforcement agency and the State Oceanic Administration, and two small privately owned Chinese fishing trawlers.

China has a huge official commercial fishing fleet, with some three hundred thousand motorized vessels, by far the biggest such fleet in the world. Most of the fishing boats are just that—fishing boats—but an unknown number of trawlers and other merchant ships are actually controlled by the Chinese navy and used as reconnaissance vessels, electronic signals intelligence gatherers, and so on; their crews are specially trained and often wear military uniforms. (The Soviets also made extensive use of such "fishing trawlers" in the Cold War to shadow U.S. Navy ships, especially off the California coast.) Other civilian-owned Chinese fishing trawlers and their crews serve as a kind of seaborne militia. Their primary job is fishing, but they can also be called in by the Chinese navy for special missions—such as shadowing or harassing an American ship in international waters. Using civilian trawlers for that kind of work gives the Chinese navy a certain level of deniability if and when the trawler crews do something really dangerous or stupid.

Which is exactly what trawler No. 8389 does now. The trawler, which is registered to a commercial fishing company on Hainan Island, closes to within fifty feet of the *Impeccable* while crewmembers shout at the American ship; one of the Chinese crewmembers is waving a People's Republic flag. The *Impeccable* crewmembers turn a fire hose on the Chinese trawler to brush it back, soaking some of the trawler's crewmembers, but to no avail; the fishermen strip to their underwear and the trawler closes to a mere twenty-five feet off the *Impeccable*'s stern. One of the Chinese sailors seems to be trying to grab the *Impeccable*'s towed sonar array cable with a boat hook—a foolish attempt, given that the towed array gear weighs thousands of pounds. In a video of the incident, crewmembers on the *Impeccable* are heard predicting that the guy with the boat hook is "gonna be gargling saltwater" if he's not more careful.

The boat hook guy doesn't manage to snag the cable, but at this point the *Impeccable* has had enough. The commanding officer radios to the Chinese ships that he's leaving the area and requests safe passage. But the Chinese aren't cooperating. The two trawlers swing around in front of the *Impeccable* and drop large pieces of wood in its path, and then park themselves a hundred yards in front of the larger ship. To avoid a collision the *Impeccable* has to do an emergency stop, which isn't too difficult when you're only going 4 mph. Now, as one of the *Impeccable* crewmembers says, "We're DIW"—dead in the water, and surrounded by hostile Chinese ships.

Few if any of the *Impeccable* crewmembers are old enough to personally remember an earlier incident involving an unprotected American spy ship, the USS *Pueblo*, but they've certainly heard about it. In 1968 the *Pueblo* was in international waters off the

North Korean coast when it was shadowed and harassed by North Korean gunboats and fishing trawlers. The next day the *Pueblo* was fired upon by the North Korean vessels. (Some sources suggest it was the Chinese who encouraged the attack.) With no means of defending his ship—its two machine guns were stowed away—the *Pueblo*'s captain surrendered. One crewmember was killed and eighty-two others were captured; they were starved and tortured for eleven months before being released after the U.S. issued an apology—an apology that was immediately rescinded after the prisoners' release. Little of the classified material and gear on board the *Pueblo* was destroyed before its capture, which gave the North Koreans—and presumably the Chinese—an intelligence bonanza. The North Koreans later turned the *Pueblo* into a floating anti-capitalist-running-dog museum, and although generations of U.S. sailors have fantasized about restoring its honor by blowing it up, it remains parked today on a river in Pyongyang.

Now, with the *Impeccable* in possible danger of being boarded or fired upon—it's not likely, but it's possible—it conceivably could be another *Pueblo*-style situation. Crewmembers are wondering aloud if they'll have to perform an "emergency destruct"—that is, destroy the classified documents and gear aboard the ship.

In the end it doesn't come to that. Finally the trawlers move off and the *Impeccable* sails away. But it's the most serious clash between the U.S. and China since the EP-3E was forced down on Hainan Island in 2001.

Ever since the standoff over the downed EP-3E, China had seemed to want to play nice on the world stage—in its own fashion—even as it continued its dramatic naval buildup. After the 9/11 terrorist attacks, China offered diplomatic support for the U.S.-led war in Afghanistan, and cooperated in antiterrorism efforts.

In the decade's early years there were numerous diplomatic visits and contacts by the highest-level civilian Chinese and American

leaders. In 2002 President George Bush visited China—one of four
trips to China during his presidency—and later that year Chinese
president Jiang Zemin visited Bush's ranch in Crawford, Texas,
where the Chinese leader put on a cowboy hat. High-level U.S.
military officers met with their Chinese counterparts on numerous
occasions—known as "mil-to-mil" contacts—and got tours of each
other's bases and ships during port calls or through official visits.

True, it wasn't all sweetness and light; there were a few incidents at sea during the period. For example, in September 2002,
the USNS *Bowditch*, an unarmed "oceanographic research vessel,"
was operating in the Yellow Sea when it was repeatedly buzzed
by a Chinese plane while a Chinese patrol boat came in close and
ordered the *Bowditch* out of China's EEZ; later, in May 2003,
the *Bowditch* was harassed again, this time by Chinese fishing
trawlers. In October 2006, a Chinese Song-class diesel-electric
sub, likely armed with torpedoes and anti-ship missiles, managed
to slip through the escort screen of the carrier USS *Kitty Hawk*
while it was operating off Taiwan, closing to within five miles
of the carrier before popping to the surface. Some navy officers
interpreted it as a "Gotcha!" move, a warning from China that U.S.
carrier groups could no longer expect to operate with impunity.

And then there was the Chinese antisatellite missile incident
of 2007. After years of calling for a ban on "militarizing" space,
the Chinese fired a missile armed with a kinetic "kill vehicle"
(that is, not an explosive warhead) at an old Chinese weather
satellite falling to the Earth from a low orbit about five hundred
miles up. The kill vehicle shattered the satellite into thousands
of pieces, creating a potentially dangerous debris field that could
harm other satellites or space vehicles. It was an astonishing
accomplishment—no one had thought China had that technical
capability—and a worrisome one. The U.S. military is critically
dependent on satellites for everything from communications to

reconnaissance to GPS-guided weapons targeting; any future mass attack on the U.S. satellite system could render the U.S. military both blind and deaf. The U.S., which hadn't tested an antisatellite missile in twenty years, filed a formal protest with China, which claimed the test was not military in nature. In 2008 the U.S. followed the Chinese antisatellite missile shot with one of its own, firing a missile from the cruiser USS *Lake Erie* to destroy a reportedly malfunctioning spy satellite in low orbit, but without creating an extensive debris field.

Still, for the most part, the post–Hainan incident Bush administration years seemed to be a high-water mark in Chinese-American relations. Yes, there were disagreements over Taiwan and Tibet and the South China Sea, and human rights violations in China; there was also grumbling in Congress that the mil-to-mil contacts were a little too chummy. But with wars in Iraq and Afghanistan stumbling along, the U.S. was only too happy to avoid confrontations with China.

But now, with the 2009 assault on the *Impeccable*, the Chinese "charm offensive" seems to be ending. Now they suddenly seem intent on getting into the U.S. Navy's face.

And it's not just the *Impeccable*. At about the same time the fishing trawlers are harassing the *Impeccable*, a thousand miles away in the Yellow Sea there's a similar drama being played out with another Military Sealift Command surveillance ship, the USNS *Victorious*. The *Victorious*, a slightly smaller version of the *Impeccable*, is operating 120 miles off China's coast when a patrol boat assigned to the Chinese Bureau of Fisheries—in reality an arm of the People's Liberation Army Navy—looms unannounced out of the darkness and lights it up with a high-intensity searchlight; for the *Victorious* crew it's startling, like having a stranger walk up and shine a flashlight in their eyes. The next day a Y-12 turboprop buzzes the *Victorious* eleven times at an altitude of about four hundred feet—low enough to rattle nerves on the American vessel. Then, two months later, still in the Yellow Sea, two Chinese "fishing trawlers" go after the *Victorious* again, closing to within thirty yards and then parking themselves in front of the American vessel, forcing it to stop; another Chinese ship orders the *Victorious* to leave China's "sovereign" waters.

A month after that, the U.S. guided-missile destroyer USS *John S. McCain* is steaming in the South China Sea off the Philippines—again, in what China claims is its exclusive economic zone—when a Chinese submarine collides with the *McCain*'s towed sonar array, damaging it. U.S. officials publicly announce that the collision appears to be unintentional; after all, they say, a submarine intentionally ramming into a destroyer's sonar cable would be dangerous to the submarine if the cable got wrapped around its prop. But some navy officers aren't so certain. Sure, no American sub commander would pull such a stunt—but that doesn't mean a Chinese sub commander wouldn't. To some, it's a case of assuming that an opponent thinks and acts the same way you do—a dangerous assumption for any military force to make.

The *Impeccable*, the *Victorious*, the *McCain*. After almost eight years of more or less peaceful relations with China, that's four dangerous incidents in four months, all in areas that China claims as its sovereign waters. For the first time, the Chinese seem serious about confronting the U.S. Navy over their claims of sovereignty in disputed waters.

And although the newly installed Obama administration doesn't realize it, it's the beginning of a trend.

After the *Impeccable* and *Victorious* incidents the U.S. lodges a formal protest with Beijing, calling the Chinese harassment unlawful and dangerous. A Chinese Foreign Ministry spokesman responds that the U.S. accusations are "totally inaccurate" and that by conducting operations in the EEZ the *Impeccable* "broke international law and Chinese laws and regulations." It's the sort of diplomatic dickering that basically means nothing.

The navy is allowed to send a guided-missile destroyer into the South China Sea to escort the *Impeccable*—the destroyer is the USS *Chung-Hoon*, named after a Chinese-American U.S. Navy admiral and World War II hero—but essentially, the Obama administration acts as if the incidents never even happened. In a White House meeting with the Chinese foreign minister, President Obama talks about "cooperation" and "the importance of raising the level and frequency of the U.S.-China military-to-military dialogue in order to avoid future incidents."

In other words, *Can't we just talk this over?*

At the highest echelons of the U.S. Navy there certainly are senior officers willing to do that. They believe that if they can develop closer relationships with their Chinese counterparts, the U.S. can help shape China's military policies and restrain its aggressive tendencies. They believe that cooperation and gentle persuasion, not shows of military force, will change the arc of Chinese behavior.

In short, they believe that the U.S. can actually *trust* China.

CHAPTER 5

Panda Huggers

There's an air of tense anticipation aboard the aircraft carrier USS *Carl Vinson* as the admiral is brought aboard at the San Diego Naval Base. Sailors line the quarterdeck rails and the gangway, their loose black ties carefully draped over spotless white uniforms, their white sailor hats—known as "Dixie Cups"—positioned just so. As they stand at attention and salute the admiral's arrival, some can't resist turning their heads to steal a glance at him.

Of course, having an admiral aboard a carrier like the *Vinson* isn't unusual. When a U.S. Navy carrier is operating at sea, there's always at least a one- or two-star admiral on board in command of the entire strike group, and visiting delegations of high-level military and civilian brass are frequently stopping by—congressmen, senators, even a president. Among the more experienced sailors who serve on carriers, the sight of a senior admiral doesn't excite too much attention.

But this admiral isn't just any admiral. This four-star admiral is the CNO—the chief of naval operations—the navy's highest-ranking uniformed officer. He's a member of the Joint Chiefs of Staff and military advisor to the secretary of the navy, the secretary of defense, the National Security Council, and the president of the

United States—and to the 430,000 officers, sailors, and reservists of the U.S. Navy, he is the earthly equivalent of God in summer whites.

And on this particular morning aboard the *Vinson*, in September 2013, the God in summer whites is Admiral Jonathan Greenert.

Appointed to a four-year term as CNO by Barack Obama in 2011, Greenert has forty-two years behind him since he reported for plebe summer at the Naval Academy, including tours as commander of the Seventh Fleet and vice chief of naval operations. A steelworker's son from blue-collar Butler, Pennsylvania, raised in modest circumstances, Greenert was one of those striving kids— altar boy, high-school swim team and baseball team, president of the Latin Club, National Honor Society. A lot of kids back then had paper routes; Greenert had *two* paper routes, one in the morning, one in the evening. At the Academy he was known for his quick wit, engaging personality, and for what was somewhat mysteriously referred to in the class yearbook as his "colorful weekends"; he graduated in 1975 with a degree in ocean engineering.

Now age sixty, Greenert is tall, lean, angular, with short-cropped, thinning salt-and-pepper hair. Still outgoing and personable, he is quick with a joke, able to put even awestricken junior officers and enlisted men at ease, and able also to smile when dealing with foreign military leaders who are being difficult—which, as we'll see, is now a big part of his job as CNO. Nine times out of ten he's the smartest person in the room, but he's careful to hide the fact that he knows it. He has a habit of prefacing a discussion with a self-deprecatory "I don't know much, but . . ."—and then he goes on to demonstrate that he knows very much indeed, rattling off complicated facts and figures and concepts from his head without ever looking at a note.

The "twin dolphins" badge on his uniform identifies him as a submariner, although at six-foot-three he's taller than the average "bubblehead." When he was first starting out in the cramped confines of subs, he probably bumped his head a lot. Still, he has a submarine officer's bearing, and a submariner's methodical, analytical mind. Ask him a question and there's always a very slight pause before he answers, as if he's running through all the possible permutations. He's the first submariner in a decade and a half to occupy the CNO's Pentagon office.

In the 1970s the submarine service was even more of an elite and secretive culture than it is today; the submarine fleet was a kind of a navy within the navy. Much of that had to do with the irascible and controversial Admiral Hyman Rickover, the "father" of the nuclear-powered navy. Rickover's utterly unforgiving standards concerning attention to detail and quality control left a mark on almost every navy officer who ever served under him—Greenert included. Even now, decades after Rickover was finally forced to retire from the navy at the unprecedented age of eighty-two, Greenert still tosses out "Rickover-isms." One of his favorites is—Trust what you *in*spect, not what you *ex*pect.

After extensive training in nuclear propulsion systems, Greenert earned his submariner's badge as a junior officer aboard the nuclear-powered attack submarines USS *Flying Fish* and USS *Tautog*. (This was before the *Tautog* collided with the Soviet sub.) He also served as engineer officer aboard one of the most unusual submarines in navy history—"Submarine NR-1." Although it was retired from service in 2008, the NR-1, nicknamed the "Nerwin," deserves a special mention.

Just 145 feet long, the smallest nuclear-powered sub ever built, the NR-1 was never formally named or even commissioned because Rickover didn't want it subjected to normal navy oversight; that's the kind of power Rickover wielded. Launched in 1969, the NR-1 was designed to dive to a depth of up to three thousand feet—far deeper than any normal navy sub—and use mechanical arms to recover objects from the ocean floor. It actually had retractable wheels to creep along the bottom, making it the only American sub in history to come equipped with tires. It was manned by a handpicked crew of only ten officers and enlisted men, who ate frozen TV dinners, bathed out of a bucket once a week, and burned chlorate candles to produce oxygen; as you can imagine, after a week or so it got pretty funky in there. Most of NR-1's Cold War missions are still classified—don't even ask—but there are a few we know about: Among them were retrieving missiles that had fallen off an aircraft carrier and searching the seafloor for pieces of the space shuttle *Challenger* after it blew up in 1986. It says something about Greenert that being crammed into the tiny *Nerwin* for up to a month at a time more than half a mile below the ocean's surface was one of the high points of his career.

After a tour as executive officer aboard the USS *Michigan*, Greenert got his first sea command in 1991 as commander of the USS *Honolulu*, a first-generation Los Angeles–class fast-attack sub based at Pearl Harbor. More than 350 feet long, with a crew of just over a hundred, and armed with torpedoes and horizontally launched Tomahawk cruise missiles and tube-launched Harpoon missiles (later Los Angeles–class subs would be equipped with vertical launchers), the *Honolulu*'s primary mission was to quietly patrol alone in the far reaches of the ocean, to find and track enemy submarines and ships—and if it came down to it, to kill them.

It was *Hunt for Red October* stuff, and Greenert was considered "shit-hot" at it (that's a compliment). Except that by the early 1990s, with the Soviet Union fallen and its Pacific fleet mostly rusting at the docks, and with the Chinese and North Korean navies' antiquated ships hugging their own coasts, there wasn't a lot of red in the hunt. Although the navy launched aircraft strikes and fired Tomahawk missiles in support of the American campaign in the First Gulf War, at the end of the twentieth century nobody expected the navy to actually slug it out with other naval forces in the Western Pacific. There really weren't any.

In fact, although the navy played fighting roles in both the Afghanistan and Iraq wars—air and missile strikes, SEAL teams, and of course the marines, which are part of the navy—as the twenty-first century began it also tried to project a kinder, gentler, less warlike image. For example, in 2007 the navy codified its new outlook in an official mission statement titled *A Cooperative Strategy for 21st Century Seapower*. In the statement, the first of its kind in two decades, the navy announced that its traditional "core missions"—projecting American power worldwide, protecting the sea lanes, and so on—would remain the same. But it also added "humanitarian assistance / disaster relief" as a navy "core mission," and it stressed that in the future the navy would put as much emphasis on preventing conflict as it would on preparing for conflict. One way to do that, the navy said, was to "foster and sustain cooperative relations with more international partners."

Disaster relief? Prevention of conflict? Cooperative relations? All well and good. Certainly the U.S. Navy had long played an important role in international disasters, sending carrier strike groups and hospital ships to deliver supplies and aid to victims of earthquakes and tsunamis and other catastrophes around the globe. And the navy has always had a diplomatic function, sending fleets around the world to show the flag and reassure friends—and remind potential enemies—that the U.S. would be there if they needed help. Certainly the navy had provided a deterrent to conflict simply by being the biggest, most powerful naval force in the world.

But to make disaster relief and fostering cooperative relations part of the navy's core mission, on an equal level with preparing for combat operations, and to divert war-making resources to accomplish them—well, it wasn't the U.S. Navy of World War II, or even the Cold War.

It wasn't that the navy had become a pacifist institution. But to employ an overused but instantly understood term, there was (and still is) a certain "political correctness" among many navy officers, a reluctance to acknowledge—publicly, at least—that the ultimate purpose of all those expensive guns and missiles and airplanes and torpedoes aboard navy ships is to kill people if killing became necessary. That attitude probably reached its apogee in early 2013, when the head of Pacific Command, Admiral Samuel Locklear, told a reporter that the most serious security threat facing the U.S. in the Pacific region was not North Korean missiles or China's growing ambitions and naval capabilities. No, the admiral said, the biggest security threat facing the U.S. in the Pacific region was *global warming*—and the U.S. and its Pacific partners should commit military resources to prepare for it. (Locklear also said he thought that "Sometimes . . . the Chinese get handled a little too roughly" by other nations over territorial disputes in the region.)

As you might expect, not all high-ranking navy officers were on board with the new, less aggressive trend. There's a story about one navy admiral—not Greenert—who asked a group of junior surface warfare officers aboard a ship what they thought the navy's primary mission was. The young officers hemmed and hawed, trying to come up with the correct answer, and finally they suggested that the navy's primary mission was to "help people," or (cribbing a line from a navy recruiting commercial) "to be a global force for good." "No!" the admiral barked, and then he led the young officers to the main deck and pointed at a five-inch gun. "This is a gun!" the admiral said. "It shoots bad people! It kills bad people! That's what we do!"

It was pure Bull Halsey stuff. (World War II admiral William "Bull" Halsey was beloved by the press and public for his aggressive character and comments, famously saying after Pearl Harbor that "by the time we're finished with them, the Japanese language will be spoken only in hell.") The problem was that by the beginning of the second decade of the twenty-first century most U.S. foreign policy decision-makers didn't want Bull Halsey stuff from military leaders, at least not when it came to China and the Pacific region; they wanted peace-talkers out there, not war-talkers.

(That's not to say there aren't U.S. operational plans for a military conflict with China. Of course there are. There are plans for everything, probably including plans for the invasion of Canada and a nuclear war with France. But even in wargames or training exercises, there are Red forces [them] and Blue forces [us], but never Red *Chinese* forces, at least not publicly; in training simulations that involve a military asset specifically associated with a certain country—say, for example, a simulated Chinese Jin-class Type 094 ballistic-missile sub—the nationality of that asset is always off the record.)

The navy's efforts to portray itself as a nonaggressive, cooperative player in the Western Pacific became even more pronounced after the Obama administration unveiled its aforementioned Pacific pivot in 2011 and 2012, the "rebalancing" of American focus and more of its military force away from the Middle East and back toward Asia and the Pacific. On the diplomatic side that involved establishing closer relationships with nations that had felt slighted or ignored during the U.S. preoccupation with the Middle East. On the economic side it included the (now aborted) Trans-Pacific Partnership or TPP, a twelve-nation trade deal that involved the U.S., Japan, Malaysia, Vietnam, Singapore, Brunei, Australia, and New Zealand but not China.

On the military side, the rebalancing involved shifting assets—including navy ships—to the region; eventually 60 percent of the U.S. fleet would be assigned to Pacific Command. But the U.S. Navy in the Western Pacific and the Indian Ocean region also had the delicate task of establishing closer working relations with the navies of nations who were nervous about China's military and especially naval expansion—which is to say, almost all of them—and to do it without alarming China. To accomplish that, U.S. Navy commanders would meet regularly with those countries' navy commanders, and their fleets would conduct extensive joint exercises to learn how to communicate and work with each other. The ultimate goal would be to achieve what Greenert calls "interoperability," the ability of one nation's navy to conduct actual operations at sea with the ships of another nation's navy. That may sound easy, but it's not. Multi-ship exercises at sea are essentially combat without live ammo, and they're difficult enough when all the ships and aircraft are in the same navy. When you throw in ships and planes from other navies, with people who speak other languages and follow different procedures and have different equipment, they're even more difficult—and dangerous.

Underlying this interoperability idea was what was once dubbed "the thousand-ship navy" concept. The theory was that if the U.S. Navy had three hundred ships, and if it were able to achieve interoperability with the navies of ten other countries that had seventy ships each, then the U.S. Navy–led coalition would have a thousand ships to draw on. (An actual thousand-ship U.S. Navy has been the impossible dream of generations of American admirals. The last time that dream was a reality was in 1955, when the navy had 1,030 ships.) The U.S. wouldn't necessarily have to have formal treaties with those other nations; all they would need is a common interest and goal, such as protecting sea lanes, combating piracy, responding to a natural catastrophe—or, say, preventing China from gaining naval hegemony in the Western Pacific and the Indian Ocean.

Of course, like most things in the Asia-Pacific region, in actual practice it isn't that simple. Just because most countries in the region share a fear of China's military rise, and just because most look to the U.S. as a check on China, it doesn't mean those countries necessarily share the same interests or are eager to work together. Among the various nations there are trade issues, arguments over disputed islands, seething ethnic and historical hatreds. And that's especially true when it comes to the U.S.'s most powerful ally in the region—Japan.

Every nation, America included, has events in its history that can only be regarded with shame and regret. But in terms of recent Asia-Pacific history, Japan has more to answer for than most. Japan's occupation of the Philippines in World War II culminated in the rape and slaughter of tens of thousands of civilian Filipinos. Its forced-labor construction projects like the Burma railway killed hundreds of thousands of conscripted Southeast Asians. Its decades-long occupation of Korea was marked by repression and an effort to stamp out Korean culture. The list of Japanese atrocities against its fellow Asian countries could go on. Americans may have long forgiven, and even forgotten, Japan's wartime behavior, but some Asia-Pacific nations have longer memories. They all have diplomatic and economic ties with Japan, and in most Asia-Pacific countries Japan gets generally positive ratings in public opinion polls. But in some countries—South Korea is one in particular—there's a lingering distrust of Japan's long-range intentions, especially since Japan began building up and modernizing its "self-defense" forces. The fear is that notwithstanding its constitutional ban on war, a nationalistic, militarized Japan could one day reprise its World War II aggression.

As for China's view of Japan, sometimes it's almost as if World War II ended yesterday. Japan's invasion and occupation of China from 1931 to 1945 left an estimated 20 million Chinese dead as a result of starvation, battle, and outright murder, and Japan's failure—in Chinese eyes—to adequately apologize for its actions still inflames passions and stokes nationalistic outbursts. According to one recent poll, 81 percent of Chinese have a negative view of Japan, while 86 percent of Japanese have a negative view of China. The same poll found that almost 80 percent of Chinese believe that Japan has not apologized sufficiently, while 70 percent of Japanese believe they've apologized enough or that no apology is even necessary. It's why Chinese fans routinely boo during the playing of the Japanese national anthem at soccer games. There are other military, economic, and diplomatic issues between the two countries, but it's clear that history still plays a significant role.

So it's not surprising that China would see the military side of the U.S.'s Pacific pivot as a threat. Here the U.S. was, strengthening its military ties with historical Chinese enemies like Japan, South Korea, and Vietnam and striving to eventually achieve "interoperability" with their growing navies. To China it smacked of containment, in the same way that NATO and other U.S.-led alliances had tried to "contain" the Soviet Union during the Cold War. Historically China has had a fear—a phobia—of being encircled by hostile nations that could invade its territory by land or sea. Now, as a world economic power, it also had to worry about being encircled by nations that in conjunction with the U.S. Navy could threaten the distant sea lanes on which its market economy depended.

(Although China has trade and diplomatic ties with other Asia-Pacific nations, it has almost no military allies other than North Korea—and North Korea is more of a headache than an ally.)

Of course, the Obama administration insisted that the military aspect of the Pacific pivot was not directed against China, that the U.S. wanted to improve U.S.-China relations, not damage them. But how could the U.S. help prevent China from feeling threatened? Or at least make them feel a little less threatened?

The answer, according to the Obama administration and some elements of the navy leadership, was to *bring China into the game*.

You'll recall that after the *Impeccable* and *Victorious* incidents in 2009, President Obama personally stressed "the importance of raising the level and frequency of the U.S.-China military-to-military dialogue." As a result of the Pacific pivot, that became part of the U.S. Navy's mission and mantra: More ports-of-call by U.S. Navy ships to China and vice versa, more mil-to-mil visits and contacts by top U.S. and Chinese military commanders, even holding joint exercises with the Chinese navy. Greenert announced that the U.S. Navy's ultimate goal was to achieve interoperability with the Chinese navy.

True, U.S.-China mil-to-mil contacts had been going on for decades, fitfully at times. But now the tempo and level increased. In 2010 there were only six significant meetings between high-level U.S. and Chinese military and civilian defense establishment officials; in 2011 there were ten, and in 2012 there were fourteen. (It was a degree of high-level military interaction that would have been inconceivable with the Soviet Union during the Cold War. For example, when the chief of the Soviet general staff visited the Pentagon for the first time ever, in 1987, shortly before the collapse of the Soviet Union, it made headlines across the country; by 2013 a visit to the U.S. by a top Chinese military commander, or vice versa, was so common it hardly rated a mention.)

The theory behind the increased mil-to-mil contacts was that if the U.S. military treated China as a partner and not a potential adversary, then China would *act* like a partner, and curb its aggressive actions in the South and East China Seas and elsewhere. In fact, U.S. military officers were ordered not to publicly refer to China as a potential military threat or even as a competitor—and just to make sure there was no misunderstanding on that point, top officers like Greenert were required to have any planned public statements on China vetted by the State Department and the National Security Council.

The vetting part annoyed Greenert—and in fact, he didn't really need his public statements to be vetted. As CNO he was fully on board with the administration's nonconfrontational policy on China. He truly believed that personal relationships between military commanders could prevent conflicts and help shape China's long-term military and national policies.

Here's Greenert on China: "If conflict occurs out there, first of all, we've failed. The job is not just to prepare for conflict; clearly we have to do that. But our main job is to preclude it. If we focus only on what we're going to have to do to fight China, that's not good. We need to figure out how we're going to engage with and influence China, and bring it as an emerging power into what we have shaped [in the Asia-Pacific region]. Some say you can't do that, you're foolish to try. But I say we'd be foolish not to try."

Maybe. But most American allies and partners in the region weren't at all sure that China would respond to soft words and gentle persuasion—and they had good reason to think that way. China's maritime forces had avoided direct confrontations with the U.S. Navy after the 2009 *Impeccable* and *Victorious* incidents; although its ships continued to shadow U.S. Navy ships in the South and East China Seas, they generally did so at a decent distance. But that wasn't the case with other, smaller nations' vessels. China seemed determined to put them in their place.

There were a host of incidents. In 2010 a Chinese "fishing trawler" collided—seemingly intentionally—with a Japanese coast guard patrol ship just off the Senkaku Islands in the East China Sea, after which the Japanese arrested the boat's captain. (Japan has administered the tiny, unpopulated islands since 1971, but their ownership is also claimed by both China and Taiwan.) The incident sparked major street demonstrations in China and

Japan, and the Chinese government halted exports to Japan of rare earth minerals used in electronics manufacturing. That same year in the Yellow Sea there was a seaborne melee between South Korean coastguardsmen and Chinese fishing boat crews armed with knives and broken beer bottles—a fracas that ended with one of the Chinese boat captains being shot and killed by the Koreans, reportedly an accident. In 2011 a Chinese navy frigate fired on Philippine fishing boats near the disputed Jackson Atoll in the South China Sea, and later that year Chinese patrol boats cut the sonar cables on two Vietnam-sponsored oil and gas survey ships just off the coast of Vietnam. In 2012 Chinese navy ships began chasing away Filipino fishing boats near the disputed Scarborough Shoal in the South China Sea—an action that continues to this day, and which we'll discuss further in a later chapter. In 2013 a Chinese navy frigate locked its weapons radar on a Japanese navy destroyer in the East China Sea, a hostile act just a step away from actual combat.

And those are just a few examples; there are scores of others, many unreported. Japan, South Korea, the Philippines, Vietnam, Indonesia—all had repeatedly clashed at sea with the Chinese navy or its subsidiaries. Again, the almost decadelong Chinese "charm offensive" was over. And while they wouldn't necessarily admit it publicly, for fear of annoying China, most of those countries looked to the U.S. Navy to act as a check on Chinese aggression. To them, the U.S. Navy's getting chummy with the Chinese navy sent the wrong signal—and more than a few high-level U.S. Navy officers agreed.

Of course, as he walks up the gangway of the USS *Carl Vinson* on this September morning in 2013, Greenert is well aware of the dismissive term some navy officers and other defense officials have for people who think China will play nice if given the chance. But that's the policy, those are the orders, and Greenert agrees with them. So although he would never put it this way, on this day that's what Admiral Jonathan Greenert is doing.

He's hugging a panda.

There are three senior Chinese navy officers accompanying CNO Greenert as he boards the USS *Carl Vinson*, all dressed like Greenert, in the Chinese navy equivalent of summer whites.

One is Captain Zhang Zheng, the aforementioned commander of the Chinese aircraft carrier *Liaoning*—the same *Liaoning* that in a few months will be the quarry of the USS *Cowpens* in the South China Sea. Zhang is friendly, charming, well educated; the son of a former Chinese naval officer, he has a master's degree from the Dalian Naval Academy, and having spent two years studying at the Joint Services Command and Staff College in England, his English is perfectly precise. Another Chinese officer is Captain Dai Ming Meng, the pilot who was recently the first to land a J-15 fighter on the *Liaoning*'s deck—an accomplishment that made him a celebrity on state-controlled Chinese media. Unlike Zhang, Captain Dai is noticeably arrogant, and more than a bit cocky—but then, he *is* a fighter pilot.

And then there's the leader of the Chinese delegation—Admiral Wu Shengli, the top commander of the People's Liberation Army Navy, a ranking member of China's Central Military Commission and Greenert's Chinese navy counterpart. Of medium height, a bit pudgy, and bald under his gold-braided white peaked cap, Wu has been described as tough, smart, calculating, cagey, ruthless—but no one on the American side, including Greenert, would ever call him charming.

Wu grew up as a son of privilege, but in murderous times. He was born in August 1945, the month that Japan ceased hostilities in World War II. (Wu's given name, Shengli, is Chinese for "victory.")

His father was a well-known People's Army political commissar in the war with Japan and during the civil war with the Chinese Nationalists; he later held several important political posts. As a result, young Wu was considered one of the "princelings," the sons of high-level Communist Party members who always seemed to have the first shot at cushy jobs and quick promotions.

Wu's family connections no doubt spared him from the worst effects of Mao Zedong's Great Leap Forward, a process of forced collectivization and ill-planned industrial expansion that resulted in widespread famine and the deaths of millions of Chinese in the late 1950s and early 1960s. Wu joined the People's Liberation Army in 1964 and, again most likely through connections, won admission to the PLA's Surveying and Mapping College to study oceanography. As a student at a military school, Wu escaped being directly caught up in another of Mao's mad schemes, the Great Proletarian Cultural Revolution of the 1960s and early '70s—an orgy of anarchy and violence that saw more than a million people murdered and tens of millions more beaten, tortured, humiliated, or banished to hard labor on collective farms. But even if not directly involved, it seems unlikely that Wu could have grown up in such times and not developed a pretty hard-eyed view of the world.

They were hard times for the Chinese navy as well. The navy had always been a poor cousin to the People's Liberation Army, and conditions aboard navy ships were primitive at best. Wu would later recall serving as a young officer aboard Chinese navy frigates and destroyers and seeing conscript sailors stay aboard ship when in port because at least on the ship they could get something to eat; Chinese sailors would eat their meals on deck, Wu remembers, and slept on sheets of metal siding. Conditions in the Chinese navy gradually improved, but even two decades later, as Wu steadily rose in the senior ranks, that same Chinese navy still found itself shockingly outclassed and overwhelmed by the U.S. Navy.

It's different now, of course. Now Wu is the commander of an increasingly modern and expanding navy, a navy that no longer accepts the idea that the U.S Navy will remain the dominant naval power in the Asia-Pacific region. As he and his retinue accompany Greenert into the *Vinson*'s hangar deck, Admiral Wu wears the hard look of a man who's willing to talk, but not necessarily willing to compromise.

This isn't the first time Wu has visited the U.S. and met with high-ranking military officers; he was last here in 2007, shortly after being named commander of the Chinese navy. But it's the first time he and Greenert have met, and outwardly, at least, the two couldn't be more different: Greenert the small-town American guy, warm, outgoing, personable, dedicated to democratic-with-a-small-d principles; Wu older, reserved, even cold, a Communist-with-a-capital-C. And on this day they have different agendas. Greenert wants to start up a personal relationship, to demonstrate that he, Greenert, and by extension the U.S. Navy, can be trusted. And Wu wants to learn about American aircraft carriers. What it took the Americans decades to learn he wants his navy to master in a few short years.

Ever since they started work on the *Liaoning*, the Chinese have had an intense interest in learning about U.S. Navy aircraft carrier operations. The reason for that is simple: No one is better or more experienced at launching and recovering aircraft on a pitching, rolling deck than the U.S. Navy. So when planning his visit to the U.S., Wu initially asked for a tour of a U.S. carrier conducting air operations at sea.

But U.S. officials quickly nixed that idea. People may think that movies and news reports have already shown everything there is to know about aircraft carrier operations, but in fact there are some technologies and operational details that remain classified and by U.S. law can't be shared with the Chinese military. The U.S. wants to show the Chinese some leg, but not that much leg. So instead they chose the *Vinson*, which is safely docked at its home port, its air wing off the ship and its reduced complement crew performing routine maintenance.

(Wu also repeatedly asked for a demonstration of an F-18 simulator for himself and his entourage, but that was nixed as well. Wu isn't a pilot, but Captain Dai certainly is, and giving him access to the simulator would be like handing him the keys to an F/A-18E/F Super Hornet, the U.S.'s mainstay carrier fighter, and letting him take it for a spin over San Diego.)

So after a brief greeting in the hangar deck from the *Vinson*'s commanding officer—despite the honor guard of sailors on the bridge and gangway this is a nonformal affair—Wu and his retinue start their tour of the carrier's unclassified areas and systems: flight deck, ready room, air operations control room, officer and crew berthing areas, galley, catapult control room, arresting gear section.

Actually, this isn't entirely new to Wu. He toured another docked carrier, the USS *Harry S. Truman*, during his U.S. visit in 2007. But back then the Chinese navy didn't have an aircraft carrier, and now it does—the *Liaoning*. So Wu and Captains Zheng and Dai are particularly interested in the *Vinson*'s catapults and Mark7/Mod3 arresting gear systems.

The *Liaoning* doesn't use a catapult system—more on that later—and its relatively short flight deck makes having efficient arresting systems to slow down a landing aircraft particularly important. (There are reports, denied by the Chinese, that two pilots have been killed while testing the J-15 jets deployed aboard the *Liaoning*.) But future Chinese aircraft carriers could be flat-decked and catapult-equipped. The problem for the Chinese is that catapults like those on the *Vinson* are extremely complicated and difficult to maintain; it takes a long time to learn how to operate them efficiently and safely. The more they can learn about them from the undisputed experts the better.

Speaking through an interpreter (Wu speaks a little English, and probably understands more, but they use an interpreter anyway), the Chinese admiral snaps questions at the American sailors who operate the various equipment: How does this work? What do you do? What is this for? The sailors, dressed in working blue coveralls, are a little ill at ease—not because they're talking to a Chinese admiral but because the CNO is there. But they answer the admiral's questions in a general way.

Actually, in a way it's too bad for Admiral Wu that he doesn't get to see an aircraft take off from and land on the *Vinson*. Because as anyone who has witnessed it firsthand will attest, it's extremely cool.

Almost everyone has seen film of jets taking off and landing on an aircraft carrier flight deck. But to actually see and hear and feel an airplane being flung into the sky with a catapult and then see it snag an arresting wire and come to a full stop two seconds after landing—well, it's a heart-racing experience.

Pick a plane—say, an F/A-18E Super Hornet fighter. It's about sixty feet long, weighs about fifty thousand pounds loaded, has a top speed of about 1,200 mph, a combat range of about four hundred miles without in-air refueling, and can be armed with a host of air-to-air and air-to-surface missiles and precision-guided bombs. The pilot strapped inside the single-seat cockpit is probably in his or her late twenties to midthirties, and depending on rank and years in the service, he or she probably earns about $90,000 a year including flight pay and other allowances. The pilot is one of the small minority—about 20 percent—of would-be navy aviators who are skilled enough and lucky enough to make it through the ever-narrowing "pipeline" from initial flight training to flying fighters.

During launch and recovery operations, crewmembers on a carrier flight deck scurry about wearing different colored shirts: red-shirts are bomb loaders and firefighters, blue-shirts move the planes, purple-shirts ("grapes") handle fueling, yellow-shirts and green-shirts handle the launch. A typical carrier has four catapults or "cats," two to launch off the bow and two to launch off the angled deck at the ship's waist. The cat relies on a metal slide or "shuttle" that fits into a three-hundred-foot-long slot on the carrier's deck. To launch the plane, deck crews attach a metal hook or "launch bar" to connect the plane to the shuttle, and also attach a "holdback" bar to the rear of the plane's nose gear (front wheel); the holdback allows the pilot to throttle up for launching without moving forward or burning out his or her brakes.

Each catapult is powered by two pressurized steam pistons situated below deck. The amount of pressure in the pistons has to be precisely synced with the aircraft's weight and various other factors—wind speed over the deck, outside air pressure and humidity, and so on. Too much steam pressure and the catapult's initial jolt will rip off a plane's nose gear; too little pressure can produce a "cold shot"—that is, the plane never gets up to takeoff speed and may plunge off the flight deck, at which point the pilot has to eject and an $80 million airplane is in the drink. When the steam level is set and the plane is up to full power, the pilot gives an "OK" salute to the catapult officer—known as the "shooter"— who hits a button that releases the holdback bar. At that point the catapult starts dragging the plane down the flight deck at about 165 mph, and three hundred feet and a little over one second later the cat flings the fifty-thousand-pound plane off the carrier's bow. The entire launching process takes only about a minute per plane.

It's all pretty dramatic, and even sailors who've seen it a thousand times still get a thrill from the spectacle: the deck crews dancing around, jet engines screaming, steam billowing from the cat, the smell of fuel and jet exhaust, the fighter plane quivering like a hunting dog straining at the leash, and then the explosive release of power as the cat is let go.

Getting that plane safely back on deck is pretty dramatic as well. Central to that task is the "arresting gear," a series of two-inch-thick steel cables stretched across the deck and attached at each end to other cables that lead below deck to a hydropneumatic "arresting engine." A returning plane comes down to the deck at about 150 mph and its eight-foot-long tailhook snags one of the cables, which plays out like a giant bowstring as the arresting engine dispels the plane's kinetic energy; the Mark 7/Mod3 arresting gear can stop a fifty-thousand-pound plane in about 350 feet and in about two seconds. If the pilot misses all the cables, the plane becomes a "bolter," but because pilots are trained to accelerate to full power as soon as the jet's wheels touch the deck—just in case the aircraft fails to catch any cable—he or she should be able to get airborne off the deck again. The embarrassed pilot is likely to survive, but given navy humor is also likely to find a giant metal bolt hidden under the pillow when the pilot climbs into his or her bunk. (As we'll see, future U.S. Navy carriers will have new and improved catapult and arrester cable systems.)

But even though Admiral Wu doesn't get to see actual carrier flight operations, he does get to see the *Vinson*'s and the U.S. Navy's most powerful weapon—that is, the senior and master chiefs, the experienced noncommissioned officers without whom the navy could not function.

The role and status of U.S. military NCOs is sometimes difficult for civilians to understand. In the navy there are six levels of petty officers: petty officers third, second, and first class (pay grades E-4 to E-6); chief petty officer (E-7); senior chief petty officer (E-8); and master chief petty officer (E-9). (In the other U.S. military branches, E-5s and above are various ranks of sergeant.)

Technically the lowest-ranking navy officer, an ensign, outranks the highest-ranking NCO, the master or command master chief petty officer. The master chief will call the ensign "sir" or "ma'am," and when appropriate he or she will salute the ensign first. If a young ensign gives a master chief an order, the master chief is legally required to obey it.

But that's just military courtesy. In practice a master chief has far higher status than a new young officer, and is valued accordingly; a master chief with twenty years' service is actually paid twice as much as an ensign fresh out of the Academy—about $6,000 per month base pay for the chief versus about $3,000 for the ensign. (Military pay is based not just on rank but on years of service.) An ensign may give a master chief an order to carry out, but if it's a stupid order the ensign is going to get some counseling from the master chief—or the XO. And no sane ensign would dream of chewing out a senior or master chief; even admirals invariably treat senior chiefs with professional courtesy and respect.

That's because chiefs and senior chiefs and master chiefs are the ones who really know how all the navy's stuff works—engines, airplanes, computers, sophisticated electronics systems. Sure, commissioned officers know the theory and can plan the strategy. But officers come and go, skipping between sea and shore duty, changing ships as they advance in rank. A senior chief, meanwhile, may stay aboard the same ship or type of ship for years, learning its idiosyncrasies, figuring out the work-arounds and quick fixes needed to keep old and temperamental equipment operating and making sure sailors do their jobs. And becoming a senior chief is not just the result of on-the-job training; in today's navy promotions to senior petty officer ranks are partly based on education levels, so in addition to advanced in-house navy training in their specialties, most senior chiefs have at least a college associate's degree, and many have bachelor's or even master's degrees.

Again, the Chinese navy doesn't have anything remotely like the U.S. Navy's senior petty officer class—although it's been trying to change that. In 1999 almost all of the Chinese navy's non-officers were conscripts with ninth-grade educations or less. Later the Chinese navy started recruiting better-educated enlistees and making them petty officers, so that by 2009 about a third of its non-officer ranks had some college education that qualified them for appointments as mid- or senior-level petty officers. But you can't take someone with a college education and overnight turn him or her into a competent petty officer. A good senior petty officer combines education with experience—years and years of experience. It takes decades to build up a corps of solid, competent NCOs, and the Chinese navy still isn't there yet.

So when Admiral Wu sits down for a question-and-answer session with dozens of senior chiefs aboard the *Vinson*, he really can't relate. Of course, being senior chiefs, they aren't awed by having a Chinese admiral in their presence—and even if they were, they wouldn't show it. Having the CNO aboard is something special, but a Chinese admiral? No big deal. Still, they're polite in their own "been-there-done-that-seen-it-all" way. For example, when Wu asks them through the interpreter how they interact with junior commissioned officers, they try to explain it—see above—but it's clear that Admiral Wu doesn't get it. In fact, he seems a bit stiff and uncertain about having an informal discussion with non-officers; he is, after all, an admiral in the Chinese navy.

One thing the chiefs make clear to Wu and his team about carrier operations: This is risky business if you go fast. It's unforgiving. Safety takes time. Without safety you risk losing support—internal and external.

In any event, after his three-hour tour of the *Vinson*, Admiral Wu gets to take a look at the unclassified sections of the Los Angeles–class attack sub USS *Jefferson City*, also docked in

San Diego. Again, it's nothing new—Wu visited the docked attack sub USS *Montpelier* in Norfolk during his 2007 visit to the U.S.—but the sight of a Chinese admiral aboard a U.S. nuclear-powered attack sub still raises some eyebrows. Some navy admirals wonder privately if the U.S. is giving up a little too much of the secret sauce.

But following the sub visit, Admiral Wu does get to see something new. In planning the trip he asked for a tour-at-sea of one of the navy's newest ships, a littoral combat ship, or LCS. And since there's little about the controversial class of ships that hasn't already been made public, Admiral Greenert and the navy said sure.

So the next day Greenert and Wu and their various entourages climb aboard a navy Seahawk helicopter and fly out to the USS *Fort Worth*, which is conducting sea trials in the open ocean off San Diego.

And this time, it is Admiral Wu who is utterly unimpressed.

The navy's littoral combat ships are just that—ships designed to operate near the world's littorals, or coastlines, and carry out the navy's expanding missions there.

LCSs are small (about four hundred feet long) and designed to be fast (up to 50 mph), with a shallow draft (less than fifteen feet), making them useful for combating near-shore threats such as pirates and terrorists and drug runners; they also have unusually wide flight decks capable of handling multiple helicopter and un-manned drone operations. Also, if there's a disaster relief mission, they can carry more supplies than a destroyer and get them to the scene in a hurry. With small crews of about a hundred personnel to run the ship and "operate" the mission modules, they can show the flag in foreign ports without leaving a big, domineering footprint in local and regional politics like a visiting carrier strike group sometimes does. And best of all from a budgetary point of view, they're supposed to be relatively cheap, about $400 million or so, or about half the cost of an Arleigh Burke–class guided-missile destroyer hull—although in practice it hasn't worked out that way.

To some top navy leaders on this day in 2013, the LCSs represent the golden future; they envision building as many as forty of the new ships and deploying at least half in the Western Pacific. The goal is to demonstrate U.S. "presence" without offending any nation's sensibilities—especially China's—and also without breaking the bank. Greenert, for example, calls the LCS the "poster ship" for the Asia-Pacific navy of the twenty-first century—and he's proud to show one off to Admiral Wu.

But a lot of top navy commanders see the LCSs a little differently. They think the LCS program is one of the dumbest things the U.S. Navy has done in decades.

There are two classes of navy LCSs, named after the first ships of each class to be commissioned: the Freedom class—of which the USS *Fort Worth* is one—and the Independence class. (All of the Independence-class LCSs are slated to be deployed to the Pacific.) Of the two, the Independence-class LCSs are definitely sexier looking, with a trimaran (three-hulled) design, a long, sleek bow, and an unusually large landing deck at the stern; they look sort of like small aircraft carriers coupled with destroyers. The smaller single-hulled Freedom-class littoral combat ships are more conventional looking, but they can still turn an eye. At full speed the ships' diesel-powered generators, turbines, and water-jet propulsion systems produce an impressive twenty-five-foot-high "rooster tail" of white water that can swamp a small boat; they're sort of like giant Jet Skis.

But visual appeal aside, both classes of LCS have issues.

Take the USS *Freedom*, the first of its class. Built by giant defense contractor Lockheed Martin—which is primarily an aircraft and aerospace company—and commissioned in 2008, the ship was plagued with cost overruns and literally thousands of production and design discrepancies; during its navy certification trials, it failed twice, and miserably so. In March 2013, USS *Freedom* departed San Diego for a ten-month deployment to Changi Naval Base in Singapore, the first step in the navy's plan to establish a permanent rotating LCS presence in the South China Sea. Unfortunately, it's a long way from San Diego to Singapore, and the *Freedom* barely made the trip; the power plant equipment kept cutting out, causing the ship to lose all power until backup generators kicked in—a disquieting experience for a navy ship in the middle of the ocean.

True, the *Freedom* was a big hit at Singapore's 2013 International Maritime and Defence Exhibition, a gathering of naval officers and experts from around the region and the world. Greenert, who was there, later said that when the navy commanders of India and Malaysia toured the ship they were impressed; they said the Freedom-class ships would "resonate" better with their own navies than would bigger U.S. ships. Still, during its Singapore deployment the USS *Freedom* continued to suffer embarrassing power plant breakdowns.

As for the Independence-class LCSs, they also had cost over-runs and serious deficiencies, although not nearly as many as the Freedom-class ships. But both ship classes have the same funda-mental conceptual problems.

For one thing, the LCSs aren't multipurpose ships like de-stroyers or frigates. Instead they have a modular design in which different "mission modules" can be switched in and out to perform different tasks—antisubmarine warfare, mine detection, potential Special Forces operations, anti-ship surface warfare. The problem is that you can only change out the different mission modules in port, and it can take a lot of time—currently up to a month or so. So, for example, if you urgently need an LCS that can do antisubmarine operations, but the only one available is fitted out with an antimine mission module—well, the shooting's probably going to be over before that LCS can get switched out.

That's one fundamental problem. But a bigger one is that LCSs can't take a hit, and they really can't give a significant hit, either.

Neither LCS class is designed to take a missile strike and be able to keep on fighting; they'd be lucky to be able to limp back to port, assuming they don't sink outright. The Independence-class LCSs are particularly vulnerable; their trimaran hulls are built of lightweight aluminum that could crumple like tinfoil if they took a missile hit. True, in any major naval conflict the LCSs might be able to hide in some protected area along a coast. But if you're hiding, if your weapons systems and radar are shut down to avoid enemy electromagnetic detection, then by definition you're not fighting—which the LCSs weren't meant to do in the first place. That's because the LCSs are notoriously under-gunned, with only a small fraction of the firepower of a Burke-class guided-missile destroyer. In fact, that's what Admiral Wu notices most as he and Greenert tour the USS *Forth Worth* off the coast of California.

The Freedom-class LCSs are hard to get around in, with narrow passageways and narrow, steep ladders and stairs; it's no problem for Greenert, who spent years in cramped submarines, but the aging, out-of-shape Chinese admiral is struggling a little. Still, he takes the standard tour—bridge, engine room, flight deck, crew quarters, main deck gun. And by the time it's over, Admiral Wu is almost—not quite but almost—laughing. It's as if he's thinking—"This is what the U.S. Navy has been making such a fuss about?"

"It doesn't look like a powerful ship," Wu says, a bit undiplomatically. And the Chinese admiral is right. The USS *Fort Worth* isn't a powerful ship; none of the LCSs are. The *Fort Worth*'s main gun is an MK 110 57mm gun that can lob a five-pound shell about five miles, and it has a few machine guns—good enough to sink some pirate motorboats but useless against bigger targets. And that's it. No missiles, no torpedoes, just a popgun on the deck and some machine guns. (True, eventually some LCSs will be equipped with missiles, but not on the *Fort Worth* on this day.) Combine the lack of offensive and defensive firepower with the LCS's low "survivability" rating and what you have is a ship that probably would be a sitting duck in any hot conflict at sea.

And Wu knows it. He starts comparing the *Fort Worth*—unfavorably so—to the Chinese navy's new Jiangdao-class (Type 056) corvettes, which bristle with 76mm guns, torpedo launchers, and YJ-83 long-range anti-ship missiles that can strike a target a hundred miles or more away. They're small but they're powerful—and the Chinese navy plans to churn them out by the dozens in the next few years. The new corvettes are multi-mission platforms that can be built quickly and in quantity without costing an arm and a leg. While the U.S. has been pouring billions of dollars into LCSs, which many see as glorified sea scooters, China has been investing in actual warships.

It's pretty clear to Wu which navy is getting the better deal. And the irony of it is inescapable: While China has been expanding from a brown-water (inland/coastal) to a green-water (mostly coastal toward the sea) to a blue-water (deep sea) navy, with the LCS program the mighty U.S. Navy has been throwing much of its resources into creating a brown-water naval force in the Western Pacific.

So as he and Greenert fly back to San Diego after the USS *Fort Worth* tour, Wu is probably feeling like a coach who has just scouted out the opposing team's star players—and likes his own team's chances.

Admiral Wu's U.S. visit doesn't end with the tour of the *Fort Worth*. After a stop at Marine Corps Base Camp Pendleton, north of San Diego, Greenert and Wu fly to Washington, D.C., for more discussions. There's a brass-band-and-red-carpet honors ceremony at the Washington Navy Yard, at which Greenert is expansive about future relations between their two navies.

"Admiral Wu is the head of a great and a growing navy," Greenert says. "They are actively modernizing, and the relationship between our navies is increasing as well. The purpose of his visit here this week has been to continue our military-to-military relations, and evolve and mature our relationship, looking for great opportunities to share common interests and move ahead in our cooperation."

It's pretty chummy stuff.

Over the coming few years Greenert and Admiral Wu will have numerous personal meetings, telephone calls, video conferences—four face-to-face meetings in 2014 alone. (Greenert even gives Wu his personal cell phone number—sort of a call-me-anytime thing—but Wu doesn't reciprocate, saying his bosses on the Central Commission wouldn't approve.) And through it all, Greenert will continue to pound the theme of close cooperation and understanding between his navy and Admiral Wu's. But at the same time, Greenert never really figures out what to make of the guy.

They'll never be bear-hug buddies, but Greenert respects Wu professionally, and he understands that Wu has to answer to his bosses, just like Greenert has to answer to his bosses. He also understands that Wu's job is to protect Chinese interests, just as Greenert is dedicated to protecting American interests. At the most basic level, it's important for them to each know exactly where the other is coming from. Still, Greenert comes from a navy culture that values honesty and straightforwardness when dealing face-to-face with allies and partners and even potential partners. You may not be able to tell them everything, but if you want them to trust you and work with you, you don't out-and-out lie to them.

But Admiral Wu seems to have a different operational concept when it comes to accuracy and trust and truth.

Take the pig thing. At one point, during the obligatory small talk that precedes a meeting, Greenert casually mentions to Wu through the interpreter that he and his wife have gotten a new dog. But through mishearing or misinterpretation Wu somehow gets the impression that Greenert has gotten a pig. A pet pig! Wu isn't exactly known for his finely tuned sense of humor, but apparently he thinks it's hilarious that the U.S. chief of naval operations is walking around with a pet pig. So even after Greenert tells him no, it's a dog, not a pig, Wu can't let the pig thing go. He keeps talking about it, telling other people that Greenert has a pet pig, and no one can ever convince him otherwise.

And in another canine-related "misunderstanding," somebody tells Greenert that Wu has a pet water dog, like a Portuguese water dog, so at their next meeting Greenert gives Wu a glossy coffee table–style book about water dogs as a gift. Wu accepts the book, not very graciously, and then he tells Greenert that he doesn't have a water dog, or any dog. Greenert is a little embarrassed; he doesn't like getting caught operating on bad information. But then one of Wu's aides later admits to one of Greenert's aides that yes, Admiral Wu does indeed have a water dog, and everybody knows it. It could be Wu just doesn't want to admit that the top admiral in the Chinese navy would have time for a pet dog. For Wu it could be a loss of face.

Sure, those are small, inconsequential things. But they give some insight into what U.S. Navy officers are up against as they try to implement the Obama administration's policy of friendly military engagement with the Chinese. Again and again, truth will be elusive, facts will be ignored, lies will be told.

And what happens after the cruiser USS *Cowpens* meets the Chinese aircraft carrier *Liaoning* in the South China Sea is only one example.

CHAPTER 6

Crashback

A hundred miles out from Hainan Island, just hours away from the *Cowpens's* planned interception of the Chinese navy carrier *Liaoning* in December 2013, Captain Greg Gombert issues another order to the officer of the deck—and again the captain's will is instantly broadcast throughout the ship.

Assume Condition EmCon Delta. Assume Condition EmCon Delta.

"EmCon" is short for "emissions control," and "Delta" means emissions control at the highest, most secure level. What the order means in practical terms is that throughout the *Cowpens*, radars are shut down, active sonars are turned off, radios go silent. Almost everything that gives off an electromagnetic signal suddenly goes dead.

The idea is simple. The *Cowpens* is trying to make itself invisible—or as close to that as possible—and sneak up on the Chinese carrier task force undetected.

It might just work. The *Cowpens's* superstructure has a somewhat reduced radar cross-section, compared to large American warships of decades past, making it at least marginally more difficult for an opposing force's over-the-horizon radar to pick up. And at EmCon Delta the ship presents a very low electromagnetic signature, one not associated with a U.S. warship. The

South China Sea is a busy place, filled with container ships and tankers and cruise ships and bulk freighters and fishing vessels large and small. The hope is that the radar operators aboard *Liaoning*'s escort ships, staring at display screens dotted with dozens of circles, squares, and triangles that indicate ships, will miss the *Cowpens* in the crowd.

Going to EmCon Delta is a risky maneuver, though. It effectively renders the *Cowpens* blind to incoming aircraft or missiles. And in such a crowded sea, it increases the chances of accidental collision. The last thing Gombert wants to do is run over a fishing boat. So every few minutes he orders a quick radar snapshot on the Furuno, a small, commercially available radar system that's used by many small commercial vessels. It gives Gombert some situational awareness, and if the Chinese do pick up the radar signal, maybe they'll think the *Cowpens* is just another fishing trawler.

A few hours later, twenty-five miles off Hainan Island, home of the largest Chinese navy base in the Asia-Pacific, this crowded sea gets a little more crowded. The *Cowpens*'s passive sonar picks up a series of underwater whirrs, clicks, and clanks that form an identifiable acoustic signature. They're very faint, but they're there. The sonar officer reports to the bridge.

"Captain, I think we've got a Chinese submarine out there."

This is interesting. The *Liaoning* isn't in sight yet, but from satellite data and other intelligence Gombert knows that it's close. And if the aircraft carrier is conducting joint operations with a sub—it could be a Type 039 Yuan-class sub, one of the new superquiet diesel-electrics—it indicates a higher level of operational capability than the U.S. Navy expected.

And now, suddenly looming up over the horizon, there it is—the *Liaoning*.

The *Liaoning* began its life with the Chinese navy as a secret. Built in the Ukraine for the Soviet navy in the late 1980s, it was still unfinished when the Soviet Union went belly-up and construction ceased. Using a Chinese travel agency as a cover, China bought it in 1998 for a mere $20 million and had it towed to China. Not wanting to alarm anyone with its plans for a carrier force, China initially claimed the ship would be converted into a floating hotel/casino in Macao. But obviously, on this day, the *Liaoning* isn't armed with slot machines; its hangar and flight deck are occupied by J-15 fighter jets.

By U.S. standards the *Liaoning* is an unusual-looking aircraft carrier. U.S. aircraft carriers are "flattops" that use powerful steam-driven catapults to hurl their aircraft off the flight deck. But as we've seen, catapult systems are complicated, and expensive, so the *Liaoning* uses a different method. At the bow the *Liaoning's* flight deck curves up in a graceful arc some three stories high. An aircraft taking off powers up to full throttle, releases the brakes, and screams along the flight deck to that arc and then soars into the air like an Olympic ski jumper. The ski-jump launch method means the *Liaoning's* aircraft can only carry limited weapons loads, but the method is elegantly simple.

From the *Cowpens's* bridge Captain Gombert can see that the *Liaoning* has at least five amphibious ship escorts steaming in formation around it. The amphibs, which are designed to carry troops, amphibious assault vehicles, and helicopters, are relatively small—175 to 250 feet long—and are dwarfed by the carrier. But they range around the *Liaoning* like a pack of shepherd's dogs guarding one very large gray sheep.

If the *Cowpens* can see them, they can see the *Cowpens*. No need for EmCon Delta anymore. The ship's radars, active sonars, and communications systems light up again. On the bridge, the *Cowpens's* radio receivers suddenly pick up an explosion of furious Chinese coming from the escort ships' bridge-to-bridge communications systems. Gombert can't understand what they're saying, but he can easily read the tone. The Chinese escort ship's commanders are *yelling* at each other.

"I need the translator up here," Gombert says. Moments later, a young Asian-American sailor appears on the bridge, looking more than a little nervous. This is unaccustomed territory for him.

The young sailor is not an official navy translator. His rate is fireman (E-3), meaning he's a sailor of the third-lowest rank in the navy. But he happens to be a native Mandarin speaker, and he was tracked down while on shore leave from another ship and dragooned onto the *Cowpens* specifically for this mission. He's a good man, a good sailor, but English clearly remains his second language. He monitors the escort ships' radio transmissions.

"They are surprised by you," he tells the captain. "They don't know where you come from, why they didn't see you."

"We caught them with their pants down," Gombert says. It's a small triumph, but it's also a danger. The *Cowpens* is still twelve miles from the *Liaoning*, and the Chinese are already pissed off.

It's time for some eyes in the sky. Gombert orders the *Cowpens* slowed to a helicopter launching speed of five knots, and the Seahawk pilot expertly lifts his helo off the ship's lurching flight deck and heads in the carrier's direction. Gombert reminds the *Cowpens*'s air boss to keep the helo five miles away from the carrier—close enough to grab some good pictures with high-tech cameras, but far enough away not to interfere with the carrier's air operations. The *Liaoning* is zigzagging through the sea at flank speed, about thirty-two knots, testing its rudder controls and getting ready to launch and recover aircraft. And its captain is not happy to see the *Cowpens* bearing down on him.

The young sailor/translator on the *Cowpens*'s bridge is still monitoring the Chinese ships' radio transmissions. He turns to Captain Gombert and says, "The big ship, he's telling the little ships to take care of you. He has undersea operations."

Undersea operations—in other words, the carrier is operating in conjunction with a submarine. That confirms it. But it also complicates things. In these shallow waters over the continental shelf, Gombert will have to be careful not to bring the *Cowpens* too close to the Chinese sub. There's a danger of a collision, or maybe the sub commander will just freak out when his sonar picks up a U.S. warship bearing down on him. This is that kind of situation.

Suddenly two of the smaller escort ships break formation and head for the *Cowpens* at top speed, about eighteen knots. They appear to be Type 074 landing ships, each about 175 feet long.

And now it starts. The *Cowpens*'s radios crackle with heavily accented and unmistakably angry English coming from the *Liaoning*.

"You are violating China security space! You must leave the area!"

Through his radio communications officer, a young lieutenant with the calm, unflappable voice of a 9-1-1 operator, Gombert answers.

"This is the U.S. Navy warship *Cowpens*. We are in international waters."

"You must leave area!"

"We are in international waters."

"Leave now!"

"International waters."

It goes back and forth like that as the amphibs close in on the *Cowpens*, which in turn is still steaming directly toward the carrier, now about ten miles away. One amphib is about a hundred yards off the port bow, the other off the starboard, matching the bigger ship's speed. They've got the *Cowpens* bracketed, and the distance between them is diminishing. It's obvious what the amphibs are trying to do. They're trying to turn the *Cowpens* off its course, to herd it away from their carrier.

The *Cowpens* is an agile ship, but it's still almost six hundred feet long. As large ships go it can turn on a dime, but at sea that dime is several hundred yards across. And the bulky Chinese amphibs are even less maneuverable. One small miscalculation, a couple seconds of bad seamanship, and one of those amphibs could slam into the *Cowpens* like a seaborne train wreck, or vice versa.

And it seems like these amphibs don't care. The one on the starboard side suddenly turns and cuts across the *Cowpens*'s bow at an oblique angle, so close that it's in the *Cowpens*'s "forward shadow zone," part of it disappearing from his line of sight under the front end of the cruiser. Gombert can't believe it.

While startled sailors get out of the way—"Make a hole!"— Gombert dashes from the bridge, swings down some ladders (stairways) to the main deck, and sprints to the bow. From there he sees that the *Cowpens*'s bow has missed the amphib's stern by fifty feet. Fifty feet! He stares at the amphib, while a couple of hard-eyed Chinese sailors on its bridge deck stare back. Gombert runs back up to the bridge, stunned at what the Chinese amphib has just done.

Okay, sure, the *Cowpens* is trying to spy on their carrier, just as Chinese navy ships have spied on American ships. But there are *rules* for these things—and there's common sea sense, too. What the amphib skipper has done is an incredibly aggressive and hostile act, an act that under the laws of the sea is a felony, not a misdemeanor. Gombert has to wonder—"Are these guys nuts? Are they suicidal? Are they actually *looking* for a fight with an American cruiser?"

It's possible. Gombert knows full well that in years past the Chinese navy has opened fire and killed people to enforce its claims to sovereignty in these waters. They haven't killed any Americans, at least not in recent decades, although they've come pretty close. Maybe today is the day it starts.

Gombert returns to the bridge, where the Chinese radio messages are continuing—urgent, angry, almost hysterical.

"Leave area immediately!"

"We are in international waters."

"Leave now! You put yourself at risk!"

Gombert almost smiles at that one. Risk? No kidding.

Given the Chinese ships' aggressiveness and unpredictability, the OOD asks the captain if the *Cowpens* should modify its weapons status, just in case the Chinese go completely batshit and open fire. Ordinarily, as a safety measure, it requires three separate orders to fire a missile or open up with the five-inch guns. Under modified status it requires only one: The captain tells the weapons officer to fire, and half a second later the missiles or main gun rounds are on their way.

Gombert thinks it over, and quickly decides no. If he lights up his weapons systems' radar, the Chinese might electronically pick up on it; it would be like a fighter pilot locking his air-to-air missile guidance systems onto another plane. It could rattle them—maybe even rattle them enough to open fire first. The Chinese escort ships aren't heavily armed, packing only a few 25mm guns. But this close to the coast there could be some small Houbei-class Chinese missile gunboats lurking near the shore, not to mention some land-based missile batteries. Again, given the aged state of the *Cowpens*'s Aegis Combat System, the ship simply can't handle an incoming swarm of Chinese missiles. There's also that Chinese submarine out there he has to worry about. Besides, Gombert's orders are to maintain a "de-escalatory posture." But the fact that he even considers modifying his weapons status indicates just how tense the situation is.

And now it gets tenser. The Chinese amphib that cut across the *Cowpens*'s bow swings around and starts moving directly into the *Cowpens*'s course about five hundred yards ahead. Gombert orders a slight course correction to get around it, but the amphib shifts to block that course as well. It's like the amphib's commander is daring the *Cowpens* to ram him—and if that happens, if the *Cowpens* T-bones that little amphib, it's going to be like an eighty-thousand-pound semitrailer T-boning a minivan. People are going to die.

The amphib is only two hundred yards away now, and a ship as big and fast as the *Cowpens* takes a long time to stop—and that's only if Gombert is *willing* to stop. By every rule of the sea, the *Cowpens* has the right-of-way; if the Chinese amphib gets cut in half, it's their own damn fault. The *Cowpens* is moving closer, closer, closer . . .

It's like a moment frozen in time. In the Command Information Center, radar operators scan the skies for the first sign of incoming missiles, and sonar operators strain to hear the sound of the Chinese sub getting ready to launch its torpedoes or anti-ship missiles.

Radios squawk out angry English—"Leave the area! Leave the area!" On the decks, sailors who can see what's going on are giving each other "Holy shit!" looks. On the bridge, the junior officers are looking desperately at Captain Gombert, who stares out at the rapidly nearing amphib, knowing he has to make a decision—and that there's no good decision to make.

In the end, he has no choice.

"ALL BACK EMERGENCY FULL! BRACE! BRACE! BRACE!"

In an instant the massive gears deep in the ship go from full ahead to neutral to full reverse, while the cruiser's four twenty-thousand-horsepower-each engines are screaming to provide full power. The effect is like a jumbo jet landing on a too-short runway; the bow pushes down, the stern rises up. Throughout the ship, sailors and officers have to grab the nearest handholds to keep from being tumbled forward. The collision warning alarm bounces off metal bulkheads throughout the ship, like the flailing of a gong. It's not at all certain that the ship will be able to stop in time.

Above, the cruiser USS *Cowpens,* whose crew found itself at the center of the U.S.-China clash, launches missiles at an airborne drone during a live-fire weapons shoot. *Courtesy of the U.S. Navy.*

The *Cowpens* was badly in need of a general overhaul or major upgrade at the end of this century's first decade. Instead the navy performed only cosmetic maintenance and rushed it back out to sea. Both the vessel and its crew were subsequently ill-prepared for an encounter with a Chinese carrier-led armada. *Courtesy of the U.S. Navy.*

With the launch of its first aircraft carrier, the *Liaoning,* the Chinese navy entered the realm of the world's naval elite. Thus were the seeds planted for its encounter with the USS *Cowpens. Courtesy of Navy.81.cn.*

EP-3E Aries II flights near the military-sensitive Hainan Island in the South China Sea—conducted for the purpose of gathering intelligence—have always rattled the Chinese, who use facilities there for submarine, surface-combatant, and other major military operations. In 2001, a Chinese fighter collided with an Aries aircraft, killing the pilot of the combat jet and forcing the EP-3E to make an emergency landing on the island. *Courtesy of the U.S. Navy.*

One of the U.S. Navy's most important intelligence-gathering aircraft—and a potential successor to the Aries—the P-8A Poseidon has been the target of Chinese criticism and aerial military harassment. Designed to detect and track submarines, the Poseidons have also helped detail Chinese military expansion and fake-island building. *Courtesy of Boeing.*

Fiery Cross Reef in the Spratly Islands group is just one of the new South China Sea military outposts developed by the Chinese in recent years. China has built up islands, or in some cases created its own artificial islands, to build a "Great Wall of Sand," warns Admiral Harry Harris, the commander of the U.S. Pacific Command. More literally, the islands are used to assert territorial rights and as airstrips to stash aircraft that can be called on at short notice. *Courtesy of CSIS Asia Maritime Transparency Initiative/DigitalGlobe.*

Another example of China's growing military might has been the DF ballistic missile series, which reportedly can be guided to strike a moving aircraft carrier. While the missile has never been truly tested operationally, even the possibility that America's carriers may be vulnerable has forced U.S. military strategists to rethink the navy's posture. *Courtesy of* Business Insider.

Armed with Tomahawk missiles, guided-missile destroyers like the USS *Preble* can launch land attacks from several hundred miles away. But the expansion and improvement of Chinese naval and missile capability has forced the U.S. Navy to seek technological upgrades. *Courtesy of the U.S. Navy.*

The USS *Hopper* tests an upgrade of the Standard Missile-3 Block IB off the coast of Hawaii. *Courtesy of the U.S. Navy.*

Facing an increasing threat of missile-salvo attacks, American destroyer crews train constantly until operating the Aegis Combat System becomes second nature. Live-fire exercises like this one conducted by the guided-missile destroyer USS *Chung-Hoon* are vital to keeping the ships and sailors prepared. *Courtesy of the U.S. Navy.*

In an effort to bring China into the international naval community, the U.S. invited the growing navy giant to the Rim of the Pacific (RimPac) training exercise in July 2014 off the coast of Hawaii. China violated naval protocol, though, by sending its intelligence-gathering ship to "spy" on the event. *Courtesy of GlobalSecurity.com.*

To conduct coastal operations more effectively, the U.S. Navy developed shallow-water-penetrating littoral combat ships such as the one pictured here, the USS *Freedom*. Unimpressed by the LCS's striking camouflage paint scheme, the Chinese dismissed the new vessel as being undergunned and overhyped, while U.S. admirals searched for ways to arm their new creation with over-the-horizon missiles. *Courtesy of the U.S. Navy.*

LCS USS *Coronado*'s first test shot of a Harpoon Block 1C missile, during the 2016 RimPac exercise in the Pacific. By arming LCS vessels with such missiles and using sensors on other ships, aircraft, or even satellites, U.S. strategists feel they can penetrate enemy defenses more easily. *Courtesy of the U.S. Navy.*

While Congress bemoaned the price tag of the USS *Gerald R. Ford*—at least $13.2 billion—the U.S. Navy touted the ship's technological advances in launching and landing aircraft, incorporating directed-energy weapons, and conducting operations with significantly fewer sailors. *Courtesy of the U.S. Navy.*

Two F-35B Lightning II Joint Strike Fighters (JSFs) land on the flight deck of the amphibious assault ship USS *America*. Extremely hard to find and track with radar, the new aircraft are packed with state-of-the-art sensors, processors, and communications systems. *Courtesy of the U.S. Navy.*

The futuristic USS *Zumwalt* is the largest and most powerful guided-missile destroyer built by the U.S. Navy. Its futuristic shape is meant to confuse radar and it has the energy-producing capacity to power lasers, electromagnetic guns, and other next-generation weapons. *Courtesy of the U.S. Navy.*

The Office of Naval Research has sponsored the development, deployment, and testing of the U.S. Navy Laser Weapons System (LaWS) in the Arabian Gulf. With a laser and enough power, a ship's captain never has to worry about "going Winchester"—running out of ammunition. *Courtesy of the U.S. Navy.*

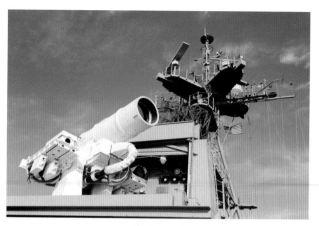

The U.S. Navy has come to rely on subsea drones to countermine and intelligence gather. But China views drone operations as intrusions into sovereign waters. Chinese resentment led to a seizure of an unmanned American submersible just before Donald Trump became president. *Courtesy of the U.S. Navy.*

Captain Gregory W. Gombert
Courtesy of the U.S. Navy.

Admiral Harry B. Harris, Jr.
Courtesy of the U.S. Navy.

Admiral Jonathan W. Greenert
Courtesy of the U.S. Navy.

Rear Admiral Michael C. Manazir
Courtesy of the U.S. Navy.

Vice Admiral Thomas S. Rowden
Courtesy of the U.S. Navy.

Finally, after it's traveled two ship lengths, about twelve hundred feet, the *Cowpens*'s reversing screws generate enough counterforce to slow the cruiser's forward momentum and bring it to a full stop, a mere one hundred yards short of the amphib.

And in that moment, just before the screws start pulling the ship backward, the mighty USS *Cowpens* is DIW, lying dead in the water in the South China Sea.

Old navy surface warfare sailors have a word for this kind of unusual emergency at-sea stopping maneuver. They call it a "crashback"—and for a U.S. Navy warship, and its captain, having to execute a crashback is never a good thing.

Given his "de-escalatory" orders, Captain Gombert really had no alternative. It was like being a car driver confronting a guy who intentionally jumps in the street ahead of the speeding car. Sure, the car has the right-of-way. But the driver has to at least try to avoid splattering the guy all over the asphalt—and it's the same on an ocean. The rules of the sea say you do everything you can to avoid a collision, no matter who's at fault.

Still, Gombert knows the score. A crashback is potentially dangerous for a ship's crew, and hard on the ship's mechanical systems; it's like throwing a speeding car into reverse. And by navy standards, in almost every circumstance, a captain who has to order a crashback is, at minimum, guilty of poor seamanship.

Maybe he failed to spot a looming reef or shoal. Maybe he misjudged his ship's course and speed relative to other ships and he had to execute an all-back full emergency to avoid a collision. And even if the crashback was prompted by an adversary's deliberate action—such as parking his vessel directly in the ship's path—there's always the question: Why didn't the captain anticipate that, and maneuver his ship accordingly? Why did he allow himself and his ship and crew to be put in that dangerous position?

So Gombert knows there will be criticism, second-guessing,

a lot of why-did-he-do-this or why-didn't-he-do-that chatter in navy wardrooms and officers' clubs. That may not be fair, but again: Anything that goes wrong on a navy ship is more than the captain's responsibility. It is the captain's fault.

And there's one other indignity that the *Cowpens* and its captain still have to suffer. As Gombert backs his ship away from the amphibs, the radio crackles with a new voice coming from the carrier. It's Captain Zhang Zheng, commander of the *Liaoning*, the same Captain Zhang whom Admiral Greenert and others found so charming when he toured the USS *Carl Vinson* with Admiral Wu just a few months earlier. He seems less charming now.

"Warship 63, this is the Chinese carrier," Zhang says. "Warship 63, this is the carrier requesting to speak to your Charlie Oscar [commanding officer]."

Gombert takes the radio mic.

"This is Charlie Oscar 63. Roger. Over."

"I didn't care for how you were talking with my colleagues," Zhang says in his crisp, commanding voice. "I don't like what's going on over there. I don't know what you are doing, but we are busy conducting our own operations. I don't see why this is being so difficult. You don't have to be so rude. You can just get out of the way. We are two professional seagoing officers and this situation requires natural decorum for the sake of everyone's safety."

Gombert can hardly believe it. He was half expecting an angry harangue, like he got from the amphib skippers; what he's getting is a headmaster quietly lecturing a schoolboy. And it pisses him off. Under the carrier captain's orders the amphib crew came *this close* to getting killed out there—and now this guy is acting like it's the *Cowpens*'s fault.

Gombert would like to set this guy straight, to give him a thorough ass-chewing concerning a ship commander's duties and responsibilities not to put sailors under his command in a suicidal position. But he has his orders. His orders are to be "cordial and respectful."

So what Gombert says to Captain Zhang is this: "I am very sorry for what's happened. I didn't mean to disturb your operations. I know our helicopter is bothering you, but we're just doing some surface-search surveillance. This is what we do every day. I'm just executing my air plan. Our helo will be leaving your location shortly. Why don't you tell me where you are going next so I know not to go there?"

"That really is none of your business," Zhang says, curtly. "Just get the helo out of the way, please."

Gombert off-keys the mic and contacts the *Cowpens*'s helo pilot over the direct radio link.

"You guys get what you need?"

"Yeah, Captain," the pilot says. "We're good."

Gombert puts out an order to prepare for aircraft recovery and then keys the mic.

"The helo will be leaving your location shortly and we'll be on our way, Captain."

"Fine, have a nice day."

Have a nice day! The undertone of contempt in the carrier captain's voice is unmistakable.

To civilians back home all this might not seem like a big deal, a mere seagoing traffic dispute in a faraway place most of them couldn't find on a map. But everyone on the *Cowpens*'s bridge, Gombert included, understands what just happened. This wasn't a Chinese interceptor jet "thumping" an Aries, or the Chinese navy harassing an unarmed navy surveillance ship. For the first time the Chinese navy has openly confronted a U.S. Navy combatant ship on the high seas—a cruiser, no less—and forced it to back down.

The *Cowpens* is still being pinched by the amphibs, so after the

Seahawk lands on the flight deck Gombert pulls a hard rudder and then orders full ahead, sailing away from the Chinese carrier. One of the amphibs follows, but the *Cowpens* is faster, and the Chinese ship gradually starts to fall behind. It's a ridiculous spectacle, the little amphib chasing the massive cruiser like a yapping dog chasing a car—and like the dog, the amphib probably thinks the American cruiser is afraid of it.

Which in a sense it is. In following his orders and the rules of the sea, Gombert has demonstrated that the U.S. Navy is unwilling to kill—or to die—to protect its rights and interests in the South China Sea. And at the same time, the Chinese amphib skipper has demonstrated that the Chinese navy *is* willing to see its sailors die to protect their country's contrary interests. For both sides, it's a lesson that will be remembered.

Captain Gombert is actually prepared to give the *Liaoning* another go, maybe drop down below the horizon for a while and then shift course and close with the carrier task force from another direction—and then hope that the amphibs won't sally forth on another suicide mission. But the brass back at Seventh Fleet wave him off. They've been kept generally apprised of the situation by encrypted text messaging, with an officer on the *Cowpens*'s bridge describing what's happening, and they've heard enough. They order the *Cowpens* to "resume routine patrol."

So the *Cowpens* turns southeast, away from Hainan Island, away from the *Liaoning*, with the little amphib still doggedly in pursuit—chasing the U.S. Navy out of the South China Sea.

"A cruiser!" the young navy surface warfare officer says bitterly. "They did this to a cruiser! Jesus!"

The young officer is nursing a beer in an Irish pub called Siné, just a short walk from the Pentagon. Like so many other navy officers, he's thinking about what happened ten thousand miles away in the South China Sea—and he's not happy about it.

"We should at least act like we're the most powerful navy in the world," he says, swirling his pint before taking a gulp. "You do things like that, and everybody thinks you're a pushover. They think you're all talk. That's not good for anyone."

Sure, he admits, he wasn't there on the bridge of the *Cowpens*. And yes, he's currently a chairborne sailor commanding a desk—a very small desk—buried in the deepest recesses of the Pentagon. Still, he's been out there, he served on destroyers, he knows how the Chinese navy operates.

"You show this kind of weakness to the Chinese—you give an inch—they'll take a mile," he says. "You have to show them strength or they'll run right over you—literally. He [the *Cowpens*'s CO] had the right-of-way. I can see him slowing his speed, maybe altering course a little. But he should have kept going and let the Chinese get out of the way."

It took about a week for the story of the *Cowpens*'s near collision in the South China Sea to break publicly. And as the most serious confrontation in years between the U.S. and China in the disputed sea—one even more potentially dangerous than the USNS *Impeccable* in 2009—it got a lot of attention.

But judging from the American and Chinese explanations of what happened, you had to wonder if the two sides were even talking about the same ship.

"On December 5th, while lawfully operating in international waters in the South China Sea, USS *Cowpens* and a PLA navy vessel had an encounter that required maneuvering to avoid a collision," a navy spokesman said. "This incident underscores the need to ensure the highest standards of professional seamanship, including communications between vessels, to mitigate the risk of an unintended incident or mishap." U.S. Secretary of

Defense Chuck Hagel called the Chinese actions "unhelpful" and "irresponsible," and State Department officials announced that formal protests over the incident had been lodged with Beijing.

Officially, the Chinese government response was muted. In a statement on its website, the Defence Ministry said only that the Chinese ship involved was conducting "normal patrols" when the two ships "met." The statement added that "during the encounter, the Chinese naval vessel properly handled it in accordance with strict protocol. The two defense departments were kept informed of the relevant situation through normal working channels and carried out effective communication."

Okay, fair enough. But unofficially, in the Chinese news media, the response was far different—and you have to remember that in China, "unofficial" news stories often offer better insight into what Chinese Communist Party leaders are thinking than official statements from the government; every word of every story is vetted by Party censors, which allows the leadership to say something without actually saying it. So officially/unofficially, the line was that the incident was all the Americans' fault—and they'd better be careful.

Here's what China's state-run news agency, Xinhua, had to say in an English-language article:

"On December 5, U.S. missile cruiser *Cowpens*, despite warnings from China's aircraft carrier task group, broke into the Chinese navy's drilling waters in the South China Sea, and almost collided with a Chinese warship nearby. Even before the navy training, Chinese maritime authorities [had] posted a navigation notice on their website"—that is, the twenty-eight-mile safety zone mentioned earlier—"and the U.S. warship, which should have had knowledge of what the Chinese were doing there, intentionally carried on with its surveillance of China's *Liaoning* aircraft carrier and triggered the confrontation."

The *Global Times*, a subordinate publication of the Communist

Party's newspaper *People's Daily*, also insisted that the Americans had caused the incident, huffing, "Bad guys always claim innocence first."

Chinese navy rear admiral Yin Zhuo, a highly respected and influential voice in Chinese government circles, was even more aggressive in commenting on the incident, saying, in an article in the *People's Daily*: "You can sail freely and we can too, but your freedom to sail cannot impact our freedom to sail. The instant you interfere with our sailing, sorry, but we will block you."

We will block you! To some, that seems to sum up the Chinese navy's new attitude toward the U.S. Navy and toward America in general. And that young officer swilling a beer in Siné Irish Pub isn't the only one in the navy who thinks the U.S. has suffered a serious loss of face—not only in relation to the Chinese but in relation to U.S. allies and partners in the Western Pacific.

But at the moment it doesn't really matter what they think. Because their boss—the CNO—takes a different view.

Not long after the incident in the South China Sea, Chief of Naval Operations Admiral Jonathan Greenert is sitting in an electronically secure room in the Pentagon, drinking a cup of coffee and waiting for a teleconference with Chinese Admiral Wu Shengli in Beijing. Greenert has been fully briefed; he knows what happened out there with the *Cowpens*. He's not angry about it, at least not publicly. He's not going to pound the desk and demand that the Chinese navy knock that crap off—which is what some navy officers think he should do. That's not his style, and in his view, that's not his job, either. Instead, his job is to calmly work with his Chinese counterpart to try to avoid such incidents in the future.

So after Wu comes up on the screen, and after the obligatory pleasantries—of the "How's the weather in Beijing?" variety; the pet pig thing hasn't come up yet—Greenert gently brings up the subject of the Chinese navy amphib parking itself in front of the *Cowpens* and forcing the crashback.

And what Admiral Wu tells him, apparently with a straight face, through the translator is this:

"That wasn't our ship."

Greenert isn't sure he heard him right. "How's that again?" he says.

"That wasn't a Chinese navy ship," Wu says. "It was an *army* ship. It was a People's Liberation Army amphibious ship that was not under navy control; it reported up a different chain of command."

In other words, Wu is saying that "we, the Chinese navy, had nothing to do with it."

Of course, it's an old dodge for the Chinese to blame incidents at sea on "rogue operators" or other Chinese government agencies; it offers them a level of deniability, a way to not lose face by admitting any official or personal error or responsibility. A Chinese Bureau of Fisheries patrol boat harasses the USNS *Victorious* in the Yellow Sea while a Chinese navy ship is lurking nearby? Hey, the navy had nothing to do with it. A Chinese fishing trawler almost collides with the USNS *Impeccable* in the South China Sea while a Chinese navy surveillance ship is standing by? Not the Chinese navy's problem. A Chinese navy vessel lands troops and building materials on a disputed small island? It was a rogue group of overly patriotic young officers acting without official permission. And so on.

And Wu's not just denying any Chinese navy involvement in the incident; he also claims that the Chinese navy actually stopped the amphibs' dangerous actions. He claims that Captain Zhang Zheng, CO of the *Liaoning*, got on the radio and ordered the Chinese amphib ship skippers to stop harassing the American cruiser, after which he and the *Cowpens*'s skipper had a cordial chat over the radio and the U.S. cruiser quietly departed the area. That's his story and he's sticking to it.

Well, that certainly doesn't quite square with what Gombert and others saw and heard that day. And when Wu's version of the incident inevitably gets around the Pentagon and the Pacific Fleet, it causes more than a little eyerolling among some senior navy officers. They wonder—"How can we ever trust these guys?"

But again, it's Greenert's job, as he understands it, to trust the Chinese—or at least to believe they're capable of being trusted. That's the policy. So on the teleconference with Wu, Greenert lets the *Cowpens* incident slide and moves on to what he's really interested in—which is to say, CUES.

In 1972 the U.S. and the Soviet Union signed a document called the Incidents at Sea Agreement, which was designed to head off conflicts between American and Russian ships and aircraft. The agreement banned—or at least it was supposed to ban—such things as simulated attacks on the other side's ships, or surveillance ships coming so close as to "embarrass or endanger the ships under surveillance." As we've seen, that U.S.-Soviet agreement wasn't particularly effective. Still, for years Greenert and others pushed for a similar international agreement, with China included as a signatory. The long-awaited result was CUES—Code for Un-planned Encounters at Sea—a proposed naval agreement that spells out signals and procedures to be used when one nation's naval warships or naval aircraft encounter another nation's warships and aircraft on or over the high seas.

The precise signals and ship-handling procedures in CUES are pretty complicated, but its basic provisions are not. The pro-posed agreement suggests that naval ships should maintain a "safe distance"—one nautical mile—from foreign naval ships, that they shouldn't interfere with other navy ships' formations or try to disrupt their exercises at sea, and so on. More specifically, the pro-posed CUES agreement suggests that the "prudent commander" should avoid such things as simulating attacks with missile radars, illuminating ships' bridges with powerful spotlights, conducting aerial acrobatics over ships or other aircraft—all of which the Chinese navy or its proxies have been doing to U.S. and other nations' ships for years in the Yellow, South, and East China Seas.

Until now, in early 2014, China has been noncommittal about signing on to CUES. But now Greenert amps up his pitch to Admiral Wu, telling him that incidents like the one with the *Cowpens* are exactly what the proposed CUES agreement is designed to prevent, and that signing it would go a long way toward reducing tensions in the South and East China Seas. It could keep a potentially deadly confrontation like the *Cowpens* incident from getting out of control, Greenert insists.

The key word here is that the proposed agreement merely "suggests" that these rules be followed; it doesn't require them to be followed. The proposed agreement is not legally binding on any nation that signs it; it's a guideline, not an international treaty or law. Nor does it necessarily cover navy-to-navy encounters in ocean areas where a country claims sovereign rights—which in China's case is much of the South and East China Seas.

But despite all that, Greenert is convinced that if the Chinese sign on, it will indicate that they're ready to join the stable, rules-based system of conduct at sea that the U.S. has advocated—and sometimes enforced—in the Western Pacific for decades. It will be another step in bringing China and its navy into the game. So he's pushing it, hard.

Of course, Wu can't make a decision on his own. But four months later, after being reassured that the agreement is just a guideline, not a legally enforceable code, the Chinese are ready to sign on. Greenert flies to China for the 14th Western Pacific Naval Symposium in Qingdao, a biennial conference of some two dozen countries' top naval commanders that this year is being hosted by Admiral Wu and the Chinese navy. Twenty-one nations sign the

CUES agreement, China included—although the Chinese make it clear that the agreement will not affect their right to defend sea territory they claim as their own.

"With a document like this, we can avoid those incidents in the future," Greenert tells reporters at the conference. "To get every country that is involved and that has a stake in the economy out here and in the security [of the region] to sit down and agree to a foundational document, that's really important. Without that foundation, you can't get started."

As for Admiral Wu, U.S. Navy officers who've had dealings with him know that there are times when he is tough, stubborn, and unyielding, and other times when he's at least a little more open and accommodating. In other words, there's a good Wu and a bad Wu—and on this occasion, he's the good Wu.

Calling the CUES agreement a "milestone document," Admiral Wu says that "we need to respect history and take history as a mirror and continue to resolve maritime disputes and conflicts through peaceful means, as well as avoid extreme behavior that may endanger regional security and stability."

It certainly *sounds* good. One thing is clear, though: The *Cowpens* won't be involved in any more confrontations with the Chinese navy in the South China Sea, at least not for a long time. Because as the admirals in Qingdao are signing the CUES agreement, the *Cowpens* is dockside in San Diego, preparing for a three-year refit and modernization.

And its captain is in serious trouble.

News spreads quickly in the close confines of a navy ship, and secrets are hard to hide. So it isn't long before the word starts getting around the USS *Cowpens*:

"There's something strange going on with the captain."

There's been no official criticism of Captain Greg Gombert's actions during the run-in with the *Liaoning* escort amphib, no black mark on his heretofore spotless record. And he's convinced that he handled the whole thing professionally and in compliance with his orders. But again, he's been in the navy long enough to know that there'll always be somebody willing—even eager—to second-guess. Maybe that knowledge has something to do with what happens to him, and to the *Cowpens*.

It starts while the *Cowpens* is on a routine port call in Singapore, and Gombert is feeling sick. He goes to a hospital ashore, where he gets some antibiotics for strep throat, but he's still feeling lousy. Then it gets worse. He develops a case of Bell's palsy, a partial paralysis of the muscles on one side of the face that is often associated with recent upper respiratory infections. It usually goes away by itself after a couple of weeks, and in its mild forms it isn't physically debilitating; a navy doctor rules that Gombert is physically able to command the ship, and Gombert himself refuses to request a temporary relief for medical reasons.

But Gombert still feels awful, so while the *Cowpens* is at sea he takes to his cabin to rest—and then he stays in there for almost three months, barely coming out for more than a few minutes each day while the ship is at sea.

Actually, the cabin that Gombert takes to isn't technically his cabin—or at least it's not supposed to be when the ship is at sea. On a ship like a cruiser (or a carrier) there are, in fact, two captain's cabins. One is the "at sea" cabin, a relatively modest living space located conveniently near the bridge and the CIC; the other is the "in port" or "unit commander's" cabin (UCC), a much more plush suite situated on a lower deck, far away from the bridge. When a cruiser is in port, the captain may live in the fancier cabin and use it to entertain visiting dignitaries. When the cruiser is at sea as part of a task force of several ships, the commander of the task force (usually an admiral) may use the cruiser as his flagship, in which case the admiral will stay in the unit commander's cabin. So it's a little odd that Gombert is using the UCC while the *Cowpens* is at sea.

In fact, Gombert's decision to live in the UCC has already caused him some trouble. Just before the *Liaoning* incident, when the *Cowpens* was part of the task force providing humanitarian relief for victims of Typhoon Haiyan in the Philippines, the rear admiral commanding the task force was annoyed that Gombert's things were still in the UCC when he, the admiral, boarded the ship. It was the sort of breach of navy etiquette that does not endear someone with the rank of captain to someone with the rank of admiral.

Nevertheless, with the *Cowpens* at sea, Gombert is living in the UCC—and hardly ever leaving it. Which raises the question, who's running the ship?

Normally under these circumstances it would be the XO, the executive officer, but at this point the *Cowpens* doesn't have an actual XO. Recall that after taking command Gombert lost confidence in his XO, calling him a "significant leadership team weakness." In early December that XO left the ship and his replacement hasn't arrived yet. So with the navy's concurrence, Gombert names the *Cowpens*'s chief engineering officer, a thirty-three-year-old female lieutenant commander, as the temporary XO. It's only supposed to be for about three weeks, until the new permanent XO arrives— but as it turns out, she will serve as XO for the next four months.

Sure, the lieutenant commander is considered competent, but she only has eleven years in the navy, with not nearly enough experience or training to be an executive officer on a cruiser—even if the captain is there to keep an eye on things, which in this case he mostly is not. The captain is mostly in his cabin, sick. What that means is that the lieutenant commander, who is still serving as chief engineering officer, is now not only the acting XO—the person responsible for the day-to-day operations of the ship—but also the acting captain of the ship while Gombert is in his cabin. It's way too much for any one officer to handle.

So while the *Cowpens* is going through various potentially dangerous maneuvers at sea—navigating shoals, transiting high-traffic areas, undergoing fuel replenishments in heavy seas with an oil tanker just fifty yards away—you have an inexperienced officer on the bridge giving orders to even more inexperienced officers, with a billion-dollar ship and the lives and safety of four hundred crewmembers in the balance. True, Gombert can monitor some of those things on the video and computer system in his cabin—but he really should be on the bridge.

Meanwhile, the ship is falling apart. The *Cowpens* already had equipment problems when it left San Diego, and now those problems are exacerbated. Without a full-time XO to constantly monitor every department head—and if necessary to kick some butt—maintenance suffers, inspections aren't being properly performed, logs and repair reports are being "gun-decked" (fudged or even falsified). It's a mess—and it gets even messier.

Even before he got sick, officers and crewmembers had noticed something about the captain and the new temporary XO. It seemed like they were spending a lot of time together—in his cabin, with the door closed. Of course, there's nothing inherently wrong with that; there's a conference table in there, and COs and XOs have to work closely with each other. But this is almost every evening. And it gets more troubling. The XO starts storing some of her toiletries in the captain's medicine cabinet, and fixing meals for the captain in his cabin's adjoining galley. People notice that when the ship is in port for liberty, the captain and the XO leave the ship together and return together. At one point a crewmember on liberty in Brunei sees the CO and the XO together ashore—and in the rather prim phrase of a later official navy report, "they were holding hands with their fingers interlocked." When they realized they had been seen, the report said, "their hands immediately parted."

Pretty soon it's all over the ship. The other officers, the senior chiefs, the enlisted crewmembers—they're all talking in the wardroom about the thing between the CO and the XO. Eventually another officer approaches the XO and warns her about the talk, at which point she denies there is "anything going on" between her and the captain, adding "If [I] were a man, this would not be an issue"—which may or may not be the case. Gombert also denies any sexual contact.

But you have to understand that in the military, you don't have to actually have sexual contact to be guilty of illegal fraternization; the mere appearance of such conduct is enough, especially if it is "prejudicial to good order and discipline," which this certainly is. A navy ship's captain is supposed to be the professional, moral, and ethical compass for the crew. Now the CO and the acting XO are doing things that could land an ordinary seaman in the brig—and the crew doesn't like it. Morale is at rock bottom.

Still, the *Cowpens* continues on its patrol schedule. There are stops in Japan, the Philippines, an exercise with a destroyer squadron off the coast of Guam. Finally, in April 2014, the *Cowpens* returns home to San Diego after its seven-month-long deployment—and suddenly, Greg Gombert's navy career is over.

It starts when Gombert asks a "post-deployment safety assessment" team to inspect the *Cowpens*. The team quickly discovers that, among other serious deficiencies, firefighting systems have fallen into disrepair, conditions on the flight deck make helicopter operations unsafe, and records have been falsified; some people think it's a miracle that the *Cowpens* made it home without a serious accident.

And the crew isn't in much better shape. The wife of one un-named senior chief later tells a newspaper, "My husband never comes home from deployment depressed. He's usually upbeat and excited to talk about all the fun things he did on the cruise and the port visits. But this time was different. He just came back, sat on the couch and had this sad look on his face. He said 'I'm just glad we made it home.'"

The shocking condition of the ship results in Gombert being summarily relieved as CO—the third *Cowpens* CO to be relieved for cause in just four years. And during a subsequent investigation, it doesn't take long for the navy to also learn about Gombert's extensive absences from the bridge—or about the relationship between the captain and his acting XO. The resulting official re-port fairly drips with condemnation of the *Cowpens's* commander, describing his behavior as "deliberate, conscious misconduct" that put his ship and his crew in peril.

"The violations revealed by the investigation, especially the blatant abdication of command responsibility on the part of the [commanding officer], are among the most egregious I have en-countered in my thirty-two-year career," one admiral writes. "In my experience they are beyond rare; they are unprecedented."

As you'd expect, the navy's shocking investigative report makes headlines across the country. "Navy Skipper Retreated to Cabin for Weeks, Left Crew Leaderless," one headline reads. "*Cowpens'* Bizarre Cruise," says another. "Navy Skipper Abdicated Com-mand," says another. And so on.

No navy officer's career can survive something like that. In the end Greg Gombert is found guilty of fraternization and failure to perform his duties and is forced to retire. The female lieutenant commander is also disciplined for conduct unbecoming an officer and forced out of the navy. The *Cowpens's* command master chief, the ship's highest-ranking NCO, is also disciplined for failing to notify higher authorities about what was going on aboard the ship.

To this day Greg Gombert can't fully explain the breakdown that cost him his career. The effects of his illness? The knowledge that his decisions on that day in the South China Sea would inevitably be second-guessed? Or was it simply the crushing pressure of being the captain of a U.S. Navy warship at sea? Greg Gombert readily admits that he failed; he's just not sure why.

It's hard not to infer from all this that what happened to the USS *Cowpens* in the South China Sea was a reflection of a modern U.S. Navy that seems unsure of its mission in the Western Pacific, unsure who its primary opponent is—or if it even has an opponent. It's a navy that rushed an unprepared ship and an unprepared crew into a dangerous confrontation with the Chinese navy, and then, at the very top, seemed to deny that a confrontation even took place. It's a navy and an American defense establishment whose most senior commanders seem unwilling or unable to acknowledge that China's growing navy even poses a threat.

Of course, not *all* senior navy officers look at it this way. They know from long experience that cooperation and dialogue with a demonstrably ruthless opponent are useless unless backed up by force—and by the will to use that force if necessary.

CHAPTER 7

Dragon Slayer

I t's a cold, oh-dark-thirty morning in January 2014 as Harry Harris walks across the tarmac at Kadena Air Base on Okinawa. A compact man with graying black hair, he's dressed in a green flight suit and a well-worn brown leather flight jacket—which is also a well-*earned* leather flight jacket. As a naval flight officer, Harris has already logged 4,400 hours in the air—and now he's about to make it 4,408.

The aircraft Harris will be flying in on this mission is a P-8A Poseidon, one of a half dozen Poseidons recently deployed to the Western Pacific. The Poseidons are the navy's new multi-mission airplane that eventually may replace the various versions of the old P-3 Orions, including the EP-3E Aries version that was involved in the Hainan Island midair collision discussed earlier. The land-based Poseidon has a cruising speed of about 500 mph, a range of about twelve hundred miles with a four-hour on-station window—that is, how long in patrols once it reaches its mission range—and a price tag of about $200 million each. "Multi-mission" means just that: Able to be armed with an array of anti-ship missiles, depth charges, torpedoes, and sonobuoys, and packed with latest-generation electronic gear, the Poseidon can be configured to perform antisubmarine warfare missions, anti-ship strikes, antimine operations, ground strikes on land targets, and electronic signals intelligence-gathering—all while cruising as high as forty-one thousand feet.

Although the Poseidon is based on the Boeing 737 design, no one would mistake it for a commercial airliner. For one thing, except for an observation porthole near the cockpit, there are no windows along the sides; for another, under the wings there are cigar-shaped pods the size of kayaks for the aircraft's electronics gear and mounts for Harpoon anti-ship missiles. In the cabin there are a couple rows of high-backed seats and six consoles arrayed along the left side to manage the aircraft's electronics: radar, acoustic sensors, powerful high-resolution and infrared cameras; the cameras can capture the logo on a sailor's cap from twenty thousand feet up, while the infrareds can actually see through new paint that may have been slapped on to disguise a suspect ship's name and hull number. The P-8A even has a hydrocarbon sensor to detect exhaust fumes from submarines cruising at snorkel depth; in other words, this plane can *smell* submarines.

The Poseidon crew is much smaller than the crews of the older P-3s, just nine officers and enlisted personnel, including two pilots and a tactical coordinator (TACCO) to manage the mission; the pilots fly the plane while the TACCO analyzes the data and controls the plane's weapons. This particular Poseidon is manned by members of Patrol Squadron (VP) Sixteen, the "War Eagles," and the mission today is simple: head out over the international waters south and east of China and see what they can see: ships, aircraft, electronic chatter, submarines—especially submarines.

It's simple, but that doesn't necessarily make any mission routine—particularly not this one.

One reason this mission isn't routine is because Harry Harris is on it. Harris, you see, is Admiral Harris, as in four-star Admiral Harris, and he is the commander of the U.S. Pacific Fleet—which means he's in direct command of every navy ship and every navy sailor and every navy plane in the entire Pacific Ocean, including this P-8A Poseidon.

It's pretty unusual for the Pacific Fleet commander to fly an operational reconnaissance mission. But then, Harris isn't your usual admiral.

For one thing, he's the first Asian-American to make four-star rank in the U.S. Navy. His father, Harry Sr., was a navy petty officer from Tennessee who served on the aircraft carrier USS *Lexington* during World War II; later, while stationed in Japan, he met Harris's mother, Fumiko, who was working on a navy base, a member of a once-prosperous Japanese family who had lost everything in the war. After Harris was born, his father retired from the navy and moved the family to a hardscrabble farm in rural Tennessee and later to Pensacola, Florida.

As you might guess, being a half-Japanese kid in the American South in the early 1960s wasn't easy; memories of the war against the "Japs" were still fresh. His mother refused to teach him Japanese, wanting him to be "one hundred percent American," which he certainly is. But he's also proud of his Japanese heritage; one of the few times anybody has ever seen him get choked up in public was at a ceremony honoring Japanese-American World War II vets. (His favorite movie is the 1951 film *Go for Broke!*, about the Japanese-American 442nd Regimental Combat Team fighting in Europe.) On the surface Harris is a polished, urbane senior navy officer, with two advanced degrees, one from Harvard, one from Georgetown, and he studied international relations and the ethics of war at Oxford. And yet, underneath that there are elements of a plain-speaking good ol' country boy whose accent recalls the hills of Tennessee.

Sometimes it's hard to read him—even to tell when he's kidding. For example, if you ask him what kind of music he likes, he'll tell you with an absolutely straight face that he likes all forms of good music—that is, he likes country *and* western. Or take the superstition thing. Harris insists that all navy fliers are superstitious, and that he differs only in being willing to admit it. He won't walk under a ladder; if a black cat crosses in front of his car, he'll turn around and head back home; he carries a good luck charm or talisman—which he won't identify—in the pocket of his flight suit whenever he flies. Then there are the MREs (meals ready to eat) that navy fliers often eat on long recon missions. Harris's favorite is chili and macaroni, chili-mac, but he refuses to eat anything with chicken or turkey in it—which is to say, when he's flying he won't eat anything that had wings. Seriously.

But make no mistake. Behind the occasional folksy casualness and self-deprecating humor there's a tough, demanding commander and a relentless competitor. Unlike a lot of navy senior officers, Admiral Harry Harris has a hunter's eyes.

Harris's rise to higher command was as unusual as his background. After winning admission to Annapolis, in his senior year he asked for navy pilot training, only to find that his eyesight wasn't quite good enough to make the cut. So before he graduated from the Naval Academy in 1978—he majored in engineering and was on the varsity fencing team—he chose instead to take the naval flight officer (NFO) track.

NFOs undergo some of the same initial training as pilots do, including flying solo in small fixed-wing aircraft, but after that the paths diverge. NFOs train to serve on multi-crew aircraft as weapons officers, electronic warfare officers, navigators, and radar intercept officers or RIOs; think Goose, Tom Cruise's RIO in *Top Gun*. As a seasoned TACCO aboard P-3s, Harris had to master pretty much all of the above.

In NFO training Harris selected the P-3 Orion as his plane of choice, and after earning his gold NFO wings he flew on Orions on missions around the world—the Atlantic, the Pacific, the Indian Ocean, the Mediterranean. This was at the height of the Cold War, so the primary reconnaissance target was Soviet submarines. They'd be flying missions out of, say, the Azores islands in the North Atlantic, and intelligence would get a report that a Soviet sub was coming around Africa from the Indian Ocean. So they'd send Harris and the Orion crew out to look for it—dropping sonobuoys, flying search patterns. That was the game; if you knew where the Soviet subs were, you could track them and destroy them if it came down to it. Harris never had to drop a depth charge or a torpedo on a Soviet sub, but you get the impression he wouldn't have hesitated for a second if that was what the mission required. He was a Cold War warrior—and in some ways he still is.

Harris flew on Orion missions in the First Gulf War, Afghanistan, and Iraq, racking up four hundred combat flight hours as the navy diverted its sub-tracking aircraft to hunt terrorists in deserts and mountains; even as he rose in rank and started being a commanding officer, he still flew missions whenever he could—partly to keep up his flight status and partly for the fun of it.

That's right, the fun of it, the thrill of the competition. Here's Harris on what it takes to be a naval aviator:

> You have to have a sense of competitive aggression. We're all about dropping bombs on bridges or dropping bombs on islands or firing Mavericks or Harpoons at a ship, or a torpedo at a sub. The outcome is going to be death, and you've got to have the willingness to do that.
>
> More than that, you've got to look for that dangerous place and put yourself in it. You have to know that the combination of your own skill and everything you've been taught and everything you've learned is all going to come together—and you're going to win. You're a fighting guy, and you've got to go fast and hit hard.

That's what I look for as a fundamental quality in navy aviators. I want the guy or gal to be really competitive. If you don't live in that environment, maybe you should find another line of work. Everything to me is a competition. You know that saying, "It doesn't matter whether you win or lose, but how you play the game?" Whoever said that probably lost.

That should make it pretty clear. Gandhi this admiral is not.

Every rising navy officer has to serve some desk time, and Harris excelled at some highly political jobs, including chief speechwriter for the chairman of the Joint Chiefs of Staff and the chairman's direct representative to U.S. Secretary of State Hillary Clinton. He knows his way around Washington.

And yet, he also has a reputation for being—well, some might say outspoken, some might say blunt. For example, in 2006, when Harris was commander of Joint Task Force Guantánamo, three prisoners held on terrorism allegations simultaneously hanged themselves in their cells. Harris immediately ordered an investigation, but he didn't take the politically correct route of wringing his hands and regretting the terrible loss of life. Instead, he publicly described the mass suicide as "an act of asymmetrical warfare waged against us." The man knows who his enemies are.

Patrol aircraft NFOs don't have quite the glamour and panache that navy fighter pilots do—if they did, Goose would have been the star of *Top Gun*—and therefore they've traditionally had a harder time breaking into the high-level ranks. So when Harris took over command of the Mediterranean-based U.S. Sixth Fleet in 2009, he was the first member of the land-based navy patrol aircraft community ever to command an entire U.S. fleet—and he's the first of that community to command the Pacific Fleet. That's another thing that makes today's Poseidon mission unique: Not only is the Pacific Fleet commander coming along, but he's the first Pacific Fleet commander who knows from experience exactly what long-range recon missions are all about.

And there's something else. As Harris climbs up the ladder to the Poseidon crew compartment and greets the crew, everybody on the plane understands that things could get tense up there. They know that the Chinese interceptors are out there, waiting.

Just six weeks earlier, with no public warning or discussion, the People's Republic declared an "air defense identification zone" (ADIZ) over much of the East China Sea, including the Senkaku Islands that are controlled by Japan but whose ownership is disputed by China. The Chinese government insisted that any aircraft flying through the ADIZ, military or commercial, would have to file a flight plan and get permission from China—this despite the fact that most of China's new ADIZ covered international waters and airspace.

Of course, the U.S., Japan, and South Korea all protested, condemning the Chinese declaration as an "air grab" of international airspace. To stand up for the "freedom of the skies" principle, the U.S. promptly sent two air force B-52s from Guam through the new Chinese ADIZ without notifying China or asking permission— and without prompting any significant action by the Chinese.

Still, the Obama administration appeared to waffle on the issue. While the U.S. said that none of its military aircraft would observe the new Chinese rules, it advised commercial aircraft to comply—or, better yet, to avoid the area if possible. On the other hand, the administration did make it clear that any attempt by China to forcibly take over the Senkakus would trigger a U.S. military response under the provisions of the U.S.-Japan mutual security treaty. That may have given the Chinese some pause about actually trying to take the islands, but it didn't stop them from sending military aircraft into Japan's airspace; every year Japanese air self-defense fighters scramble hundreds of times to intercept Chinese planes flying into the airspace around the Senkakus.

China, for its part, feigned shock that anyone would object to its ADIZ, noting that some twenty countries, the U.S. and Japan included, also had long-standing air defense identification zones extending outward from their coasts. The *People's Daily* condemned the "alarmist warnings" and "arbitrary attacks against China" by the U.S. and Japan in particular, and accused both countries of trying to enforce a double standard against China—which, as usual, wasn't exactly true. Yes, the U.S. does have its own air defense identification zone, and it has since 1950. But the U.S.'s ADIZ requirements only apply to aircraft planning to land in U.S. territory, not to any and all aircraft just passing by in international airspace.

It's hard to figure out what China is up to with this East China Sea ADIZ business. Obviously, they want to stop the U.S. surveillance flights and expand their control over more and more swaths of ocean in the Western Pacific. But is it a bluff? Or are they serious? And if they are serious, how far are they willing to go to enforce the unilateral ADIZ declaration? So as the P-8A Poseidon rolls down the runway at Kadena and lifts off into the still-dark sky, no one, Harris included, really knows what to expect.

Harris's heart will always be with the P-3 Orions; the license plate on his personal car in Hawaii reads "IFLYP3." But he knows their time is past. First introduced in 1961, when Harris was only about five years old, the old Orions have already far outlasted their projected thirty-year life spans; some have as much as twenty-six thousand hours of flight time. During the Cold War the navy had more than two hundred Orions, but now there are fewer than a hundred left—and they're expected to all be gone by 2020 and replaced by the Poseidons.

And as he settles into the seat by the observation porthole, Harris has to admit that the Poseidon is, as he puts it, "a super airplane." Not only are its electronics superior to the Orion's, but it's more crew-friendly. Some of the old Orions rattle and shake like flying jackhammers, but the Poseidon has a much smoother ride, which is important when you're staring at a computer screen for hours at a time. It's a quieter aircraft, too; compared with the Orion's, the Poseidon crew compartment is like a library.

Today's mission is primarily reconnaissance, looking at the ships passing below, seeing who's who and where they're heading, soaking up ELINT (electronic intelligence). If they detect a submarine, especially somewhere where the sub isn't supposed to be—say, near Japanese waters around the Senkaku Islands—they might drop some sonobuoys to try to identify and track it. Figuring out where to drop them and what the data means is the TACCO's job; it's partly science and partly art.

(Poseidons can carry more than a hundred sonobuoys of various types. Basically they're tubes about three feet long that are parachuted into the water and then float on the surface, playing out hydrophones to preset depths up to several hundred feet. Once in place they start transmitting data back to the Poseidon— acoustics, water temperature, bioluminescence caused by a passing submarine, and so on—that the Poseidon crew can use to locate and track a sub. Once deployed the sonobuoys are not recovered; they self-destruct after a preset time.)

But so far on this mission, no subs. All normal, just the usual stuff.

And then the Chinese fighters show up.

There are two of them, both Chengdu J-10s, known as "Vigorous Dragons" in China and "Firebirds" in the West. Fifty feet long, with large "delta"—triangle-shaped—main wings and canard mini-wings, they're armed with air-to-air missiles and a double-barreled 23mm "autocannon" that can spit out more than three thousand rounds a minute. The fighters are capable of Mach 2 speeds but are more agile and easily controlled at lower speeds—such as, say, the 500 mph speed of a Poseidon. You'll recall that the Chinese J-8 interceptor that collided with the American EP-3E near Hainan Island in 2001 had control problems when flying at the American plane's slow speed; that, along with the Chinese fighter pilot's aggressive stupidity was a primary cause of the collision. The Vigorous Dragons don't have that low-speed control problem. But it remains to be seen if they have an aggressively stupid pilot problem.

So far, at least, they seem to be acting professionally. They take up position under the Poseidon's right wing, at a respectful distance. There's no coming in close, no "thumping," no effort to make the U.S. plane alter course. They just sort of hang there, watching, as the Poseidon continues its mission.

The Poseidon crew isn't worried about the Chinese fighters—it's all part of the game—and certainly neither is Harris. He's been intercepted and shadowed many times before, by Russian fighters, Warsaw Pact fighters, Chinese fighters, you name it. No big deal.

Still, Admiral Harry Harris has to wonder about what the Chinese are doing, not just here over the East and South China Seas but throughout the Indo-Asia-Pacific. Sure, he understands the administration's policy of not antagonizing China, and as a military man he's honor bound to carry out that policy. He even agrees with it, up to a point; no one wants a military conflict with the Chinese.

But Harris knows this region, knows the players, knows the cultural and historical forces at work. Not only was he born here, and has served numerous deployments here, but his postgraduate studies were focused almost entirely on Western Pacific security issues. He understands that, yes, trying to build a cooperative relationship with the Chinese is all well and good. But he also knows that in this region, American cooperation with China has to be backed up by credible American combat power and resolve—and the cooperation has to be returned in kind. Anything less will be viewed as a sign of American weakness, not only by the Chinese but by every nation in the entire neighborhood.

And so far, the Chinese haven't been all that cooperative. The harassment of U.S. and other countries' ships in the South China Sea, the provocative East China Sea air defense identification zone declaration, the incident with the USS *Cowpens*. Harris knows exactly what happened out there in the South China Sea about a month earlier, and while he hasn't publicly criticized the *Cowpens*'s skipper for what happened that day, it's clear he wouldn't have objected if the American cruiser and the Chinese amphib had exchanged a little paint—that is, if the *Cowpens* had "shouldered" the amphib out of the way.

"I'm a product of the Cold War," he says later. "No [commander] would get relieved for doing that."

His view is: "We should cooperate with China where we can, but confront China where we must."

The point is that as far as Harris is concerned, the Chinese are pushing—and so far the U.S. isn't pushing back. As a result the U.S. has actually made China seem more powerful than it really is. "China is not ten feet tall," he finds himself constantly reminding military leaders in the region.

Given all that, and given his personality, as the Vigorous Dragons shadow the Poseidon, it's easy to guess what Admiral Harry Harris is probably thinking about the Chinese. He's probably thinking—"We're going to have more trouble with these guys."

And if that is what he's thinking, he's right.

The officers and sailors on the bridge of the carrier USS *Ronald Reagan* can hardly believe it. It's July 2014, and the *Reagan* is steaming off the coast of Hawaii with its protective screen of escort ships, getting ready to practice flight operations. And there, coming over the horizon and bearing down on the *Reagan* carrier group, is a Chinese navy ship.

"Is that a Chinese AGI?" a junior officer on the *Reagan*'s bridge says aloud as he stares at the Chinese ship through binoculars. The question is strictly rhetorical. One look at the massive electronics radomes mounted on the ship's superstructure is enough for him to know that the Chinese ship clearly is an AGI—auxiliary general intelligence—ship, which is to say, a spy ship. More specifically, it's the People's Liberation Army Navy AGI ship *Beijixing*, here to vacuum up the *Reagan* carrier group's electronic signals and secrets. The only reason the junior officer poses the question is because he still can't quite believe it.

"What the hell are they doing?" he says, shaking his head in astonishment.

Of course, having a Chinese spy ship crash a U.S. Navy party on the high seas isn't all that unusual; it has happened lots of times before, to the *Reagan* and other navy ships. But what's unusual about this particular spy ship, and what is so confounding to the crew of the *Reagan* and to the U.S. Navy in general, is that this time the Chinese navy is crashing a party to which it's already been invited.

The party in question is the aforementioned biannual Rim of the Pacific (RimPac) naval exercise held in Hawaii and San Diego. Hosted by the U.S. Navy since 1971, RimPac is the biggest joint naval exercise in the world. This year almost two dozen countries have sent a total of forty-eight ships, hundreds of aircraft, and twenty-five thousand personnel for the monthlong exercise.

The RimPac exercise is part military, part social, part diplomatic. At sea the various navies will practice underway maneuvers, ship-to-ship communications, helicopter operations, and so on. In port at Pearl Harbor or San Diego there are briefings, receptions, seminars, formal dinners for the international naval brass, soccer games between ships' crews, "open ship days" in which sailors and civilians get a chance to tour other countries' ships. It's a chance for sailors from navies large and small to get to know each other, to eyeball the other guys' stuff, and to show off the best of their own.

Along with countries from the Americas and even Europe, most of the major nations (and some of the nonmajor ones) in the Indo-Asia-Pacific region are represented here—although there are some exceptions. North Korea wasn't invited for obvious reasons, and for various international-political reasons Taiwan was also excluded. Vietnam isn't here, either; although Vietnam and the U.S. have started to conduct some small-scale joint naval exercises—they call them "naval engagements"—Vietnam's navy isn't quite ready for a large-scale exercise like RimPac. Thailand, the U.S.'s oldest treaty partner, was supposed to send a contingent, but it was disinvited by the U.S. at the last minute following a military coup and a crackdown on dissidents in that country. (Morally it may make sense for U.S. concerns about civil and human rights to override important military partnerships and potential partnerships, but it often baffles and annoys the countries involved—not to mention complicating the lives of U.S. military planners.)

Still, most of them are here. There's a submarine from the Royal Australian Navy, a frigate from the Indian navy, a guided-missile destroyer and several other ships from Japan, a multi-mission amphibious ship from the Royal New Zealand Navy. There's a landing platform dock ship from Indonesia, a platoon of marines from the Royal Malaysian Navy, a couple of destroyers and a submarine from South Korea, an offshore patrol ship from Brunei. Singapore has sent a stealth frigate, the Philippines has sent a navy staff detachment, and even tiny Tonga has offered up an infantry platoon from the Tonga Defense Services. And of course the U.S. Navy is represented by a host of ships large and small, including the carrier USS *Ronald Reagan*. There are so many ships, and so many powerful naval radars in operation, that it sometimes causes garage-door openers to malfunction in Honolulu.

And now, for the first time ever, the Chinese navy is at RimPac as well, represented by the aforementioned *Haikou* destroyer and three other ships. The planning for the Chinese participation has been going on for more than a year, and the Obama administration and some top navy brass—including CNO Admiral Jonathan Greenert—have hailed it as a milestone in China-U.S. cooperative military relations. The Chinese government, too, has described it as a recognition of China's and the Chinese navy's growing importance in world maritime affairs.

Other senior navy commanders aren't quite so excited. For example, Pacific Fleet Commander Admiral Harris believes it's better to have some interaction with the Chinese military than to have no interaction at all. But at the same time, that doesn't necessarily mean he trusts the Chinese.

"I've been watching them," he says later. "And I have a darker view of China than I used to have."

And others in the halls of Congress and at conservative D.C. think tanks are even less enthused. Congressman J. Randy Forbes, a Virginia Republican who chairs the House Armed Services Committee's Sea Power and Force Projection Subcommittee, is one of them. A few days before RimPac begins, he says this in an interview: "Given Beijing's belligerent behavior towards its neighbors across the Asia Pacific in recent months, it gives me pause that they would be rewarded with the opportunity to participate in such a prestigious exercise. . . . Beijing has demonstrated a hostility toward its neighbors and U.S. interests that must be met with real consequences."

(Forbes knows China, and the U.S. Navy, and shipbuilding. His congressional district encompasses Newport News Shipbuilding, the only shipyard in the country that can build aircraft carriers. As a founder of the Congressional China Caucus, Forbes was one of the first to warn about China's naval growth in the early-to-mid 2000s, when almost everyone else was fixated on the Middle East. During many trips to China he visited Chinese steel industries and noticed the thickness and quality of the steel plates—to an experienced eye a dead giveaway that the Chinese were building aircraft carriers. Almost no one, including most experts in the Pentagon, believed it until satellite photos proved Forbes right. Forbes is a strong navy advocate, and has formulated a plan for a 350-ship navy. As you might guess, he's no fan of the Obama administration's accommodationist policy toward China's military.)

Forbes isn't alone in his wariness of the Chinese. To cite another example, Congressman Dana Rohrabacher, a California Republican, asks, "Why do we want a potential adversary to [be able to] catalogue our weaknesses?" And more than a few defense establishment analysts liken inviting the Chinese navy to RimPac to inviting a fox into a henhouse.

But the U.S. Navy top brass don't report directly to a couple of congressmen and some defense analysts. They report to the president of the United States—and the administration policy is to cooperate with the Chinese, to bring them into the game. So that's the theme at RimPac 2014: Relations are supposed to be friendly, and for the most part they are. But there are some tense undercurrents.

For one thing, U.S. law prohibits Chinese participation in any U.S. military exercise that might give away classified methods or techniques. So the navy has to deny Chinese requests to participate in a special operations "opposed landing" drill against a ship at sea, and also deny their participation in any live or simulated missile firing and tracking exercises—including the firing of their own missiles or deck guns. Some of the Chinese navy officers at RimPac chafe at the restrictions; they want to show off their hardware. And some senior navy officers also think those rules are too restrictive, that China should be given more access—but that's the law.

Also, many of the other countries attending the RimPac exercises have tangled with the Chinese at one time or another—and it's hard to keep the simmering resentments completely hidden. For example, after more than a century of constant enmity, and amid ongoing territorial disputes in the East China Sea, the Japanese and Chinese contingents have tacitly agreed that their ships will stay away from each other during RimPac maneuvers at sea; China also withdrew from a planned humanitarian relief exercise after it learned the exercise would be commanded by a Japanese navy officer. RimPac participants from the Philippines, which in 2014 is also involved in long-standing turf disputes with China in the South China Sea—the Filipinos pointedly call it the West Philippines Sea—also notice a certain strain in the air when Filipino and Chinese officers encounter each other at social functions.

No one talks much about these and other tensions between China and regional countries. But no one denies they're there, either.

Still, the four Chinese ships at RimPac—the destroyer *Haikou*, the frigate *Yueyang*, the replenishment ship *Qiandaohu*, and a medical ship named *Peace Ark*—are all a big hit. Visitors crowd aboard them on the "open ship days" in Pearl Harbor; U.S. Navy officers line up for guided tours; and journalists write disproportionately about them. When the ships steam out of Pearl Harbor to conduct actual at-sea exercises with U.S. and other navy ships, the mood surrounding China's first participation in RimPac is upbeat, positive.

And then, just as at-sea maneuvers get fully under way, the Chinese navy spy ship *Beijixing* pops up uninvited a few miles away from the USS *Ronald Reagan* carrier strike group.

Again, spying on another navy's ships in international waters doesn't violate international law; on the contrary, it's almost expected, on every side. The USS *Cowpens*, remember, was dispatched to the South China Sea to gather intelligence on the Chinese carrier *Liaoning*. So the U.S. Navy has no real complaint there;

in fact, the *Beijixing* spy ship also turned up at the RimPac 2012 exercise two years before.

But this time it's different. In the four decades since the RimPac exercise began, no invited participant has ever brought along an uninvited intelligence ship to spy on the other participants. And now, first time out of the box, the Chinese are doing exactly that. In American eyes, it's—well, it's just downright rude.

And it's in-your-face rude, to boot. It's not as if the Chinese have secretly sent a submarine to monitor the exercise while trying to escape detection, or as if they've parked a spy ship disguised as a fishing trawler near the exercise area. The *Beijixing* spy ship is clearly visible to everyone on the *Reagan*'s bridge, so it couldn't hide or disguise its purpose even if it wanted to. The ship is four hundred feet long, with a crew of about 250, and those large gray radomes on the superstructure—they look like giant volleyballs—make the ship's purpose undeniably obvious.

Of course, news of the Chinese spy ship party crasher quickly gets out, which in turn prompts more than a few "I-told-you-so"s from critics of the administration policy of getting chummy with China's military.

"They have chosen to disrespect the other international participants by sailing an intelligence-gathering ship directly into the middle of the exercise," the aforementioned Congressman Randy Forbes says in an email statement. "RimPac participation should be reserved for US allies and partners . . . who share our interests in a free, stable, and prosperous Asia-Pacific region. It was already a stretch to reward Beijing with an invite. It's clear that their first trip to RimPac should be their last."

As a result of the spy ship incident, there's also an amendment to a bill in the U.S. House of Representatives to defund any future U.S. military exercise with the Chinese military. It loses, but it still garners 137 votes.

But senior U.S. Navy commanders downplay the spy ship incident. In fact, they argue that the spy ship's uninvited visit could actually be a good thing—because, they say, it establishes a precedent about the law of the sea.

Remember the Chinese argument that under the United Nations Convention on the Law of the Sea, foreign naval ships shouldn't be allowed to conduct military operations within another country's two-hundred-mile exclusive economic zone, or EEZ? The Chinese government used that argument to justify Chinese harassment of U.S. ships—the USNS *Impeccable*, USNS *Victorious*, USS *Cowpens*—while those ships were operating in China's claimed EEZs in the South China Sea and elsewhere.

But now they're doing the very same thing near Hawaii that the U.S. ships were doing in the South China Sea. The *Reagan* carrier group is operating in waters about a hundred miles off Oahu, well within the U.S.'s exclusive economic zone surrounding the Hawaiian Islands, but outside the twelve-mile U.S. territorial limit. So as far as the U.S. is concerned, under the rules of the sea the Chinese spy ship is in international waters and within its rights to be there—just as U.S. warships have the right to operate within China's EEZs. As a result, the U.S. Navy makes no attempt to harass the spy ship or chase it away. It wants to show the Chinese how such things should be handled.

And the Chinese government seems to agree with that concept—*seems* to. In a statement about the spy ship incident released to the Chinese press, the Foreign Ministry says that "the People's Liberation Army Navy ships' operation in waters outside the territorial seas of other countries is in line with international law and international practice."

Again, that's exactly what the U.S. has been saying. As Pacific Command CO Admiral Sam Locklear tells reporters in Hawaii, the Chinese government's statement is "a recognition, I think, or acceptance by the Chinese for what we've been saying to them for some time. Military operations and survey operations in another country's EEZ, where you have your own national security interests, are within international law and are acceptable. This is a fundamental right nations have."

Well, maybe that's the way an American might logically see it, that if the Chinese are publicly acknowledging their right to do something, then they must also be acknowledging the other side's right to do the same thing. But no one has ever gotten rich betting on consistency of logic from the leaders of the People's Republic of China.

In any event, the RimPac exercise goes on, albeit with some events curtailed to avoid compromising U.S. Navy methods and practices. Meanwhile, the Chinese spy ship is kept under close surveillance but publicly ignored. A few weeks later the RimPac exercise is over, and there's a lot of public boilerplate talk by American and Chinese military officials about how the joint exercise has fostered a spirit of better cooperation and understanding and communication and openness and et cetera, et cetera.

But the basic question concerning the spy ship remains— that is, why? After all, the Chinese leadership had been publicly touting the invitation to RimPac as evidence of the new respect the Chinese navy is getting from the U.S. and the world. So why would they endanger future invitations to joint exercises—and Chinese-American relations in general—with such brazenly aggressive behavior? What did they really have to gain?

Back in Washington, after the RimPac exercise is over, Admiral Greenert would like to know the answers. After all, he's been pushing the bring-the-Chinese-into-the-game policy, a policy that is being seriously questioned not only by hostile members of Congress (see above) but also, privately, by some high-level navy officers. And now the Chinese do this? He is, privately, pissed off.

So in his next teleconference with Admiral Wu Shengli, Greenert asks him, not in so many words—*What the hell was that AGI
thing about?*

And what Wu tells him is—*Hey, it wasn't my idea.*

Wu explains that because the Chinese navy had been excluded
from participating in some of the militarily sensitive RimPac
events (again, see above), the Central Military Commission had
decided to send their own "representative" to observe those parts
of the exercise anyway. That's the word Wu uses for the Chinese
spy ship—it was a "representative." Wu insists to Greenert that
he argued against the idea, but he was overruled by the rest of
the CMC.

Well, Greenert knows about being overruled. And he gets the
feeling that Wu is genuinely embarrassed about the whole thing,
that he has suffered a serious loss of face. So he lets it slide and
they move on to other things.

But there's no doubt that the RimPac spy ship incident has
made Greenert's job of carrying out the administration's cooperate-
with-China policy that much tougher. The Chinese seem to view
cooperation as a one-way street—and in tense places like the South
China Sea, they're still acting as if they own that street.

It's August 2014, just a few weeks after the end of the RimPac
exercise, when a Chinese J-10 fighter closes in on a U.S. P-8A
Poseidon reconnaissance plane over the South China Sea. Pacific
Fleet Commander Admiral Harry Harris isn't on this mission (his
previously mentioned flight occurred seven months prior). Given
his zest for airborne action and excitement, though, he probably
wishes he were.

Because this thing is getting hairy.

The Poseidon is about 135 miles east of Hainan Island, in international airspace but also in China's declared EEZ. The Poseidon crewmembers are doing their standard drill: looking and listening and scooping up signals from the electromagnetic spectrum and capturing images on their high-tech cameras. Later there are reports from the Chinese side, which the U.S. Defense Department won't confirm, that on this day the Poseidon is dropping sonobuoys in the water, perhaps to track one of the four or five Jin-class nuclear ballistic subs that are based at the Yulin Naval Base on Hainan.

But whatever the Poseidon is doing, it is seriously annoying the Chinese—as the J-10 fighter pilot now makes clear.

First the J-10 pilot crosses under the Poseidon just fifty feet from the American plane. Then he makes a ninety-degree pass directly in front of the Poseidon's nose, with the J-10's belly exposed, presumably to make the point that those missiles attached under his wings are ready to go if necessary. Then he comes around and plants the fighter directly under and alongside the Poseidon with his wingtips just twenty feet away from the American plane's wingtips. Then he does a barrel roll completely around the Poseidon. Per standard operating procedure, the Poseidon pilots keep their aircraft on a straight and level course; crewmembers are also taking photos of the Chinese plane, which eventually turns away and disappears. As usual, the navy doesn't make the Poseidon pilots or crewmembers available for press interviews—but it's probably fair to say that for them this was a pretty intense few minutes of flight time.

And it's also eerily familiar. This is roughly the same area where the Chinese J-8 fighter collided with the EP-3E in 2001, the collision that left the Chinese pilot dead and the EP-3E crew locked up like POWs on Hainan Island for ten days. As noted, the J-10 may be a better plane than the older J-8, and better able to maneuver at relatively slow speeds—but judging from this guy's behavior, in terms of pilot good sense there hasn't been much improvement since 2001.

This isn't the first occasion in recent months that Chinese fighters based on Hainan have tried to intimidate U.S. recon flights out of the airspace over the South China Sea. There were several unpublicized close encounters in the same area in March, April, and June. There's also been trouble in the East China Sea, where Japan Air Self-Defense Force surveillance planes have been hassled at close range by Chinese fighters.

But this Poseidon incident over the South China Sea, this is the closest, most aggressive, and most dangerous encounter since 2001. A *barrel roll* around a Poseidon? This has got to stop.

So the U.S. government makes a both public and formal diplomatic protest. At a press conference, a Defense Department spokesman hands out photos showing the close proximity of the Chinese plane, describes what the Chinese pilot did, and then says, "It's unprofessional, it's unsafe, and it is certainly not keeping with the kind of military-to-military relationship" the U.S. is trying to develop with China.

But the Chinese government isn't having it—unofficially or officially.

Unofficially, here's what Chinese navy rear admiral Zhang Zhaozhong, a military analyst at the National Defence University in Beijing, tells Chinese state-controlled media about the incident: "We didn't give them [the U.S.] enough pressure. A knife at the throat is the only deterrence. From now on, we must fly even closer to U.S. surveillance aircraft."

More officially, at a press conference in Beijing, Ministry of Defense spokesman Yang Yujun says, "Our pilot's operation has been professional and due regard has been given to the safety issue. Our aircraft are very precious and the lives of our pilots are even more precious." Yang goes on to demand that the U.S. cease all reconnaissance flights and U.S. Navy ship forays into waters over which China claims sovereignty—which is to say, almost all of the South and East China Seas.

"These behaviors of U.S. military ships and aircraft could easily cause misperception and miscalculation or even air and sea accidents," Yang says, adding that U.S. ships and aircraft "often show up without being invited and even broke into our exercise or training zones which have been announced in advance"—an apparent reference to the USS *Cowpens* incident.

Remember, this is just a month after the Chinese spy ship crashed the RimPac party. So for the Chinese to complain about U.S. planes or ships showing up "uninvited" in their EEZ is pretty brazen. The Chinese response also throws out the window any hope on the American side that the Chinese government meant what it said during the RimPac spy ship incident—that is, that foreign military assets have a right to operate in other nations' EEZs. Again, the Chinese attitude is—*We can do it to you, but you can't do it to us.*

And there's another twist. Later, when Greenert and Admiral Wu are teleconferencing again, Greenert mentions the dangerous P-8 intercept and asks, "What's up with that?" And what Wu tells him is: "That [J-10] fighter wasn't from headquarters. That was somebody on their own. And I'll take care of that."

Somebody on their own? In other words, a rogue pilot?

There's a couple ways to look at that. It could be a lie, a way for the Chinese government to tell the U.S. government that their pilots are angry and full of nationalistic fervor, that they can't restrain them, so the U.S. had better knock off their surveillance flights before there's a tragic incident that could spiral out of control. Or it could be that Wu isn't lying, that the Chinese military really is having a hard time controlling its fighter pilots—which is a pretty scary concept.

Either way, it doesn't change anything. U.S. aircraft continue the recon flights over the South and East China Seas, and Chinese fighters still scramble to confront them—albeit at a generally safer distance.

But even as these confrontations take place, the U.S. government and U.S. military are still pursuing the policy of friendly cooperation with the Chinese military, of trying to get China to be part of a stable, rules-based, international, law-abiding system in the Western Pacific. For example, earlier in August the Pacific Fleet flagship USS *Blue Ridge* made a port call at Qingdao and conducted a CUES exercise at sea with a Chinese navy frigate. Later, in November, amid much smiling and handshaking, U.S. Secretary of Defense Chuck Hagel and the Chinese defense minister sign a "memorandum of understanding" in Beijing called "Rules of Behavior for the Safety of Air and Maritime Encounters." It's an agreement in which both sides pledge to follow already established international rules of the sea and air—and which will turn out not to be worth the paper it's written on. Still later, in December, U.S. and Chinese ships hold a joint antipiracy exercise in the Gulf of Aden.

Again, this isn't at all like the Cold War with the Soviet Union a generation earlier. But to American military officers on the ground—or rather, on the sea and in the air in the Western Pacific—it doesn't exactly feel like peace, either.

CHAPTER 8

Missile Men

Rear Admiral Tom Rowden desperately needs better missiles—and more ships from which to launch them.

After a series of armed confrontations over some obscure off-shore islands, the Reds have launched a battalion-sized amphibious invasion of the tiny nation of Guanotomo, a treaty partner of the U.S. They've backed up that invasion with a small fleet of guided-missile destroyers, frigates, amphibious assault ships, and probably some submarines. Although Guanotomo's small self-defense force is gamely resisting, it's doubtful they can hold out for long. Rowden's job is to rush an aircraft carrier strike group and a marine landing force to Guanotomo, which is situated five hundred miles away from the Red coast, and kick the invaders out before they can get too firmly entrenched.

Ten or twenty years earlier that might have been a relatively simple task. The aircraft carrier strike group could have launched its planes and sea-to-land cruise missiles from a hundred or two hundred miles away to strike the enemy ships and ground forces already on land. The carrier itself would have simply waited out at sea, secure in the knowledge that it was out of range of enemy land-based missiles and attack aircraft, and that the cruisers and destroyers surrounding the carrier would protect it from seaborne attack by enemy guided-missile ships or subs. Once the carrier group's fighters and cruise missiles had destroyed or seriously degraded the Reds on sea and land, the marines aboard an amphibious assault ship attached to the carrier group would have hit the beach, mopped up any remaining Red resistance, and then posed for pictures with crowds of happy, grateful Guanotomese.

But this isn't ten or twenty years ago—and Tom Rowden knows it. After decades of a massive military buildup fueled by the booming Red economy, the Reds now have land- and air- and ship-launched anti-ship missiles that can reach targets hundreds of miles away, guided by sophisticated land-air-space command-and-control systems. Their fleet is equipped with anti-ship missiles that have twice the range of Rowden's anti-ship missiles, which are old and slow and relatively easy to defend against. And since all of Rowden's combat power is contained in the small patch of ocean occupied by the carrier strike group, the Reds will be able to deliver concentrated missile fire against it, launching salvo after salvo of missiles that could overwhelm the carrier group cruisers' and destroyers' antimissile systems.

So unless Rowden can come up with some better missiles in a hurry, and unless he can figure out a way to disperse his offensive forces, there's a good chance the Reds are going to blow his ships out of the water.

Or rather, blow them off the computer screen. As you probably already guessed, on this day Rear Admiral Tom Rowden isn't leading his ships into actual combat to free the Guanotomese from the Red Menace. Instead, he's standing in an amphitheater at the Naval War College in Rhode Island, running a wargame that pits the U.S. Navy—the Blue Team—against the future naval forces of an unspecified enemy, the Red Team.

The precise details of such navy wargames are classified, and they're also incredibly more complex than the simplified and fictionalized Guanotomo scenario we have imagined above. But the basic choreography of a wargame such as this one is well known. In the "breakout rooms" adjacent to the amphitheater, crowds of navy officers are gathered around conference tables, Blue Team and Red Team, plotting their strategies, assessing their own strengths and weaknesses, and guessing at the "enemy's" strengths and weaknesses and intentions. Other navy officers are scurrying about, feeding mountains of data into banks of computers—ranges, assets, capabilities, everything the Reds and the Blues can put into the fight. To account for elements of chance or luck there are rolls of the dice. Then the computers in the Decision Support Center analyze and judge all the data and show the results on giant display screens, along with charts, graphs, maps, and PowerPoint presentations.

It's an exhausting, frenetic, weeklong exercise, with the Reds and the Blues fighting it out through numerous situations and scenarios. And in the end the results of the war games are simply one more confirmation of what Rowden already knows: If the U.S. Navy is to survive and triumph in future battles at sea, the navy has to change the way it goes into the fight, and the weapons it puts into it.

Rowden is in a position to help do that. He's the director of the Surface Warfare Division on the CNO staff, which means he's the top advisor to the CNO on surface warfare policy, requirements, needs, and strategy. The son of an admiral, and a 1982 graduate of the Naval Academy, over the years Rowden has served on or in command of almost every kind of surface ship the navy has—destroyers, cruisers, carriers—on every ocean and almost every sea in the world. A fit, wiry man with silver hair, he is a tough-talking James Cagney kind of guy who fully understands the core nature of his profession. Remember that earlier story about the admiral who marched a group of young officers down to a ship's main deck gun and told them that the navy's primary mission was to kill bad people? That admiral was Tom Rowden.

Rowden's guiding principle is simple: "Defense is absolutely vital," he says. "But what wins is offense. You have to control the sea, and you control the sea by holding the other guys at risk—or by sinking them."

But if your mission is to kill bad people, you have to make sure those bad people can't kill you first. That's the crux of the problem facing the U.S. Navy, especially in the Western Pacific, and especially in relation to China: How do you protect your ships against China's new generation of "ship-killing" missiles?

Ever since World War II, carrier strike groups have been the U.S. Navy's primary offensive tactical weapons, its centers of combat gravity. As noted earlier, the strike group has the carrier in the center protected by a ring of escort ships: While the carrier is launching aircraft to attack distant targets, one or ideally two cruisers in the group protect the carrier against incoming missiles, while two to five destroyers search for enemy submarines. Depending on the mission, the carrier strike group may also include an attack sub and a fast replenishment ship, and it might also be paired up with an amphibious readiness group.

That arrangement worked fine in the waters of the Asia-Pacific after the end of the Cold War, when the U.S. Navy faced almost no serious threat on the high seas—especially not from China. The Soviets had developed an air-launched anti-ship missile system directed against U.S. carriers, but obviously the effectiveness of that system—and American defenses against it—was never tested in actual combat. With the Soviet Union defunct, that anti-ship threat disappeared, at least temporarily. So American carrier groups could expect to stand out to sea and launch their aircraft or Tomahawk missiles without having to worry too much about attacks from enemy surface ships or short-range, land-based missiles. In the Middle East and Afghanistan the navy's primary mission was to project firepower and airpower from sea to land, not to prepare for an enemy attack from land or sea.

As a result, the U.S. Navy didn't spend a lot of time or money trying to develop longer-range anti-ship missiles and better defensive antimissile systems for its ships. Even today the navy's primary anti-ship missile is the 1970s-era Harpoon, which is older than most of the sailors who operate it. Although its five-hundred-pound warhead can pack a punch, the Harpoon is slow, about 500 mph, and it has a range of just seventy miles. The navy's defensive antimissile missiles have even shorter ranges. The ship-launched Tomahawk cruise missile can hit fixed land targets a thousand miles away, but currently it's not configured to locate and attack moving ships at sea.

The point is that for decades, the navy didn't think it really needed longer-range offensive missiles or better defensive missiles. Unfortunately for the U.S. Navy, the Chinese took a different approach to offensive anti-ship missilery.

As a land-based military power with a long coastline, but without a navy to speak of, China had always been interested in missiles that could reach out and destroy enemy ships off its shores. But until the late 1990s its missile array consisted primarily of line-of-sight, short-range anti-ship cruise missiles with relatively crude internal guidance electronics. In the two decades since, however, China has leaped forward in developing over-the-horizon radar technology, satellite tracking and communications systems, and miniaturized electronics—which together make it possible to precisely target a moving ship from hundreds of miles away.

(Ironically, a key figure in China's missile development was Tsien Hsue-shen, a China-born immigrant to the U.S. who was one of the founders of the Jet Propulsion Laboratory at Cal Tech. After the Chinese Communist Revolution and the beginning of the Korean War, Tsien was caught up in the McCarthy anti-Communist purges and had his security clearance revoked in 1950. After being kept under virtual house arrest in the U.S. for five years, he returned to Communist China and helped develop China's ballistic-missile program, earning him the title "Father of Chinese Rocketry.")

The Chinese arsenal is impressive, with a wide range of farther-flying anti-ship missiles. One is the land-, ship-, or air-launched "Sunburn" cruise missile, a Soviet-designed, thirty-foot-long, ninety-nine-hundred-pound monster (more than twice the size of a Harpoon) that zips over the waves at speeds up to Mach 2.5. Computer-command course updates guide it to proximity with its target, after which it uses its own radar and sensors to home in on the targeted ship and then perform supersonic dipsy-doodles to evade the defending Aegis-directed missiles and guns.

There's also the smaller "Sizzler" anti-ship cruise missile—twenty-seven feet long and forty-two hundred pounds—that can be launched from either ships or submarines. The Sizzler travels at sub-supersonic speeds early in its flight, but as it nears its target the missile splits in two, shedding the heavier half while the smaller, faster, warhead-carrying part of the missile drops to fifteen to thirty feet above the sea surface and sprints toward the target ship at Mach 2 or better, bobbing and weaving along the way. It can be fired from 135 miles away by surface ships and subs. Upgraded Sizzlers can have a range of almost two hundred miles by giving up some of the final sprint speed. The Chinese even developed a way to put a Sizzler "four-pack" into standard commercial sea-shipping containers to launch from merchant ships.

Smaller still but nevertheless lethal is the air-launched, sea-skimming YJ-91/12 "Eagle Strike," which can deliver a one-hundred-pound warhead from 250 miles away. A long-range, land-based Chinese fighter aircraft armed with Eagle Strikes can threaten ships more than a thousand miles away from the fighter's home base. Although it's impossible to get an exact count, China has thousands of anti-ship cruise missiles available for launch from land, sea, or air.

(The resurgent Russian navy also has anti-ship missile capabilities, much of it based on designs formulated by the old Soviet Union during the Cold War. The Soviets had developed an air-launched long-range anti-ship missile that could carry conventional or nuclear warheads, but fortunately it was never tested in action.)

But the big daddy of the Chinese anti-ship missile arsenal is the DF series of anti-ship ballistic missiles, starting with the DF-21D. (DF stands for *Dong-Feng*, Chinese for "The East is Red.")

Unlike cruise missiles, a ballistic missile is fired up through the atmosphere and into space, where at a predetermined point the warhead separates from the actual missile and falls back toward Earth like a cannonball to hit its target; ballistic-missile warheads are basically glorified artillery shells. Chinese missile designers have known for decades how to precisely target ballistic missiles against fixed targets on land.

But while hitting a fixed target with a ballistic missile was relatively easy, no one had ever figured out how to target one against a ship or group of ships that was moving at thirty miles per hour on the sea. The reason was simple: If a ship detected a ballistic-missile warhead coming toward it through the atmosphere, the ship could simply change course and get out of the way—and since the ballistic warhead wouldn't be able to adjust its trajectory, it would just make a big splash in an empty patch of ocean. (That's assuming, of course, the warhead was not a nuclear weapon set for an air burst, which would have a much larger radius of destruction.)

But the DF series of ballistic missiles changed all that—or so the Chinese wanted the world to believe.

The DF-21D (the latest anti-ship iterations are up to DF-26) isn't really a ballistic missile in the strictest sense of the term; it's actually a guided missile, in the sense that as its finned warhead is falling through the atmosphere at Mach 10—ten times the speed of sound, or two miles per second—the warhead's course can be altered by a system of remote and internal radars and electronic signals that guide it precisely to its target. If a ship tries to evade the warhead, it won't help, because the warhead will turn with it—and instead of making a big splash it will make a big bang on the ship's deck. With a range of about a thousand miles, a DF-21D missile launched from a hardened site or mobile launcher on the Chinese mainland could theoretically hit an American aircraft carrier operating hundreds of miles east of Taiwan; the longer-range DF-26 could theoretically hit a ship more than two thousand miles away. Armed with a conventional cluster bomb warhead, the DF missile wouldn't sink the carrier, but it certainly would destroy its flight deck and radars and communications system, accomplishing what defense experts call a "mission kill." If that carrier and its strike group had been speeding toward Taiwan to prevent a Chinese invasion, that mission would be over.

In short, the so-called "carrier killer" ballistic anti-ship missile could be a gamechanger weapon—especially when combined with other Chinese long-range anti-ship missile capabilities.

And what was the U.S. Navy doing while China was developing these long-range anti-ship missile capabilities? What was the navy doing to counter this new threat? The short answer is, not much. For one thing, much of this anti-ship missile development took place in the first decade of the twenty-first century, while China was engaged in its aforementioned "charm offensive." The 2008 Olympics in Beijing, Chinese participation in international relief operations, more relaxed diplomatic relations with the U.S. after the 2001 Hainan incident, not to mention the American preoccupation with the Middle East—they all combined to make China seem to be an unlikely threat at sea.

And there was something else. There was a widespread belief that the Chinese simply weren't capable of such revolutionary advances in anti-ship missile technology and operation, that they couldn't master the complex network of target detection and guidance systems needed to make long-range anti-ship cruise and ballistic missiles work effectively—and certainly they couldn't do it in just a little over a decade. Remember, this was the *Chinese* navy and military.

Although some defense establishment planners privately warned of the potential threat, Tom Rowden among them, it wasn't until mid-decade that the Defense Department openly discussed what it called "disruptive military technologies"—which is to say, long-range anti-ship cruise missiles—that China was bringing to bear. It raised the possibility that China could be capable of imposing widespread "anti-access/area denial"—or in the inevitable Pentagon-ese, "A2/AD"—in the Western Pacific.

The A2/AD concept is as old as war itself: Don't let the enemy enter or operate in a key piece of real estate. The idea was that with long-range missiles and land-based aircraft, China could deny U.S. Navy forces access to broad swaths of ocean simply by making it too risky for the U.S. carrier strike groups to sail into them. No longer could the U.S. send carrier strike groups into, say, the Strait of Taiwan or the South China Sea to project power during a crisis, because the large ship formations would be sitting ducks for barrages of enemy cruise and ballistic anti-ship missiles that would overwhelm their antimissile defenses—the aforementioned and indelicately phrased missile "gangbang." Even if only a small percentage of the enemy missiles got through, it would still be enough to seriously damage or even destroy the U.S. ships. And even if the carrier group did manage to destroy all the incoming missiles, in doing so it would use up most or all of its vertically launched defensive missile arsenal, forcing it to either return to port to rearm or be vulnerable to a second strike. (Navy officers refer to running out of missiles as "going Winchester," meaning your gun is empty and it's going to take a while to reload. A navy ship's vertically launched missiles can't be resupplied and reloaded at sea.)

So instead of taking that chance, the theory went, a risk-averse U.S government would have to keep the American carrier groups hundreds or even thousands of miles offshore, out of the enemy missiles' range but also beyond the range of the carrier groups' aircraft. Since carrier-launched aircraft have a relatively short combat range, about five hundred to six hundred miles without refueling, the carrier group would be unable to accomplish its core mission—that is, striking the enemy's territory.

Well, the implications of that were obvious. If the navy carrier groups can't or won't go where they're needed, why have them? Why spend $13 billion or so on an aircraft carrier that can be put out of commission or perhaps even destroyed by a few $1 million missiles?

As you'd expect, that wasn't the kind of talk the navy wanted to hear. To counter the "area denial" threat, the navy came up with an operational plan that has gone by various names but is usually referred to as "Air-Sea Battle." It's not the purpose here to explain in detail the plan's intricacies; entire forests have been consumed to write the reports arguing the pros and cons of the concept. It's enough to say that Air-Sea Battle envisions coordinated U.S. Navy and Air Force strikes by long-range aircraft and cruise missiles against enemy missile sites, command and control centers, and satellite and communications networks—everything the enemy needs to fire and control its conventional (nonnuclear) missiles.

Non-kinetic electronic warfare would also be used to disrupt an enemy's remote guidance systems. Advocates call it "Killing the archer before he shoots the arrow."

Meanwhile, the navy is confident—or at least publicly confident—that a carrier group's layered system of missile defenses would take out an incoming cruise missile barrage. Antimissile missiles, rapid-firing antimissile gun systems like the Phalanx, and electronic warfare will destroy or confuse the enemy's missiles— and if not, if some missiles get through, well, that's war, and in war there are always going to be some risks.

As for China's DF-series anti-ship ballistic missiles, the navy's attitude is that they might not be all they're cracked up to be.

For one thing, there are a number of defensive measures that are or will be available for use against the ballistic missiles. They range from the abovementioned disruption of satellite and communications networks to physically tracking and shooting down the ballistic-missile warhead with another missile; already most U.S. destroyers are or soon will be equipped with new, improved Aegis combat systems that can track and target incoming ballistic missiles.

A carrier group could also use various electronic warfare and masking techniques to confuse the incoming guided warheads. For example, there's a proposal to use 3-D printers to create hundreds or even thousands of small, lightweight drones—similar to paper airplanes—that would be fitted with signals emitters to create an electromagnetic cloud around the carrier group; it's the modern version of ships hiding themselves in smoke screens. The navy is also working on a way to project an electronic image of a ship— sort of like creating a ghost ship—that would serve as a decoy for enemy missile guidance sensors. The enemy warhead would think it was heading toward a big, fat target like a carrier when in fact it would be targeting empty water. (Those techniques could also be used against cruise anti-ship missiles.)

And there's another reason that most senior navy officers think the Chinese DF-series missiles aren't necessarily a gamechanger. There's a growing suspicion that the "carrier killer" ballistic missile may essentially be a Chinese bluff—at least for now.

After all, as far as anyone knows the DF-series missile has only been successfully tested on ship-sized targets on land, which is easy enough to do; it's never been tested against a moving ship at sea hundreds or even thousands of miles away, which is quite another proposition. Also, the anti-ship ballistic missiles require a highly sophisticated integrated system of satellites, sensors, and communications to find, track, and target ships at sea—a system the Chinese military may not yet actually have or be able to reliably operate. In five or ten years, maybe, but not now.

And then there's this: The reason the DF-series missile may not yet be a gamechanger is because the Chinese are acting like it's a gamechanger.

Ever since the Chinese anti-ship ballistic missile program first came to U.S. public attention in the late 2000s, the Chinese have made little secret of its existence or its alleged capabilities. It's been widely discussed in military seminars and publications and in the state-controlled media; the longer-range (up to twenty-five hundred miles) DF-26 has even been proudly shown off in military parades in Beijing, right along with tanks, aircraft flyovers, and ranks of high-stepping army troops. So it could be that the anti-ship ballistic missile system is sort of like a Chinese version of the Doomsday Machine in the film *Dr. Strangelove*, the device that would automatically destroy the entire Earth if Russia were attacked—that is, it's only a deterrent if the world knows that it exists.

And to the Chinese government, that certainly may be the DF-series missile's primary mission: to help force the U.S. Navy, and by extension the U.S. itself, out of a leading role in the Western Pacific. China doesn't want to actually drop one of these things on a navy carrier, which could start or seriously escalate a conflict that would probably damage China and its economy as much as it would damage the U.S. But if the fear of the anti-ship ballistic missile could force the navy to keep its ships hundreds or even thousands of miles away from China's coasts, then China would have succeeded in its strategic goal of gaining military hegemony over the Asia-Pacific region.

In other words, the combination of long-range anti-ship cruise missiles and anti-ship ballistic missiles might scare the American navy out of the region, guaranteeing a Chinese win without so much as firing a shot. It's a strategy that dates back to the ancient Chinese military philosopher Sun Tzu, who famously said, "To win one hundred victories in one hundred battles is not the acme of skill. To subdue the enemy without fighting is the acme of skill."

So could the Chinese missile gambit work? Could the Chinese system of land-launched, aircraft-launched, and ship-launched long-range missiles force the U.S. Navy's carrier groups and other surface ships out of the South and East China Seas? As of now, no. The navy routinely sends carrier strike groups into those waters.

But what about during a crisis—say, a looming Chinese attack and amphibious assault on Taiwan? The navy probably would be willing to send in its carrier groups, even at the risk of losses; as Admiral Rowden puts it, "These ships were built to go into harm's way." But what about the American civilian leadership? Would they be willing to risk the lives of thousands of young American men and women to defend a far-off ally? That's a future political question that U.S. Navy planners can't answer.

Still, it would certainly help if the navy could reduce the perceived vulnerability of its carrier strike groups. Which is why in the wargame described above, and in real life in the Western Pacific,

Admiral Tom Rowden so desperately needs better missiles, and more ships to launch them from.

Rowden, who would rise to become the commander of all U.S. naval surface forces as vice admiral in August 2014, has a formal name for the concept; he calls it "distributed lethality." And he also has an informal phrase to describe it.

The phrase is, "If it floats, it fights."

Rowden and other navy strategists recognize the problem with overreliance on aircraft carrier groups: It gives the enemy a small number of targets on which to concentrate their fire. In all the world there are less than a dozen U.S. Navy aircraft carriers, each of which is closely surrounded by half a dozen other fighting ships while operating at sea. Big ship formations like that are relatively easy to locate, track, and attack.

But what if you had scores of other, smaller navy fighting ships scattered around the ocean, alone or in two- or three-ship groups, armed with longer-range missiles and better able to escape enemy detection? Suddenly the enemy has to worry about attacks from U.S. Navy ships they don't even know are out there.

So that's Rowden's idea. He wants to put missile systems on as many navy ships as possible. Those lightly armed amphibious assault ships, the ones designed to transport marines and landing craft and helicopters? They'll still do that, but Rowden also wants to plant missile launchers on them. Those unarmed transport ships operated by the navy's Military Sealift Command? Rowden wants to do the same with them, arming them with missiles to give them combat capability. In short, Rowden wants to turn as many navy noncombatant ships into combatant ships as he can. He'd probably put missiles on shore liberty boats if he could.

"More ships with more firepower acting more independently

will increase the planning complexity and resourcing of our potential challengers," Rowden says.

"This is a relatively simple yet powerful idea. By applying the principles of distributed lethality, the surface force can help sustain and extend America's competitive advantage in power projection against a growing set of sea-denial capabilities. As we face adversaries that are becoming more technologically advanced, it makes sense to inject some uncertainty into their warfighting calculus. Should rounds be exchanged, a distributed lethality construct allows the U.S. Navy to respond rapidly, with agility, and taking an offensive posture."

And a big part of Rowden's "If it floats it fights" concept is the oft-maligned littoral combat ship.

The LCS program wasn't Rowden's idea; he was still a midlevel officer when it was conceived. But Rowden is a pragmatist. The forty or so littoral combat ships that have been built or are on the way will soon be the most numerous surface ship class in the navy—and you have to work with what you've got. As Rowden often tells his surface warfare officers, "You want destroyers, and I get that. The LCS is not a destroyer and so you don't like that. But this is the hand you've got. So stop bitching, get over it, and play the hand you have."

You'll recall that the problems with the littoral combat ships are that they're seriously undergunned and they lack "survivability" in combat—that is, one hit by even a small enemy missile warhead could put an LCS out of action or even send it to the bottom. Rowden wants to solve that first problem by arming the LCSs with deck launchers and scores of long-range missiles. And he wants to solve the second problem—survivability—by hiding the LCSs from the enemy. If the enemy can't find it, he can't shoot at it.

Consider how a missile-armed Freedom-class littoral combat

ship might be used in the fictional "battle" for Guanotomo imagined above.

The Blue Force (U.S.) carrier strike group is getting ready to
launch its attack aircraft against the Red amphibious invasion force,
which is being guarded by a small task force of three guided-missile
destroyers. Meanwhile, on a small island a hundred miles away
from Guanotomo, a shallow-draft Blue Force LCS has crept into
a small, shallow inlet and gone radio silent. It shuts down its radars
and sonars, ceases any radio transmissions, keeps its engine power
to an absolute minimum to lower its heat signature. Electromag-
netically speaking, it's as quiet as a church mouse. All it's doing
is passively listening to radio signals from the Blue carrier group.

Suddenly the Blue carrier group comes under missile fire from
the Red guided-missile destroyers that are guarding the Red
invasion force. Sunburns and Sizzlers are streaking toward the
carrier group at twice the speed of sound, and while the strike
group's missile defense systems successfully knock them down,
those defenses may soon be overwhelmed. The attacking Red force
destroyers are out of range of the carrier group's anti-ship missiles,
and because the carrier has to maneuver to try to evade incoming
missiles, it can't get its attack aircraft aloft in time.

The carrier group does have surveillance aircraft and unmanned
drones in the air, so it knows where the attacking Red destroyers
are—and they are within range of the hidden LCS's missiles. The
carrier group transmits precise targeting data to the listening LCS,
which looses a salvo of anti-ship missiles at the Red destroyers.
The LCS will have to move now, the missile launches have given
away its location, but remember, it's a fast ship, and there are
other shallow island inlets to hide in. Meanwhile, the LCS's
missiles are streaking toward the Red destroyers, whose crews
are thinking—"Whoa! Where the hell did those missiles come
from?" After concentrating all their attention on the Blue carrier

group, they're now being attacked on a completely different axis, and they have their own survivability to worry about. Three of the LCS's missiles score hits, one on each Red destroyer, effectively putting them out of the fight. The Blue carrier group launches its aircraft, the Marines land, the Guanotomese cheer, etc., etc.

Again, that's a highly simplified version of what in reality would be an incredibly complex air and naval conflict. But it gives an idea of what an LCS could do, especially in the Asia-Pacific region, which is filled with islands, narrow straits, shallow waters, places where even destroyers can't operate. Sure, the LCSs can still fulfill their other missions: searching for pirates or drug runners or terrorists, landing Special Forces teams, showing American "presence" without leaving a big footprint that could cause problems for smaller-nation allies and friends. And in a conflict, some LCSs could still fulfill their planned defensive roles of antisub and antimine warfare and helicopter-borne surveillance.

But remember what Rowden says: "Defense is important, but offense wins." When armed with effective anti-ship missiles, Rowden and other navy planners believe, the LCSs could play an important offensive role in a real fight.

Admiral Harry Harris agrees.

"We could do a lot more with the LCS platform than we have at present," Harris says. "I tell the story of when I was a tactical action officer on the [aircraft carrier] *Saratoga* back in the mid-1980s at the height of the Cold War. One of my responsibilities was to keep track of the Soviet Nanuchka, Tarantul, and Osa patrol boats. These were relatively tiny ships, but we had to track every one of them and know where they were throughout the Mediterranean. And why was that? It was because they had Styx missiles. And so they were a threat well beyond their size. They were a threat to the carrier, the cruisers, the destroyers, the whole thing. And I want the LCSs to be viewed by our adversaries in the region in the same way that I viewed Osas, Nanuchkas, and Tarantuls back in the eighties. I think we'll be able to 'up-gun' the LCS [with missiles] and turn it into a combat ship. And that will give a real punch to what the LCS can bring to the fight."

(Harris would also like to shift land-based U.S. Army missile batteries to countries around the South China Sea to provide anti-ship capabilities, but it's uncertain which countries if any would allow that level of permanent U.S. military presence.)

And what kind of missiles would give the LCSs that punch? So far the only missiles that are envisioned to be put on the navy's littoral combat ships are the relatively short-range (about seventy miles) old Harpoons. But Rowden, Harris, and others know there are better anti-ship missiles available.

One of them is a product out of Norway.

Most people might not think of Norway as a leader in naval technology development—but they'd be wrong. Norway has a long coastline, a long maritime tradition, and a small but well-trained and technologically advanced navy. That well-seasoned expertise was put on display when the Royal Norwegian Navy sent the guided-missile frigate *Fridtjof Nansen* to the 2014 RimPac exercise off Hawaii.

In addition to giving its lucky sailors a chance to enjoy some warm weather for a change, the purpose of the *Fridtjof Nansen*'s visit was to demonstrate its Naval Strike Missile—or, in Norwegian, the *Nytt sjømålsmissil*, the New Sea-Strike Missile. Despite the name, it's a sea target and land target missile that is about thirteen feet long, travels at high subsonic speed, carries a 276-pound warhead, is powered by a solid rocket booster and turbojet, and is guided by an inertial GPS guidance system. The *Nytt sjømålsmissil* had already shown that it could operate in cold climates, but the Norwegians wanted to show that it could operate in warm environments as well—which it did, splendidly.

Part of the RimPac exercise was a SINKEX, a ship-sinking exercise—which is always a satisfying endeavor for sailors. Ask any marine or army grunt why he joined up and the usual answers are: "To serve my country, to see the world, and to blow shit up." Sailors are a little less martial. They'll usually throw in "learn a skill" as number three and "blow shit up" as number four—but the "blow shit up" is still an important factor. Firing a missile, shooting the main deck gun, even squeezing off small-arms rounds from the fantail—they're always the highlight of almost every sailor's tour. And actually sinking a ship is the ultimate "blow shit up" exercise.

So after a thorough scrubbing to prevent environmental contamination, the fifty-year-old, 569-foot amphibious transport dock ship USS *Ogden* had been towed to a live-fire area some sixty miles northwest of Kauai. A variety of aircraft, subs, and surface ships let fly at it with their missiles, including the *Fridtjof Nansen*, which launched a *Nytt sjømålsmissil* at the old *Ogden* from about 110 miles away. The missile, mounted in a deck launcher about the size of a refrigerator, surged off with a ship-shaking *whoosh* and made a direct hit on the *Ogden* less than a minute later, helping to send it to the bottom. Rowden and others were convinced that if such a longer-range anti-ship missile could be launched from a small frigate like the *Fridtjof Nansen*, it certainly could be launched from a littoral combat ship, and from other types of ships as well.

There's a problem with the *Nytt sjømålsmissil*, though—not with the missile itself, but with the Department of Defense's sclerotic acquisitions program. Launching a brand-new long-range anti-ship missile program could eat up six or eight years with competitive bidding, contract challenges, testing, production, and so on. And the navy wants a longer-range anti-ship missile in its hands yesterday.

But there is a stopgap way around that. While new missile

programs are in development, the Pentagon can allow its existing missiles to be upgraded with a tenth of the red tape a new program would require. So Boeing has developed kits to lighten its old Harpoon missile warhead from about five hundred pounds to about three hundred pounds, which would increase its range to over a hundred miles—although the smaller warhead would necessarily reduce its lethality.

Meanwhile the Defense Department is speeding up its ongoing AGM-158C Long Range Anti-Ship Missile (LRASM) program, a version of the U.S. Air Force's Joint Air-to-Surface Standoff Missile-Extended Range conventional cruise missile. Equipped with a long-range sensor developed by BAE Systems that combines passive radio-frequency sensing with an electro-optical terminal seeker capable of matching a ship's imagery to a target database, the missile is designed to autonomously locate and attack a vessel within a well-defended group of enemy ships. Roughly fourteen feet long, the missile carries a one-thousand-pound warhead at high-subsonic speed up to about 580 miles. The navy is also working on modifications to the ship- or submarine-launched Tomahawk land attack missile that could give the Tomahawk the ability to hit a moving ship from a range of a thousand miles. Other improvements to existing missile systems are also being considered.

So will new or improved missiles solve the problem that China is increasingly trying to deny the U.S. Navy access to key areas in the Western Pacific through its positioning of offensive weaponry? Can deploying better missiles on more ships help counter whatever the Chinese military might throw at the U.S. Navy—or better yet, deter them from throwing anything in the first place?

Maybe for now. Again, China doesn't want conflict with the U.S. if it can accomplish its goals without it. The "return" of Taiwan to mainland control, dominance of the sea lanes of the South China Sea, pushing the U.S. military out of the Western Pacific—those are core goals for the Chinese leadership, and it's doubtful they will give up on them.

So as long as its economy can sustain it, China will continue to develop its military technology, including its anti-ship missile programs. And if the U.S. Navy wants to remain a force in the Western Pacific, it will have to keep up.

Here's how it plans to do that.

Rear Admiral Michael "Nasty" Manazir is standing on the future, looking at the past.

The past that Manazir is looking at is the USS *Enterprise*, the navy's—and the world's—first nuclear-powered aircraft carrier. When she was commissioned in 1961, she was a modern marvel, at 1,122 feet the biggest naval vessel ever built, the first of the so-called supercarriers; stand her up on her stern and she'd be almost as tall as the Empire State Building. During her more than half a century of service, the "Big E" played a role in almost every conflict and hot spot around the globe, from the Cuban Missile Crisis to Vietnam to Afghanistan and Iraq.

But she's old now, outdated, and soon to die. As Manazir looks at her across the Newport News waterfront, she's still officially a navy ship, but in the process of decommissioning. She's sitting in a drydock with her radars and antennas removed, her anchors gone, some of her passageways and hatches closed off, her insides stripped of any reusable gear. Civilian shipyard workers are in the process of preparing her eight nuclear reactors for defueling, after which she'll be ocean-towed all the way to Bremerton, Washington, for final cutting up.

Seeing the *Enterprise* like this is a sad thing for many current navy sailors. The Big E has been part of the navy far longer than any of them have been in the navy, and they hate to see her go.

Manazir is one of them. He flew F-14 Tomcats off the Big E
during her forty-three-thousand-mile "round the world tour" in
1989 and '90.

But Nasty Manazir understands better than most that the navy
and its aircraft carriers can't get stuck in the past. The navy has to
look at the future—and that's what Manazir is standing on this
day. He's standing on the bridge wing of the navy's soon-to-be
newest carrier, the USS *Gerald R. Ford,* which is under construction
dockside at the Newport News Shipbuilding facilities. And like
the *Enterprise* was in her day, the *Ford* is unlike any other aircraft
carrier in the world.

"It's the centerpiece of naval aviation," he says. "We're not just
revitalizing a program. We're not just upgrading a weapons system.
It's all about relevancy—what it brings to the nation."

Manazir knows about carriers. Raised in California, the son
of a marine, he graduated from the Naval Academy in 1981 and
won his aviator's wings two years later. (His call sign, "Nasty," is
based on his name, which is pronounced Ma-NA-zir. Call signs
are given by the pilots' colleagues, not the pilots themselves, and
they can often be insulting or ridiculous—"AB," short for "Ass
Blaster," or "Notso" for a pilot whose last name is Swift, and so
on. But Manazir likes "Nasty" and signs off his personal corre-
spondence with it.) Self-assured and plainspoken, with a rugged
square face and a prominent mustache, Manazir looks like a movie
version of a navy pilot. He's flown F-14s and F-18 Super Hornets
off carriers around the world, racking up more than thirty-seven
hundred flight hours, more than twelve hundred arrested landings—and only one crash.

In 1987, when he was a lieutenant flying a Tomcat on a training
mission from Air Station Miramar, Manazir and his backseater
had to eject at eight thousand feet and parachute into the Pacific
after both of their aircraft's engines flamed out—an experience

Manazir likens to "playing Russian roulette." Although about 90 percent of ejections are not fatal, as soon as he pulls the ejection handle or "trigger," a pilot has about a one-in-three chance of suffering a spinal injury from the g-forces of getting blown out of a cockpit, and virtually a 100 percent chance of getting bruised up—and that's assuming everything works like it should. In Manazir's case it did. He and his backseater spent twenty minutes bobbing around on a rubber raft before a couple of helicopters fished them out of the water, but neither suffered serious injury.

Now, as he's aboard the *Ford* in the spring of 2014, Nasty Manazir is the navy's director of air warfare, responsible for the development, programming, and budgeting of all U.S. naval aviation warfighting capabilities—aircraft carriers included.

It's not an easy job, especially when it's concerned with the new Ford-class carriers, of which there eventually will be at least three—the *Ford* itself, the USS *John F. Kennedy*, and the new USS *Enterprise*, which will be the ninth navy ship to bear that name over the past almost two-and-a-half centuries. For months now Manazir has been getting beaten over the head by senators and congressmen who are upset about the *Ford*'s cost overruns and delays. The price tag is up to $13.2 billion, more than initially projected, and the expected commissioning date has been pushed ahead by two years to 2017.

Manazir has gone blue in the face trying to explain that the first-in-class of any new ship design is bound to have some problems and delays, which results in cost overruns. But the navy has to have more carriers to replace the aging Nimitz-class flattops, some of which date back to the mid-1970s. Manazir insists that the more technologically sophisticated and smaller-crewed Ford-class carriers will actually save $4 billion a year in operating costs per year per ship—which over their projected forty- or fifty-year life span will make the initial development and construction costs seem like chump change.

"They choke on the number to buy the *Ford*," Manazir says. "They say, 'That's too expensive. We can't afford this.' But to get the technology we're getting on [the *Ford*], we'd have to redesign the Nimitz carriers to make them viable. And we're only paying 15 percent more for the *Ford* than we did for [the Nimitz-class USS *George H.W. Bush*]. The *Ford* will more than pay for itself."

Not everybody buys that, but Nasty Manazir is a believer. Forget all the talk going around the halls of Congress and the Pentagon about "carrier killer" ballistic missiles and the aircraft carrier being obsolete. If it's to sustain its leadership role in the world, Manazir thinks America will always need aircraft carriers as traveling air bases, able to project U.S. power around the globe whenever and wherever it's needed. And the *Ford* is intended to do that without anyone having to worry too much about new missiles and tactics that have so many people wringing their hands.

The *Ford* looks different from its Nimitz-class predecessors. The first thing you notice is that the island, which houses the bridge and the flight operations, is set much farther aft (toward the stern) than on previous carriers. Navy officials say that gives the flight deck more "acreage" and thus the ability to launch and recover aircraft in less time. The rotating radar panels of previous ships are also gone, replaced with flat panels that produce more powerful and efficient radar. The visual effect is of a leaner, sleeker aircraft carrier.

There are also things you can't see at first glance that set this carrier apart. For example, there's the 10 million feet of electronic cables that are wired through the ship, replacing miles of old steam-powered piping, valves, and other mechanical systems used on other carriers. The *Ford*'s electronic systems can be operated more safely and with fewer crew than on the older carriers; just forty-six hundred officers and enlisted crewmembers and aircrew-

men will man the *Ford* when it finally joins the fleet, as opposed
to almost six thousand on the old Nimitz-class carriers.

The *Ford* launches and recovers aircraft differently as well. As
we've seen, the old catapults use steam power to hurl planes off
the flight deck. Those cats are heavy and require a lot of maintenance, and if they aren't set just right they can beat an airplane
to death or fail to get it up to launch speed. But the *Ford* uses
a new electromagnetic catapult system with powerful magnets
lined up along the cat trough to propel the aircraft forward. The
electromagnetic systems have very few moving parts, which cuts
down on maintenance. The *Ford*'s arresting gear is also electric
powered, as opposed to hydraulically operated, which allows better
control. The new systems will also enable the carrier to handle
more types of aircraft, from smaller, unmanned aerial vehicles to
the largest manned and unmanned fighters and surveillance or
communications planes.

There are other dramatic advances that separate the Ford-class
from previous carriers: better elevators to haul more planes and
weapons to the flight deck, improved radar systems, better launch
and landing control systems, higher bandwidth and increased
access to electrical power, and on and on. But what's even more
revolutionary than the carrier itself is what the navy intends to
put on it, and on the escort ships that will accompany it at sea.

First of all there's the F-35 Joint Strike Fighter, officially dubbed
the Lightning II, although curiously no one calls it that; it's the
JSF. The navy's F-35C is a single-seat, single-engine, all-weather,
extremely stealthy multi-role fighter with a top speed of 1,200 mph
and a combat range of about six hundred miles without refueling.
The navy plans to eventually acquire about four hundred of the
carrier-launched F-35Cs, at an eventual cost of about $85 million
or more each, and go operational in 2018. (There are other variants
on the F-35 being acquired by the air force and the Marine Corps;

the marine version is designed to take off and land vertically, like a Harrier jump jet.) This "fifth generation" fighter is packed with an array of state-of-the-art electronics—electro-optical targeting systems for extended range detection and precision targeting of air-to-air threats, active electronically scanned array radar for long-range targeting. The radar will enable the F-35 JSF pilot to effectively engage air and ground targets at long range, while also providing additional situational awareness for enhanced survivability.

To feed both fuel and surveillance data to those F-35Cs and the Super Hornets and Growlers that make up the carrier's air complement, the navy is developing the MQ-25 Stingray, an unmanned, catapult-launched aircraft that looks like a flying saucer with wings. Its initial primary mission will be to serve as an in-air refueler to extend the carrier aircrafts' ranges while also providing some surveillance and intelligence capabilities; later versions will likely be equipped to perform actual air strikes on enemy targets. Launching and especially recovering an unmanned aircraft on a lurching carrier deck isn't as easy as it may sound, but the navy has successfully tested a prototype unmanned combat jet, the X-47B. The X-47B, which looks like a giant gray bat, has a range of about twenty-five hundred miles, far greater than the navy's current manned strike fighters. Without all the equipment needed to accommodate a pilot—ejection seats, oxygen systems, and so on—unmanned strike fighters can fly farther, stay up longer, and be subjected to greater risk than piloted aircraft. Although the X-47B is a demonstrator aircraft, its unmanned strike fighter successors could give American carriers more of the long-range punch they need.

As for all those Chinese long-range anti-ship missiles that everyone says will make the supercarriers obsolete, the navy is working on that as well, with weapons systems that a few decades ago would have seemed like fantasy. Those systems include high-energy lasers, "railguns," and hypervelocity projectiles (HVPs).

In general, high-energy laser beams would counter incoming missiles by burning holes in their skins and causing thermal damage to their interiors. Lasers can also be used to "dazzle" the electro-optical sensors on a missile, in effect blinding it. Although laser guns may sound like weapons of the future, in fact the navy has already installed a laser weapon on the converted amphibious ship USS *Ponce*. A high-energy laser is generally considered to be a laser with a beam power of at least ten kilowatts; the system on the *Ponce*—straightforwardly known as the Laser Weapons System, or LaWS—has a reported thirty kilowatts of power, which can bore a hole through two inches of steel. The LaWS, which looks like a short, fat missile launcher, has been successfully tested against unmanned drones and small attack-type boats.

But the navy is thinking bigger than just thirty kilowatts. Boosting laser beam power up to 200 kW or 300 kW could permit a laser to counter at least some anti-ship cruise missiles. Even stronger beam powers—on the order of one megawatt or more—could improve a laser's effectiveness against anti-ship cruise missiles and enable it to counter anti-ship ballistic missiles; the laser systems could even be mounted on aircraft carriers themselves as a last-ditch defensive weapon. True, there are some problems to get around, including the effects of weather on the laser system's capability. But using laser weapons against incoming missiles would be a lot cheaper than using million-dollar antimissile missiles against them. It would also give a navy ship a "deeper magazine"—that is, more shots could be fired from a laser than could be fired with missile systems. Lasers are line-of-sight weapons, not over-the-horizon weapons, so they wouldn't replace missile systems on navy ships. But they could add another layer of antimissile defense.

Same thing goes for the electromagnetic railgun, or EMRG,

which the navy has been working on for more than a decade. The railgun is a cannon that uses electricity rather than gunpowder or other chemical propellants to fire a projectile; it looks sort of like a giant potato-gun, those long-piped backyard cannons kids sometimes build to fire spuds. Magnetic fields created by high electrical currents accelerate a sliding metal conductor, or armature, between two rails—hence the name—to launch projectiles at speeds of up to 5,600 mph, or about one-and-a-half miles a second, at ranges of over a hundred miles. At that speed even a small, nonexplosive solid projectile produces enormous kinetic energy; getting hit by one is like being hit by a small asteroid. Like laser weapons, railguns are cheap to fire. Each shot only costs about buck's worth of electricity, and the solid-shot railgun projectiles are basically just hunks of steel. Also like the lasers, railguns would provide deeper magazines for navy ships. A navy destroyer can only carry about a hundred missiles, but it could carry thousands of railgun projectiles.

The problem is that railguns require enormous electrical power sources to operate them—about twenty-five megawatts to fire at full range and rate of fire—and most of the navy's current combatant ships can't spare that much juice. A carrier has enough electric power reserves to fire a railgun, and laser weapons as well, but that could interfere with the carrier's primary mission of launching and recovering aircraft. Instead you'd probably want the railguns to be mounted on the carrier's escort ships to provide antimissile defense for the carrier. Some navy contractors are working on special lithium-based "energy magazines" that could be housed in special cabinets about the size of a large home entertainment wall unit and provide enough power for sustained power bursts. Another idea is to put the railguns on Spearhead-class expeditionary fast transport ships (EPFs), of which the navy has eight. (They were formerly known as joint high speed vessels.) The EPFs are small, only about three hundred feet long, but they can be outfitted to generate a lot of electrical power, and with their catamaran-style hulls and a top speed of almost 50 mph they're fast enough to keep up with a carrier strike group. The navy already has plans to install a railgun on an EPF for testing purposes.

Hypervelocity projectiles are another method of countering the anti-ship missile threat. HVPs are small artillery shells, just two feet long and with a fifteen-pound explosive payload. Their advantages are that they're extremely fast, about twice the speed of a conventional artillery shell, and they can be GPS-guided to hit their targets; they're like "smart" cannonballs. The downside is that they're expensive—anywhere from about $25,000 to a whopping $800,000 each, depending on the type. The naval HVPs were originally designed to be fired out of the new railguns, but then the navy realized they could be adapted to be fired from the five-inch deck guns currently mounted on navy cruisers and destroyers. They also can be adapted to fire from the larger 155mm (about a six-inch barrel diameter) guns that are mounted on the navy's newest platform—the Zumwalt-class destroyer.

The *Zumwalt* (DDG 1000) is undoubtedly the strangest-looking—some say the coolest-looking—navy ship in modern times. Ironically, with its slope-sided superstructure it looks a lot like the old Confederate ironclad CSS *Virginia* (better known as the *Merrimack*) that duked it out with the USS *Monitor* ironclad in the Civil War. Unlike the *Merrimack*, though, the sloping shape of the *Zumwalt* is not designed to deflect cannonballs but rather to deflect radar. The *Zumwalt* has no deck rails, no external ladders, no bridge wings, no external masts or antennas to speak of; everything about it is designed to reduce its radar signature to an absolute minimum. It's not exactly invisible to enemy electronic detection, but it can come pretty close. The *Zumwalt* may be the stealthiest big ship ever made.

And it is big, six hundred feet long and with a fifteen-thousand-ton displacement; it's actually bigger than a navy cruiser. It's arguably more powerful than a cruiser as well. It has eighty vertical launch cells for surface-to-air, sea-to-land, and antisubmarine missiles, and it's equipped with two of the bigger, longer-range 155mm deck guns previously mentioned—except that unlike other ships' guns, the *Zumwalt*'s guns can be pointed straight up if necessary. (When not in use the big deck guns are kept inside radar-deflecting compartments that pop open when needed.) The *Zumwalt*'s big flight deck can also handle two helicopters and several unmanned aerial vehicles.

But it's the future weapons that can be mounted on the *Zumwalt* that make it most impressive. Because its engines produce enormous electric power—seventy-eight megawatts, enough to power almost fifty thousand American homes—it has the capacity to operate both railguns and the higher-energy laser weapons the navy is developing. It could also be equipped with vertically launched long-range strike and reconnaissance drone vehicles. To manage all that weaponry the *Zumwalt* is packed with advanced radar, sensor, and communications systems that can track and target anti-ship cruise missiles and anti-ship ballistic missiles. Because the ship's operational systems are interconnected through what the navy calls the "Total Ship Computing Environment," the Zumwalt-class destroyers require only about 150 crewmembers, less than half of a navy's cruiser's complement. Although the navy always uses backup personnel, theoretically just three sailors could man the bridge, and just one could man the engine room.

How will the navy use such a ship? Probably not as a carrier strike group escort. Instead, it likely will become the centerpiece of so-called hunter-killer groups, small groups of two or three ships, possibly including littoral combat ships, whose stealthiness will allow them to get close to shore to attack enemy land-based missile sites as well as enemy guided-missile ships and boats. Armed with the future weapons systems described above, the *Zumwalt* could also provide long-range protection against enemy anti-ship cruise and ballistic missiles.

In short, the *Zumwalt* guided-missile destroyer is revolutionary. And it could be the perfect fit for the far Western Pacific Theater. As the top commander in that theater, Admiral Harris, puts it, "It's simply the coolest ship I've ever seen. If Batman had a ship, it would be the *Zumwalt*. With so much whiz-bang per square inch, it's like a waterborne B-2 [stealth bomber] with big guns."

True, there are some problems with the Zumwalt-class de-stroyers, the primary one being that there may not be enough of them. During the mid-2000s the navy had planned to build thirty-two of them, but that number was later reduced to just three. The numbers reduction was partly because of resistance within some of the navy's senior leadership to the ship's futuristic technology, and maybe even just the way it looks. Reducing the number of Zumwalts also had the effect of jacking up the cost per ship, which now stands at about $4 billion. Still, navy strategists believe that even one of the new ships, properly positioned, could play a decisive role in a conflict.

There are other future weapons in the works, including un-manned underwater vehicles (UUVs) that can be used for a va-riety of tasks, including minesweeping. One prototype built by Lockheed Martin is a 14,500-pound, twenty-three-foot-long beast that can drag a two-thousand-foot towed-array sonar cable behind it. The drone could be launched from a ship—say, an LCS—and then chug along on its own on a preprogrammed course while the LCS goes off on other missions. Other proposed UUVs could be launched from a pier and then head off to a preset location where they would loiter about for a month or two, seeing what they could see and transmitting that data back to ship or shore.

The bottom line is that any one of these future weapons systems—extreme high-energy lasers, railguns, hypervelocity projectiles, underwater drones, the Zumwalt-class destroyers—could be a gamechanger in a military confrontation with China. The problem is that except for the Zumwalts, none of those systems is expected to be fully operational until the early or mid-2020s.

And given what the Chinese are doing in the South China Sea, you have to wonder if by that time there will still be a game to change.

CHAPTER 9

A Great Wall of Sand

As the P-8A Poseidon flies westbound over the South China
Sea, the message is coming over the international radio net
Lima-Alpha-Charlie—loud and clear.

"This is Chinese navy, this is Chinese navy! You are approaching our military alert zone. Please leave immediately in order to
avoid misjudgment!"To which a Poseidon crewmember responds
by reading a carefully prepared statement: "I am a U.S. military
aircraft, I'm conducting lawful military activities outside national
airspace, operating as required with due regard for international
law."

This goes on a couple times, back and forth, then a different
voice comes on the radio. "This is Chinese navy, stay away from
this area, your actions are unfriendly and dangerous, your actions
are dangerous!"—after which the Poseidon crewmember reads the
same prepared response. This goes on a couple more times, same
drill, and the Poseidon crew can hear the increasingly frustrated
tone of the Chinese radio calls. Finally yet another Chinese voice
comes on and shouts, "YOU GO!"

But on this day in May 2015 the U.S. Navy Poseidon reconnaissance plane isn't going anywhere except to continue on its
mission—whether the Chinese navy likes it or not. Because the

navy and the U.S. government know what China is up to out here in the South China Sea—and now they want the world to see it. There's a news crew from CNN on the flight, the first time journalists have been allowed on an operational P-8A reconnaissance flight in the Western Pacific. And the news crew's presence is an indicator of just how angry and frustrated Admiral Harris and other defense officials are with China.

It seems that this time, China has finally gone too far.

The Poseidon's destination on this mission is the airspace near some formerly insignificant specks of coral in the Spratly Islands group, a good six hundred miles south of the nearest Chinese coastline. To understand what has transformed these insignificant specks and the Spratly Islands in general into a potential international flash point requires a little background.

The Spratlys are a collection of fourteen small, sandy islands ranging in size from one acre to just over one hundred acres; mixed in among those islands are more than a hundred reefs, shoals, and other underwater geographical "features" that are scattered over about 160,000 square miles of sea. Although known to Chinese and Southeast Asian fishermen for millennia, in the Western view the Spratlys were "discovered" in 1843 by a British whaling ship captain named Richard Spratly.

Even though the tiny islands in the Spratly group have no arable land and almost no water to support human habitation, nations have been arguing over them for almost two centuries. China, Vietnam, the Philippines, Taiwan, Malaysia, even little Brunei—over the years they have all claimed ownership of various islands and other nearby "features," with some countries sending military detachments to occupy them. The competition to occupy the islands became especially intense in the 1970s amid reports that the area might contain extensive deposits of oil and natural gas. By the mid-1980s all of the fourteen actual islands in the group had been claimed and occupied by the Philippines, Vietnam, and Taiwan.

Unfortunately for China, it came late to the island-occupying game in the Spratlys. By the time China's emerging market economy made it vital to protect its access to the sea lanes of the South China Sea, and vital also to increase its own domestic oil production, all of the Spratly Islands "features" that weren't mostly underwater were already occupied. So China decided that if it couldn't occupy the islands that were already there, it would create some new ones—starting with Fiery Cross Reef.

Fiery Cross (known as Yongshu to the Chinese) is an oval of coral about fourteen miles long and four miles across; its Western name comes from a British clipper ship that was wrecked on it in 1860. Except for one lonely, one-yard-high rock at its southern end, it's completely submerged at high tide, as are most of the reefs in the area. It's hard to imagine why anyone would kill people over such places—but they have.

In 1988, without anyone really paying attention, the Chinese government began building what it alleged was a sea- and weather-monitoring post on Fiery Cross Reef, even though the reef had been claimed by Vietnam, the Philippines, and Taiwan. Chinese ships with engineers, construction workers, and dredgers were dispatched to the reef, and in a little over a week they blasted and spread out enough coral to create eighty-six thousand square feet of permanently dry land—almost two football fields' worth—on which they eventually built military barracks and bunkers. Later the Chinese government also sent sailors to occupy Cuarteron Reef, an above-the-water reef nearby.

Vietnam was particularly angry about the Chinese reef grab. Despite receiving material aid from China during the Vietnam War with the U.S., the Vietnamese had never gotten over their fear and distrust of China, which by Vietnamese count had invaded them twenty times over the past thousand years. The latest Chinese invasion had occurred just a decade earlier, in 1979, when Chinese troops invaded Vietnam after Vietnam had invaded China's client state of Cambodia. There certainly was no love lost between the two Communist nations.

Unable to dislodge the Chinese from Fiery Cross, the Vietnamese sent two rusty transport ships and a hundred soldiers to occupy some other nearby reefs, including Johnson South Reef, an underwater-at-high-tide feature some eighty miles east of Fiery Cross. After the Vietnamese soldiers planted their flag on the reef, a couple of Chinese navy frigates showed up and sent a landing party ashore to confront them. Somehow shooting broke out—the stories differ as to who shot first—and after the Chinese landing party retreated, the Chinese navy ships opened up with machine gun fire. A video of the incident shows the crowd of Vietnamese soldiers standing knee-deep in the water while they are literally being mowed down. In the end, more than sixty Vietnamese soldiers were killed and the two Vietnamese transport ships were sunk. Eventually China wound up taking four other reefs in addition to Fiery Cross and Johnson South and building small military bunkers on them.

But they weren't finished. In 1995 the Chinese sneaked onto another unoccupied reef—aptly known in English as Mischief Reef—just 135 miles from the Philippine island of Palawan, putting up concrete bunkers on stilts atop the reef, which is submerged at high tide. When a Philippine fishing boat showed up near the reef and saw what was going on, the Chinese navy arrested the crew and held them for a week, but the takeover couldn't remain a secret forever. The Philippine government protested the Chinese intrusion, claiming the reef was part of its historic territory, but there was really nothing they could do. After being kicked out of Subic Bay in 1992, the U.S. Navy certainly wasn't going to help, and the Philippine navy consisted of a handful of World War II patrol boats. China, for its part, had two versions of the story. One was that the concrete bunkers were merely shelters for fishermen in distress. The other was that the reef had been snatched and the bunkers built by a group of "unauthorized" junior navy officers acting on their own—the old "rogue operator" excuse. Even if that were true, which it almost certainly wasn't, China didn't offer to give the reef back.

There have been other island flash points in the South China Sea. For example, in 1974, in the Paracel Islands group about two hundred miles south of Hainan Island and the same distance from Vietnam, ships and troops from China and what was then South Vietnam fought a pitched battle that left about fifty South Vietnamese dead and China firmly in physical control of most of the tiny islands. Farther south, about one hundred miles off the Philippine coast, there's Second Thomas Shoal, a thirty-mile-long collection of rocks and reefs in the Spratlys that's claimed by both China and the Philippines. To enforce its claim, in 1999 the Philippine navy ran an old World War II tank-landing ship aground on one of the rocks and stationed a small detachment of soldiers aboard it; Filipino soldiers have been living there miserably ever since, as the ship rusts away under their feet and Chinese maritime forces try to prevent them from being resupplied. There's also the previously mentioned Scarborough Shoal, another thirty-mile-long ring of guano-covered rocks and submerged reefs about 120 miles from the Philippine coast; as noted earlier, Chinese maritime forces have been turning Filipino fishermen away from the area since 2012. The list of islands, reefs, and shoals claimed and disputed by China and various other countries in the South China Sea could go on.

And why do these seemingly insignificant pieces of land and not-quite-land matter? It's partly about nationalism, the simple idea that no country should be allowed to take over a piece of another country's territory, no matter how remote. Americans would be outraged if, say, the Mexican navy showed up one day and planted their flag on Anacapa Island, a group of barren, windswept rocks off the Southern California coast; Filipinos and Vietnamese and Chinese feel the same way about Fiery Cross, Mischief Reef, and Scarborough Shoal.

But there's something else that makes the Spratly Islands and other island groups in the South China Sea important. It involves the "exclusive economic zone" issue, which as noted earlier allows nations to exercise control over the sea resources along their coasts—including commercial fishing and oil exploration and development.

Under the 1982 UN Convention on the Law of the Sea, a nation that owns an actual island—defined as a piece of land that's permanently above sea level and is capable of supporting human habitation and economic activity—is entitled to claim an EEZ of up to two hundred nautical miles around the island. If a nation possesses what the UN treaty calls a "rock"—an above-water feature that cannot on its own support human habitation or economic activity—it's still entitled to claim a twelve-mile territorial zone of sovereignty around it. Underwater geographical features like Mischief Reef don't allow a nation to claim either territorial rights or an EEZ.

So under the UN Convention rules, it would seem that the reefs China seized would *not* qualify as islands or even "rocks," and thus would do China little if any good in obtaining more exclusive economic zone territory. But China has another card it likes to play—the so-called "Nine-Dash Line."

As the name suggests, the Nine-Dash Line is a series of long dashes on twentieth-century Chinese maps that loop south just off the Vietnam coast and then north along the coasts of Malaysia,

Brunei, the Philippines, and up to Taiwan. (Because of their loop-ing shape, they're sometimes called the "Cow's Tongue.") China claims that everything within that dashed line—which is to say, virtually the entire South China Sea and all the islands in it—is historically Chinese territory. Forget about islands and rocks and EEZs. In the Chinese view, China owns the South China Sea and always has, and therefore the other nations occupying the disputed islands are trespassers who can legally be booted off at will. No other country in the region recognizes the Nine-Dash Line as valid, which matters to China not at all.

And there is one *other* reason these seemingly insignificant islands are particularly important to China: their potential value as military bases.

Only later would it seem clear that using the seized reefs as military bases was the Chinese plan all along—although the Chinese gov-ernment didn't let on about it. For most of the first decade of the twenty-first century China insisted that its intentions in the South China Sea were peaceful, that the other, smaller nations in the region had nothing to fear—just as no one had needed to fear the treasure fleets of Admiral Zheng He in the fifteenth century. China even signed a 2002 agreement with the Association of Southeast Asian Nations (ASEAN) promising that all of the countries concerned, China included, would "resolve their territorial and jurisdictional disputes by peaceful means, without resorting to the threat or use of force, through friendly consultations and negotiations."

It's worth noting that during that same decade-long period of seeming cooperation, China was rapidly expanding its military and especially naval capabilities to project power far beyond its own coasts. And the seized reefs in the South China Sea would play an important part in that.

Of course, a few bunkers manned by small detachments of Chinese troops on isolated reefs didn't pose much of a threat to anyone—except perhaps to the troops themselves. For example, some of the military detachments on Chinese-occupied reefs were so infrequently supplied that there were reports the troops might be suffering from scurvy as a result of poor diets. If the Chinese wanted to turn the reefs into militarily significant assets, the reefs would have to be expanded.

Which, beginning in 2014, the Chinese started doing.

After more than a decade of relative inactivity on the reefs, China suddenly began an unannounced crash program to "reclaim" the reefs from the sea. Dozens of ships and dredgers and hundreds of construction workers began scooping up millions of tons of sand from the seafloor and dumping it atop Fiery Cross, Subi, Johnson South, Mischief, and other Spratly Islands reefs. A little over a year later, the two football fields' worth of previously reclaimed land on Fiery Cross had grown to 665 acres, while Mischief Reef, which had never had any usable land at all, had ballooned to 1,400 acres of land. In all, China ultimately "reclaimed" more than 3,000 acres on its seven Spratly Islands reefs—and the suspicion was that they still weren't finished.

Mind you, under international rules these new "islands" aren't islands at all. You can't dump sand and coral onto a submerged reef and claim it as an island with all the legal rights thereof. But China ignored such niceties. China wanted new territory in the South China Sea, so it built some.

But what was more important than having the new land was what the Chinese military started putting on it. Fiery Cross soon bristled with sophisticated radar domes, helipads, satellite communications facilities, military barracks, artillery emplacements, and even basketball and tennis courts for the occupying troops. Fiery Cross also boasted a new airfield with a ten-thousand-foot runway.

That runway was particularly troubling. You don't need ten thousand feet of runway to launch and land small transport planes or search-and-rescue aircraft. You could almost land a space shuttle on a runway that long—and you could certainly launch and land tactical fighter aircraft on it. The eventual presence of hardened aircraft hangars by the runway seemed to confirm that China was planning to turn Fiery Cross into a military airfield.

With similar facilities being built on its other reclaimed reefs, China gained forward-deployed bases hundreds of miles from its own shores with the capability of militarily dominating much of the South China Sea region. (China already had an air base on the disputed Woody Island in the Paracels; eventually it would deploy missile batteries and tactical fighters to the island.) The combination of advanced radars, missile batteries, and tactical fighters on the islands could give China the confidence to declare a restricted air defense identification zone over the entire South China Sea—and the means to enforce it. Certainly the new island bases would give China the option of preventing, by force if necessary, other, smaller nations from exploiting resources in waters China claimed as its own. Of course, during an actual war the small bases could be quickly taken out by missile strikes. But in anything short of war, the island bases' *coercive* power would be tremendous.

The sudden expansion and overt militarization of the reefs took the world by surprise. It was a brazen disruption of the status quo, an intentional, in-your-face escalation of tensions. True, some of the other island claimants, including Taiwan and Vietnam, had also dredged and expanded their island holdings. But those only amounted to a few dozen acres, while the Chinese created thousands.

Chinese government officials insisted their new island bases and airstrips would be used for peaceful purposes, such as search-

and-rescue operations—which of course no one really believed. But they were also defiant. The Chinese foreign minister, for example, publicly declared that "the determination of the Chinese side to safeguard our own sovereignty and territorial integrity is as firm as a rock. . . . It is the people's demand of the government and our legitimate right."

Naturally, the other countries in the region with claims in the South China Sea were furious about—and frightened by—Chinese militarization of the reefs. It was as if the Chinese were anchoring a fleet of stationary aircraft carriers off their coasts; in a Cold War context, it was akin to the Soviets in 1962 putting nuclear missiles in Cuba. But unlike the U.S. versus the Soviets, none of the countries that objected to this power move was strong enough to retort with more than rhetoric.

As for the U.S. government, it had never taken an official position on the various territorial claims over the islands and reefs, declaring simply that the various parties, China included, should peacefully work out the disputes under international law. At the same time, it strongly opposed any use of the reefs or islands to impose any restrictions on freedom of navigation on the high seas.

But for many in the U.S. defense community, and especially the navy, this sudden militarization of the South China Sea reefs was too much. Even President Barack Obama, hardly a fan of confrontations with China, said this about the Chinese island-building campaign: "China . . . is using its sheer size and muscle to force countries into subordinate positions. We think this can be solved diplomatically, but just because the Philippines or Vietnam are not as large as China doesn't mean that they can just be elbowed aside."

For the Obama administration, that was strong talk. But for Admiral Harry Harris, talk would never be enough to deter China or reassure U.S. friends and allies.

Sure, Harris could talk tough as well. But he also wanted the U.S. Navy to actually *do* something.

It's March 2015, a couple of months before the P-8A flight takes the CNN crew to the Spratly Islands, and Admiral Harris is giving a speech at the Australian Strategic Policy Institute in Canberra. Although Harris is still the commander of the U.S. Pacific Fleet, he's about to move up in the world; he's recently been confirmed by Congress as the CO of Pacific Command, and will soon take over that job.

As usual, Harris starts the speech with a couple of self-deprecating gags, then he gets serious, stressing to his audience the importance of U.S.-Australian military cooperation and underlining the threat from North Korea. Finally, he turns to the Chinese artificial islands.

> We also see the misuse of maritime claims by some coastal states. The excessive nature of some of these claims is creating uncertainty and instability. These disruptions should compel us to increase cooperative efforts in this region. . . . Competing claims by several nations in the South China Sea increase the potential for miscalculation. But what's really drawing a lot of concern in the here and now is the unprecedented land reclamation currently being conducted by China.
>
> China is building artificial land by pumping sand onto live coral reefs—some of them submerged—and paving over them with concrete. China has now created over four square kilometers of artificial landmass. China is creating a Great Wall of Sand, with dredges and bulldozers, over the course of months. When one looks at China's pattern of provocative actions towards smaller claimant states . . . well, it's no surprise that the scope and pace

of building man-made islands raises serious questions about Chinese intentions. . . . How China proceeds will be a key indicator of whether the region is heading towards confrontation or cooperation.

A Great Wall of Sand! It's the perfect image, and although Harris doesn't put it this way, the suggestion is clear: China once built a Great Wall to keep out the barbarians of the north, and now it's building another Great Wall against the "barbarians" in the south. Coming from the soon-to-be highest-ranking U.S. military commander in the Indo-Asia-Pacific, that phrase alone guarantees that the speech will make headlines—which it does across the U.S. and around the world. "US Admiral: China Creating a Great Wall of Sand," says one headline. "US Blasts China's Great Wall of Sand in the South China Sea," says another.

It's the toughest statement on China to come out of the upper ranks of the U.S. military in years—too tough for some. After the Great Wall of Sand speech attracts so much attention, members of Harris's staff get a call from members of Chief of Naval Operations Admiral Greenert's staff, who politely wonder if perhaps Admiral Harris could tone it down just a bit. He doesn't—and he won't have to. Remember, the CO of Pacific Command reports directly to the secretary of defense, not to the CNO. There's never any public disagreement between Harris and Greenert on how to handle China; neither would even consider such a thing. And in any event, Greenert will retire before the end of the year.

So Harris keeps talking about the looming threat from China. Not that Harris is publicly critical of the Obama administration's policies. He's a navy officer, and firmly believes in civilian control of the military. If he is ordered to shut up, he will. But until then, he also believes that if American interests are being threatened, Americans should hear about it.

For example, at a conference for top-level national security leaders in Aspen, Colorado, Harris says this: "Most countries choose to pursue diplomatic means to address their disputes. China, on the other hand, is changing the status quo in the region through aggressive, coercive island building without meaningful diplomatic efforts toward dispute resolution or arbitration. . . . These activities are harming the environment and will not strengthen any country's legal claims to disputed areas in the South China Sea."

It's blunt stuff from a senior navy admiral who will soon command all U.S. military forces in the Pacific—and it gets blunter still. Later, while Harris is appearing at a Senate Armed Services Committee hearing, he's asked whether the artificial islands are being militarized, contrary to assurances that Chinese president Xi Jinping made to President Obama the previous fall—assurances the Obama administration appeared to believe. Harris's answer is brutally frank:

"In my opinion China is clearly militarizing the South China Sea," Harris tells the senators, "and you'd have to believe in a flat earth to think otherwise."

It's comments like that that make some top administration officials squirm. And the tough talk makes Harris an archvillain to the Chinese government.

"We have noticed that this official [Admiral Harris] is busy making comments on the South China Sea—sometimes in the U.S. Congress, and sometimes in the Defense Department—which has given us the general impression that he intends to smear China's legitimate and reasonable actions in the South China Sea and sow discord," a Foreign Ministry spokesman says. "He is finding an excuse for U.S. maritime hegemony and muscle-flexing on the sea."

But it's not just Harris's public comments that upset them. It's also his ethnicity. To a degree that almost all Americans would find offensive, from the time Harris began publicly speaking out about the South China Sea the Chinese state-controlled media have made an issue out of Harris's half-Japanese heritage. They often refer to him as the "Japanese admiral," and suggest that of course he's hostile to China—because what Japanese person isn't?

For example, the official Chinese news agency, Xinhua, has this to say about him: "To understand the Americans' sudden upgraded offensive in the South China Sea, it is simply impossible to ignore Admiral Harris's blood, background, political inclination and values."

Harris generally ignores the race-related insults. But for a man who as a kid in the Deep South had to struggle to prove that he was "100 percent American," it's a little annoying to have Chinese state-controlled media make an issue of his "blood."

Again, Harris doesn't want to just talk tough. He wants action to demonstrate American resolve in the face of China's aggressive actions in the South China Sea. His first inclination is to run a FONOP—a freedom of navigation operation—to refute the idea that China's artificial island outposts can claim to have territorial sovereignty, and can thus ban other countries' ships and aircraft from the area.

The term FONOP has been part of the navy's lexicon since 1983, but actually it's what the navy has been doing since its founding—that is, protecting the right of free passage in international waters. If a country tries to restrict free passage or illegally declare sovereignty over a patch of water, the U.S. will issue a diplomatic protest—and it may back up that protest with a show of force, sending navy ships into that patch of water to conduct operations. And if necessary, the navy will *use* that force. For example, after Muammar Gaddafi drew a line across the Gulf of Sidra—he called it the "Line of Death"—and claimed most of the gulf to be Libyan territorial waters, President Ronald Reagan sent two aircraft carrier strike groups into the gulf on a FONOP. When a Libyan fighter fired an air-to-air missile at two navy F-14 Tomcats, the American planes shot down two Libyan fighters. Other incidents followed, and the Line of Death did not stand.

The Chinese haven't exactly declared a "line of death" around their new artificial islands in the South China Sea. But it's pretty clear that they're claiming territorial sovereignty over the surrounding sea. So Harris wants to send U.S. Navy warships within twelve miles of the artificial islands with the U.S. flag flying—and to really make a statement, he'd like to have an aircraft carrier strike group do it.

"If you don't exercise your freedom of navigation rights you can lose them," Harris says. "FONOPs are a core tenet of what we do, and you have to be ready to defend them."

Unfortunately the Obama administration, ever cautious when it comes to China, isn't ready to go that far.

But Harris is allowed to send the Singapore-moored littoral combat ship USS *Fort Worth* on a "routine patrol" *near* the Spratlys—not an official FONOP, you understand, just a routine patrol. As the *Fort Worth* steams near the islands, it's closely followed and watched by Chinese maritime vessels, including the guided-missile frigate *Yancheng*. Following CUES rules, the Chinese warship maintains a respectful distance, though, and there aren't any incidents—which is good news for the *Fort Worth*.

You'll recall that when Chinese admiral Wu Shengli toured the USS *Fort Worth* off San Diego in 2013, he almost laughed at how under-gunned the littoral combat ship was. It's only a little better off now as it patrols the South China Sea. The *Fort Worth* is rigged out with a "surface warfare mission package," which includes a Seahawk helicopter and a Fire Scout unmanned helicopter. Still, the Chinese frigate could easily blow the LCS out of the water if it wanted to—which is why the navy never sends an LCS on patrol without having a bigger brother nearby. So as the *Yancheng* is tailing the *Fort Worth*, the *Yancheng* is also being tailed and watched by the guided-missile destroyer USS *Lassen*—just in case.

In the past, the *Fort Worth*'s routine patrol near the Spratlys wouldn't have been unusual; the navy has been running those kinds of patrols through the area for years, even decades. But in recent years the Obama administration instructed the navy to avoid sailing near disputed areas; now Harris wants to make such patrols routine again. Publicizing the *Fort Worth*'s patrol is also unusual. It's designed to demonstrate to friends and allies that the U.S. Navy won't be forced out of international waters anywhere in the South China Sea.

Always only able to play the hand that the Obama administration has dealt him, Harris has an idea of how to put pressure on the Chinese. He wants to "name and shame" them.

Naming and shaming is a big part of Chinese culture. On billboards, websites, TV, and even over loudspeakers, the government will identify by name people who are guilty of bad behavior: gross polluters, people who don't pay their debts, offspring who fail to care for their elderly parents, Chinese tourists who behave in an "uncivilized" manner abroad, even Chinese mountain climbers who scratch their names on Mount Everest (Chinese law deems the latter behavior vandalism). For those named it's a terrible loss of face—a concept that is much more powerful in China than it is in the West. It's not at all unusual in China for people who have been publicly shamed to commit suicide or to simply disappear.

Of course, Harris doesn't expect members of the Politburo or the Central Military Commission to actually feel any shame about the artificial island outposts; by their lights they aren't doing anything wrong. But he knows the Chinese military and civilian leaders just might be embarrassed if their activities were put under a brighter public spotlight. True, satellite images of the reef reclamation projects are already publicly available, and numerous articles have been written about them, not only about the military aspects of the island building but also about the extensive environmental damage it's causing. But Harris knows it will garner much more attention if people can actually *watch* what the Chinese are doing, on film, in close to real time.

So his public affairs office reaches out to CNN, which of course jumps at the chance to take a ride out to the Spratly Islands. In May 2015 the P-8A takes off from the old Clark Air Base in the Philippines, and as the Poseidon flies near Mischief and Fiery Cross and Subi Reefs, the CNN crew catches it all: the Chinese warnings over the radio—"GO AWAY!"—the images of lagoons filled with Chinese navy ships, the dredgers dumping sand onto what were once submerged reefs, the obvious expansion of military facilities. For good measure, Harris also releases official navy video of Poseidon reconnaissance flights over the reclaimed islands in recent months.

And it works. The South China Sea island reclamation/militarization is suddenly a major story, not only on CNN but on networks throughout the U.S. and around the world. And although the Chinese did not officially protest dozens of earlier Poseidon reconnaissance flights near the artificial islands in recent months, this one with the CNN crew clearly gets under their skin.

"The recent surveillance activity by a U.S. plane posed potential threats to China's islands and reefs, making it highly possible to lead to misjudgment which could cause maritime or air accidents," a Chinese Foreign Ministry spokesman says. "The move is very irresponsible and dangerous, putting regional peace and stability in jeopardy. . . . We urge the U.S. side to vigorously abide by international laws and relevant international rules, and abandon any risky and provocative actions."

Abide by international laws and relevant international rules? Coming from the guys who are breaking almost every international rule on the books, that's pretty rich.

Public awareness of the Chinese island-building scheme seems to have even infused key Obama administration figures with a more aggressive spirit. A few days after the CNN Poseidon flight, at a ceremony at Pearl Harbor to officially hand over Pacific Command to Harris, Defense Secretary Ash Carter says this: "There should be no mistake: the United States will fly, sail, and operate wherever international law allows, as we do all around the world. . . . China's actions are bringing countries in the region together in new ways. And they're increasing the demand for American engagement in the Asia-Pacific. We're going to meet it. We will remain the principal security power in the Asia-Pacific for decades to come."

Despite his suggestion that Admiral Harris tone down his public remarks about Chinese aggressiveness, even CNO Admiral Jon Greenert is privately alarmed at what's going on in the South China Sea. Later, after his retirement, Greenert says that "I regret I didn't take a tougher stand against China. We could have done more."

So far as the Chinese are concerned, the Obama administration always has a way of reverting to cautiousness, though. An official state visit to Washington by Chinese president Xi Jinping is coming up in September, and the administration doesn't want to do anything that the Chinese will consider provocative—which is to say, the administration doesn't want to do anything at all.

So it takes months for Harris to finally get approval for a freedom of navigation operation near the militarized artificial islands—except it's not actually a FONOP.

In October 2015 the guided-missile destroyer USS Lassen sails near the Spratlys, closely followed by a Chinese navy destroyer. The Lassen comes within six miles of one of the artificial islands, Subi Reef, well within the twelve-mile radius China claims as "territorial waters." But at the insistence of the State Department legal staff, the Lassen is sailing under at least some aspects of an "innocent passage" through another nation's territorial waters—that is, while the ship is close to Subi Reef it has its weapons control radar turned off, it conducts no drills, it doesn't put a helicopter into the air, it doesn't do anything of a military nature. In other words, the *Lassen* is almost acting as if the U.S. does in fact recognize China's twelve-mile territorial claim. The only difference is that the *Lassen* didn't request permission from the Chinese to sail near the island—a fine point of international law that allows the U.S. to insist it is not recognizing a territorial claim by China.

As the *Lassen* crosses the twelve-mile line, the Chinese Destroyer radios again and again, "You are in Chinese waters, what is your intention?" But it takes no aggressive actions. In fact, according to the *Lassen*'s CO, after the *Lassen* departed the Subi Reef area, the Chinese destroyer peeled off with a cheery message to the American ship: "Hey, we're not going to be with you anymore. Wish you a pleasant voyage. Hope to see you again." The CO doesn't think they were being sarcastic.

It's confusing. Navy officials insist that it wasn't an "innocent passage," but they won't explicitly call it a freedom of navigation operation either—although they don't discourage reporters from calling it that. It's as if the U.S. wants to reassure its friends and allies that it isn't backing off—but it doesn't want to seriously tick off the Chinese, either. It's an ambiguity that is not necessarily reassuring to allies.

Whatever the navy's goal, the publicized USS *Lassen* sail-by of Subi Reef certainly gets attention from the Chinese—specifically Admiral Wu Shengli, who is summoned to an annual meeting of Communist Party officials to account for what occurred. Shortly after the *Lassen* mission Wu participates in a video teleconference with the new CNO, Admiral John Richardson, another submariner who, unlike Greenert, publicly appears to take a sharper view of Chinese intentions. And if a statement released to the Chinese state media is accurate, Admiral Wu is furious over the USS *Lassen* excursion.

"If the United States continues with these kinds of dangerous, provocative acts, there could well be a seriously pressing situation between frontline forces from both sides on the sea and in the air, or even a minor incident that sparks war," Wu is paraphrased as saying.

Wait a minute. War? *War?* It's been common for high-level commanders on both sides to talk about potential "accidents" or "confrontations" between China and the U.S. And hawkish commentators on both sides have tossed the "W-word" around for years. But for the top commander of either country's navy to talk about actual war is a first.

Yes, there is some question about the translation. It's true also that the statement was supposedly "paraphrasing" Wu's remarks. But there's no doubt in anybody's mind that Wu's comment represents an elevated level of threat.

Out at PACOM headquarters, Harris thinks the proper response to any Chinese attempt at intimidation is to send another navy ship on a FONOP—a real FONOP—back to the Spratlys, the sooner the better; anything else will be perceived as weakness. But it's not until six months later that the Obama administration allows another guided-missile destroyer, the USS *William P. Lawrence*, back to the Spratlys to pierce the claimed twelve-mile limit around Fiery Cross Reef, which is now an artificial island. The *Lawrence* is shadowed by three Chinese ships, and two Hainan Island–based Chinese fighters scramble to overfly the American ship.

But it's strange. Although the Pentagon officially calls the *Lawrence*'s actions a "routine freedom of navigation" exercise, it also says the American warship generally performed these actions under the rules of "innocent passage"—which, as noted above, isn't exactly the same thing.

Leashed as he is, Harris still manages some successes in his efforts to show a stronger hand. In mid-2016 he brings out the USS *John C. Stennis* carrier strike group to spend two months patrolling in the South China Sea. To publicize the carrier group's presence Defense Secretary Ash Carter brings a contingent of reporters out to the carrier while it's under way and has his picture taken above the deck while aboard a Bell Boeing V-22 Osprey multi-mission, tilt-rotor aircraft. When a reporter asks Carter if the carrier group's presence is increasing tension in the South China Sea region, Carter has a quick—and strong—response.

"That's not only incorrect, it's backwards," he says. "We have been here for decade upon decade. The only reason that question even comes up is because of what has gone on over the last year, and that's a question of Chinese behavior. So, what's new is not an American carrier in this region. What's new is the context of tension which exists, which we want to reduce."

The *Stennis*'s operations in the South China Sea are a thumb in China's eye, and it seems to indicate that on the military side the pendulum is at least starting to swing back to a more aggressive U.S. posture. But in general the administration is still taking a soft line on China. Despite growing evidence that displays of force—not displays of smiles—are the most effective way to shape Chinese behavior, the Obama administration still wants to invite the Chinese military to the party. To the public dismay of some congressional leaders, not to mention the private dismay of some navy officers, the U.S. allows the Chinese navy to participate in the mid-summer RimPac 2016 exercise in Hawaii and San Diego.

So while American sailors and aviators are conducting potentially dangerous pseudo–freedom of navigation operations and reconnaissance flights, and the Chinese military is all but threatening war if those operations don't stop, the Obama administration is pursuing a concurrent U.S. effort to achieve *closer* military ties with China. It seems odd—but then, that's the way warm wars are, or at least the way the Obama team has chosen to wage this one.

But the biggest news during the RimPac exercise doesn't come from Hawaii or San Diego; instead it comes from half a world away in The Hague. In 2013 the Philippines filed a case against China with the international Permanent Court of Arbitration, arguing that the Chinese were illegally trying to occupy Scarborough Shoal even though it was well within the Philippines' exclusive economic zone. In July 2016 the tribunal unanimously rules that China's artificial islands aren't really islands, and thus not entitled to an EEZ or even territorial waters status. The court also rules that China's "historic" claim to Scarborough and other islands and reefs throughout the South China Sea is null and void; in effect, the tribunal says the Nine-Dash Line is a No-Dash Line, and not a legal line at all.

Unfortunately, the tribunal has no mechanism to enforce its ruling. And China, predictably, says the ruling matters not at all, that it will never abandon its claims to ownership of the islands.

"We will never stop our construction on the [Spratly] islands," Admiral Wu Shengli tells his counterpart, CNO Admiral John Richardson, after the tribunal's ruling. "The islands are China's inherent territory, and our necessary construction on the islands is reasonable, justified, and lawful. Any attempt to force China to give in through flexing military muscles will only have the opposite effect."

It's not exactly a conciliatory response. In fact, speaking before a packed hall at the Center for Strategic and International Studies (CSIS) think tank in Washington, Cui Tiankai, China's ambassador to the U.S., says the Chinese will not accede to a "scrap of paper." It's probably unintentional, but the comment is eerily similar to the infamous statement by the German foreign minister at the start of World War I that the treaty protecting Belgium from

German invasion was a "mere scrap of paper"—a comment that to much of the world, including then neutral America, encapsulated Germany's arrogance and contempt for treaties.

We all know how that turned out. It was the beginning of a world catastrophe. America, the world, and China itself can only hope that China's seemingly similar contempt for treaties and international rules doesn't presage another catastrophe in the South and East China Seas.

Ambassador Cui does little to nurture such hope, though, saying there were no real problems between China and the Philippines, or other Asian neighbors, before the U.S. decided to reinsert itself in the Western Pacific. "The tension started to rise five years ago, about the same time as the so-called [American] pivot into Asia," he tells the CSIS crowd. Not only does Beijing refuse to bow to a paper scrap, he says, but it won't be cowed by aircraft carriers, either.

It follows, then, that Beijing isn't about to be forced into retreat by American destroyer patrols or joint naval exercises with Japan, South Korea, and other U.S. partners—for now, the principal naval actions the Obama administration is willing to take. That summer and fall, the guided-missile destroyer USS *John S. McCain* conducts missions in the South China Sea. Packing more offensive power, the American amphibious assault ship USS *Bonhomme Richard* shoots down a target drone with a NATO Sea Sparrow surface-to-air missile off the coast of Guam before going on a South China Sea patrol with two destroyers. U.S. Marines and Japan Self-Defense Forces (JSDF) conduct ship-and-helicopter amphibious operations off Guam and Tinian, and the duo's naval forces train together in the Philippine Sea. U.S. and South Korean destroyers, submarines, and aircraft conduct joint operations in waters east of the Korean Peninsula. The U.S. Navy and the Vietnam People's Navy also have their annual Naval Engagement Activity near Da Nang.

Not everyone is impressed by America's show of strength and cooperation in the Western Pacific. New Philippine president, Rodrigo Duterte, visits Beijing in October and publicly announces his country's "separation" from the U.S. It is, he says, "time to say goodbye, my friend."

And so the warm war in the Western Pacific simmers into the fall of 2016. While there have been some American successes, over the long run the U.S. has been losing ground—or rather, losing sea.

Yes, the U.S. still remains the most powerful military force in the region. Yes, it can still send carrier strike groups into the South and East China Seas—and when it does that, when the U.S. shows strength and resolve, it reassures allies and partners and undoubtedly helps deter China from attempting large-scale aggressions. And yes, the U.S. still sends its ships and aircraft into disputed areas of sea and sky to keep the peace and enforce international law. But each day those seas and skies become more and more dangerous.

As we've seen, for years the U. S. has been trying to get China to play by the rules, to be part of the game. Through soft words and high-level military and civilian contacts it has tried to foster a sense of trust and cooperation between the two nations' governments and militaries. As part of that policy, for the most part the U.S. government has either virtually ignored or only mildly protested the People's Republic's aggressive acts—the dangerous hassling of U.S. ships and aircraft in international sea- and airspace, the *Cowpens* incident, the unilateral air defense identification zone in the East China Sea, the RimPac spy ship episode, and on and on. Despite efforts by Admiral Harris and others, even the Great Wall of Sand in the South China Sea prompted what so far has been only a limited response from the U.S. government—a response that did not change the facts on the ground at all. China still has its artificial militarized islands. With each weak response from the

U.S., China has grown more militarily aggressive, not less. And with what appears to be the almost certain election of Hillary Clinton to the presidency—or at least that's what the pollsters and pundits all say—it seems that the passive policies of the Obama administration will continue.

And then, on Tuesday, November 8, 2016, the American electorate orders a dramatic change in course.

CHAPTER 10

Course Change

E ver since the end of the Cold War the U.S. Navy had kept two sets of budgetary books.

One set of books covered what the navy wanted in order to accomplish its various missions around the world in any given year: how many ships, how many aircraft, how many sailors, how much money for new ship construction, how much for research and development—everything the navy wanted not only to meet current demands but to be prepared for new and unexpected ones. It was the navy's wish list, its fantasy budget, the sort of budget that admirals could only dream about—and as such, no one outside the navy brass ever saw it. If they had, if the civilian chain of command in the Defense Department and the halls of Congress had ever seen how much money the admirals wanted, they'd have laughed out loud.

So the navy always had a second set of budget books, the real budgets, the ones the brass thought had at least a slim prayer of getting through the White House and congressional appropriations process without being completely eviscerated. They were budgets that had to prioritize Mission A over equally important Mission B, budgets that robbed Project C to save Project D, budgets that stole from Future Weapons System E in order to maintain Current Weapons System F—and on and on. People think the

U.S. military always asks for twice what it really needs and then is satisfied when it only gets half. And in the old days that might have been true. But no longer.

The truth is that in the lean years since the end of the Cold War, as the navy has shrunk from almost six hundred ships to fewer than three hundred, it has had to fight for every ship and every dollar—and the navy has consistently lost. Even the wars in Afghanistan and Iraq didn't result in a larger U.S. fleet. Especially during the Obama administration, the navy struggled to get the most bare-boned budgets past the Defense Department and the White House—and even then the admirals would still take a beating in congressional committee hearings, from both sides of the aisle. Why does an aircraft carrier cost $13 billion? Is this new class of nuclear submarines absolutely necessary? Why is this next-generation navy fighter over budget and behind schedule? And what do we really need a navy for anyway?

Over the years the admirals had gotten used to it. And up until Election Day 2016, they figured it would go on that way.

But then, a few weeks after Donald Trump was elected president of the United States, the admirals putting together the navy budget started getting these calls from the Trump transition team. And they weren't like any calls the admirals had ever heard.

Tell us what you really need, the Trump transition guys told them. *No, wait, better yet, tell us what you really* want. *You want more ships? More aircraft? How about more money for railguns? For high-energy lasers? For unmanned aerial vehicle R&D? Just tell us. Don't worry about what you think we can afford. Don't worry about what the budget-cutters in Congress will say. Don't give us what you think you can actually get. Give us your wish list—your first set of books.*

The navy brass could hardly believe it. Were these guys *serious*? For years top navy officers had been hoping to somehow get back up to a three-hundred-ship navy. Now Trump and his team were publicly calling for a *three-hundred-and-fifty-ship* navy, not only to give the U.S. a larger naval footprint around the globe but also to stimulate the flagging U.S. shipbuilding industry. The navy hadn't heard anything like that since the Reagan administration four decades ago.

Of course, not everyone believed that the Trump administration could actually deliver the navy's complete wish list. But at the very least, White House backing for a navy expansion would give the navy brass a chance to make their case to Congress and in the court of public opinion—something they didn't really have a chance to do during the Obama administration. And even if the navy didn't get everything it needed, clearly the U.S. Navy of 2017 and beyond was not going to be the diminishing navy of 2016. Senior navy officers may not have agreed with all of Trump's policies and pronouncements; many may not even have voted for him. But it's fair to say that not a single senior navy officer disagreed with a plan to build up the U.S. Navy—no matter whose plan it was.

(As if to underscore the Trump administration's commitment to an expanded navy, Trump nominated as navy secretary Philip Bilden, a wealthy private equity manager with extensive experience in Asia. The son of a career navy officer, and himself a former army intelligence officer, Bilden wrote his college thesis on the influential nineteenth-century naval theorist Alfred Thayer Mahan, who argued that a strong navy is essential to the survival of any great power. Bilden would eventually choose to withdraw himself from consideration for the position—stymied, as Trump's first army secretary selection, Vincent Viola, had been by the task of separating himself from his business interests—but the new team in Washington was clearly sending a message.)*

---

* In June 2017, Trump tried again, nominating investment banker and retired marine aviator Richard V. Spencer for the navy job; he was sworn in on August 3, 2017.

And it wasn't just the Trump administration's views on military spending that had many senior navy officers feeling that a sea change was under way. There was also Trump's hardline vision of America's relationship with China.

Again, for eight years the Obama administration's policy had been to do nothing to rattle U.S.-China relations. In Obama's view, if the U.S. went easy on China for its seemingly small aggressions in the South China Sea and elsewhere, then maybe China would cooperate with (or at least not oppose) the U.S. on other issues—regional trade agreements such as the Trans-Pacific Partnership (TPP), global warming initiatives, cyber security, and so on.

To Trump and his team, that soft approach smacked of pre–World War II Munich-style appeasement. They believed that it only encouraged the Chinese government to commit further aggressions—and as we've seen, more than a few senior navy officers privately agreed with them. Besides, Trump didn't need Chinese cooperation on regional trade issues—three days after his inauguration Trump withdrew the U.S. from the TPP—and he'd made it clear during the campaign that battling global warming wouldn't be a high-priority issue in the Trump administration. As for trade with China, as an international businessman Trump seemed to understand that a trade war with the People's Republic would hurt the U.S. as much as it hurt China.

The point is that after his election and inauguration as president, Trump made it clear that the Obama administration policy of walking on eggshells in relation to China was officially out the window. In fact, he seemed to positively relish tweaking the Chinese leadership.

Did the president of Taiwan want to give the president-elect a congratulatory call? That was fine with Trump—and if the People's Republic didn't like it, tough. Trump not only took the call, he also publicly mused that the One China policy, which has guided

U.S.–People's Republic relations for more than four decades, might not necessarily be set in stone. (He would later walk that back a bit.) Were Chinese navy ships still harassing U.S. surveillance ships in international waters, such as occurred in December 2016 when a Chinese vessel seized an unmanned underwater vehicle being operated by the USNS *Bowditch* off the Philippines? The Obama administration had basically shrugged it off, but the Trump team let it be known that any post-inauguration stunts like that would have serious consequences—and they strongly suggested that unlike in previous harassment incidents, those consequences wouldn't be limited to soaking down a few Chinese mariners with a ship's fire hose. Were the Chinese continuing to militarize the man-made islands in the South China Sea? Trump's new secretary of state, Rex Tillerson, told Congress that the U.S. might not "allow" China to "access" those disputed islands—although how the U.S. would accomplish that access denial wasn't specified.

The Chinese reaction to all this was predictable. State-controlled media denounced the Trump administration's "rabble rousing" and accused Trump of being "as ignorant as a child." Officially, the Foreign Ministry reminded Washington that the One China policy regarding Taiwan was a "core interest" of the People's Republic—the diplomatic phrase for an issue a nation is willing to go to war over. The Chinese also sent their aircraft carrier *Liaoning* on a passage through the Taiwan Strait—sort of a Chinese FONOP. It was all tough talk, but it was also clear that after eight years of more or less benign treatment from Washington, the Chinese leadership was stunned by the sudden turnabout.

Is Trump's aggressive posture on China all bluff? Is it just bombast and bluster? Except for Trump and some key advisors, no one really knows—including the Chinese leadership. Which may be exactly what the Trump administration intends. And, indeed, as Trump takes an increasingly tougher stance with North Korea over that country's nuclear weapons posture, the new American president eases off the anti-Chinese rhetoric as he enlists Beijing's help in dealing with Pyongyang, borrowing a page from the old Republican playbook and hoping China will keep its Asian neighbors in line in return for better relations with the U.S. It's a policy that has proven to be ineffective through the decades and there's more than a little concern about what will happen—not if, but when—the relationship sours between Trump and Chinese leader Xi Jinping.

There's also a concern about what Trump is doing with what he calls "his military," flexing his own personal bombing might in Syria and Afghanistan as further evidence of the new Washington resolve.

National leaders have often found it useful to apply what's known as the "madman theory" to international relations. The idea is that if your opponents believe you're actually crazy—say, crazy enough to unleash war, even nuclear war—they'll be afraid to push you too far. President Richard Nixon famously used that approach with the Soviets and the North Vietnamese, gleefully encouraging aides like Henry Kissinger to privately suggest to their foreign counterparts that the U.S. president was mentally unstable and capable of anything. Already, there's speculation that perhaps Trump is playing the same game.

If so, it could be effective. The Chinese leadership has never doubted America's military strength; it has only doubted America's strength of will—and as we've seen, again and again those doubts were proven right. But standing up to the Chinese obviously can also be a delicate and potentially dangerous game. After all, the Chinese leadership has its own constituencies to consider. With a slowing economy and a socially restive and increasingly nationalistic population, the leadership can't be seen as kowtowing to America—and that should never be America's goal.

The issues dividing China and the U.S. are serious, and persistent. China's threats to free passage on the seas and in the skies, its lack of respect for international law, its excessive and illegal territorial claims, and its bullying of smaller, weaker neighbors—those problems pose a clear and present danger to peace and stability in the Western Pacific. And they seem no closer to resolution in 2017 than they were in 2013, when the USS *Cowpens* had its fateful encounter with the *Liaoning*.

But there's a difference. In 2013 America rushed the unprepared USS *Cowpens* and its crew into the South China Sea without really knowing what it wanted that ship and crew to do. America ordered the *Cowpens* to confront the new Chinese navy on the high seas—but to not get into a confrontation. America ordered the *Cowpens* to show that the U.S. Navy could go anywhere it wanted in international waters—except, as it turned out, where the Chinese navy decided it could not go. America told the ship and its crew to demonstrate to allies and partners that the United States was there to help protect and defend them—and then in effect it allowed the ship to be chased out of the South China Sea. And the result of that and other confrontations was a loss of U.S. prestige in the Western Pacific and the further emboldening of the Chinese leadership.

U.S. admirals now harbor no doubts about Chinese designs in the Western Pacific, which run counter to American desires, no matter who is president. Unless the U.S. Navy decides to pull all of its ships, aircraft, and people clear back to Guam, which is beyond anyone's imagining, continued confrontation with expanding Chinese naval forces is inevitable. Trump, who even his supporters concede is mercurial, may awake one morning to decide China shouldn't be provoked, a hopeful concession aimed at getting the region's superpower to play ball on North Korea or some other erupting issue, but by nightfall he may be backing a completely different policy. Such pendulum swings won't change what has become the on-the-water reality. Going forward, no matter who sits at the top of the power pyramid on either side, the fate of American-Chinese military relationships will rest in the hands and minds of those commanding ships and piloting planes in seas very far away from Washington and Beijing.

America of 2017 is not the America of 2013. And the next time the Chinese navy dangerously confronts a U.S. Navy warship on the high seas, it seems unlikely that it will be the American commander who orders the engine room to execute an "all back emergency full."

For America, and for the U.S. Navy, the era of crashbacks seems to be over.

Acknowledgments

This book wouldn't exist without the encouragement and support of so many people. I could easily fill many pages with their names, but I'll keep this brief.

First and foremost, I owe a special note of thanks to my agent, Jim Hornfischer, who recognized this project's possibilities, stood by me when all looked lost, and served as my guide and inspiration throughout. And also, my thanks to Terry McKnight for putting me in Jim's capable hands. Thanks, too, to Scribner's Rick Horgan, who also saw the book's potential and kept the faith—even through some of the roughest of seas.

I'd like to thank two teachers who gave me the encouragement early on when I needed it most: George Deal and Bob Cole.

Thanks, too, to Jefferson Morris for his support, understanding, and guidance. He kept me on track throughout my research and writing, and was a friend, counselor, and when necessary, a demanding editor. Also contributing his outstanding skills was Gordon Dillow, who took my off-course first draft and put it on the correct heading. His talent is evident on every page.

Also critical in this book's development was the assistance of many who are connected to the U.S. Navy, both those in and out of uniform. Some have asked they not be named, and I offer my sincere gratitude to those nameless sources and guides, including a special individual known to my editors and me as "Captain Dunsell."

There are others whom I must name and to whom I offer my appreciation: Michael Manazir, John Kirby, Ray Mabus, Thomas Rowden, Tamsen Reese, Richard Hunt, Jonathan Greenert, Christopher Servello, Clayton Doss, Danny Hernandez, Harry Harris, Darryn James, Patrick McNally, Hayley Sims, Caroline Hutcheson, Loren Thompson, Greg Gombert, Bryan Clark, Robert Haddick, Jim Sheridan, Mike Kaszubowski, Tony Velocci, Jim Mathews, Jim Asker, Carolyn Beaudry, Keith Little, David Kindley, Jason Scott, Craig Hooper, Bonnie Glaser, Susan Hess, Tim Wilke, Jeffrey Czerewko, Robert Myers, George Rowell, Ben Freeman, Nick Schwellenbach, David Wise, Kara Yingling, Bob Nugent, Richard Aboulafia, Alex Gray, Randy Forbes, Chris Rahmen, Bradley Perrett, Greg Poling, Brett Crozier, William Choong, William Salvin, Laurent Liu, Gary and Teresa Stewart, Ed Chen, Rick Dunham, Charles Spears, Rod Felderman, Sabrina Greaves, DeMarcus Lawrence, Javonta Smith, Russel Kates, Travis McClellan, Richard Prest, Brad Peniston, Norman Polmar, Michael Bruno, James Kirk, Matthew Stroup, Lishan Chang, and Cindy Tierney and the rest of the team at Preferred Travel.

I need to especially thank my cousin Jeanette—and T, too—for allowing me to set up my "West Coast" office in their home, and for making my stays there truly pleasurable. Thanks as well to my old mates in Australia, Tony Locke and Leah Raabe, who put up with me during my university days there—and then welcomed me back as part of their families while I researched and wrote my way through the Pacific.

I'd like to thank the people of China and Taiwan for their hospitality and warmth.

Finally, I want to mention two close friends who passed away before the book came to print: John Gresham and David Donald. They were always encouraging, and I'll miss them both.

Notes

TIMELINE

xiii *"One China"*: *On China*, Henry Kissinger (Penguin Press, 2011); private interviews.

xiii *Mischief Reef*: *The South China Sea: The Struggle for Power in Asia*, Bill Hayton (Yale University Press, 2014); *Asia–Pacific Rebalance 2025 Presence and Partnerships*, Center for Strategic and International Studies (CSIS) 2016.

xiii *closing the Taiwan Strait*: *On China*, Kissinger.

xiii *U.S. military spending*: World Bank, http://data.worldbank.org/.

xiii *Chinese GDP*: World Bank.

xv *A Chinese fighter pilot tries to intimidate*: *Born to Fly: The Untold Story of the Downed American Reconnaissance Plane*, Shane Osborn, Malcolm McConnell (Broadway Books, 2002); *China–U.S. Aircraft Collision Incident of April 2001: Assessments and Policy Implications*, Congressional Research Service (CRS), 2001.

xv *antisatellite missile*: *Defense Department Annual Report to Congress, Military and Security Developments, People's Republic of China*, Department of Defense, 2015.

xv *economic, diplomatic, and military "pivot"*: *Asia–Pacific Rebalance 2025 Presence and Partnerships*, CSIS.

xv *Scarborough Shoal*: *South China Sea*, Hayton.

xv *"Great Wall of Sand"*: Admiral Harry Harris speech, Australian Strategic Policy Institute in Canberra, 2015.

xv USS *John C. Stennis* carrier strike group: U.S. Navy release, www.navy.mil.

xv *Trump administration*: private interviews; *Countering China's Adventurism in the South China Sea: Strategy Options for the Trump Administration*, Center for Strategic and Budgetary Assessment (CSBA), 2016; "Taiwan Scrambles Jets, Navy as China Aircraft Carrier Enters Taiwan Strait," J. R. Wu, Faith Hung, Michael Martina, Reuters, January, 2017.

PROLOGUE

1 *warm war*: private interviews.
1 *It's a war*: *Asia's Cauldron: The South China Sea and the End of a Stable Pacific*, Robert D. Kaplan (Random House, 2014); *Fire on the Water: China, America, and the Future of the Pacific*, Robert H. Haddick (Naval Institute Press, 2014); *The China Dream: Great Power Thinking and Strategic Posture in the Post-American Era*, Liu Mingfu (CN Times Books, 2015); *The Hundred-Year Marathon: China's Secret Strategy to Replace America as the Global Superpower*, Michael Pillsbury (Henry Holt, 2015); *Mayday: The Decline of American Naval Supremacy*, Seth Cropsey (Duckworth Overlook, 2013).
2 *burgeoning Chinese navy*: *The PLA Navy: New Capabilities and Missions for the 21st Century*, Office of Naval Intelligence.
2 *China's four-decade transformation*: *On China*, Kissinger.
3 *observation of international rules*: *Countering China's Adventurism in the South China Sea*, CSBA.
3 *withdrawing its military*: *Fire on the Water*, Haddick.
3 *China's current leadership doesn't respond to Western concepts*: *Countering China's Adventurism in the South China Sea*, CSBA.

CHAPTER I—THE MISSION

7 *calm, almost serene day*: private interviews; Ship's Deck Log of the USS Cowpens (hull number) 63, Division NN01, Attached to COMCARSTRKGRU THREE Group, Seventh Fleet, Commencing 000(-8H) December 1st 2013 at SULU SEA, Ending 2315 (-8H) December 31st 2013 at SUBIC BAY, PHILIPPINES
7 *Cowpens is a guided-missile cruiser*: *The Naval Institute Guide to the Ships and Aircraft of the U.S. Fleet*, Nineteenth Edition, Norman Polmar (Naval Institute Press, 2013).

8 *violent missions*: U.S. Navy Fact File, www.navy.mil/navydata/fact.

9 *Captain Greg Gombert*: private interview; U.S. Navy Biographies.

9 Condition Zebra: private interviews; USS *Cowpens* daily ship log; U.S. Navy Material Conditions of Readiness.

10 *fifty-five thousand active duty officers*: U.S. Navy Fact File.

10 *sub's job*: private interviews; *Submarine: A Guided Tour Inside a Nuclear Warship*, Tom Clancy with John Gresham (Berkley Books, 1993).

10 *carriers never operate alone*: private interviews; *Carrier: A Guided Tour of an Aircraft Carrier*, Tom Clancy with John Gresham (Berkley Books, 1999); *Restoring American Seapower: A New Fleet Architecture for the United States Navy*, Center for Strategic and Budgetary Assessment (CSBA), 2017.

11 *December 5, 2013*: private interviews; USS *Cowpens* daily ship log.

12 *There's the crew*: private interviews; "USS *Antietam* and USS *Cowpens* to Complete Hull Swap," release, Commander, Seventh Fleet.

12 *ship's executive officer*: private interviews; "Command Investigation into Ship's Readiness and Leadership ICO USS *Cowpens* (CG-63)," Commander, U.S. Naval Surface Force.

13 *the ship itself*: private interviews; USS *Cowpens* daily ship log; command operations reports and related documents in Naval Historical Center.

13 *The navy decided*: private interviews; Navy News Desk.

13 *internal mechanical systems*: private interviews.

13 *The* Cowpens's *new crew*: "USS *Antietam* and USS *Cowpens* to Complete Hull Swap."

14 *the ship is actually cursed*: "Navy to Let Ousted Captain of Yokosuka-Based Ship to Get 'Honorable' Retirement," Erik Slavin, *Stars and Stripes*, January 2012; Navy News Desk.

15 *sally from its port on Hainan Island*: private interviews; "Chinese Aircraft Carrier *Liaoning* Takes Up Role in South China Sea," Minnie Chan, *South China Morning Post*, November 2013.

15 *scaring the hell out of America's Pacific friends*: *Asia-Pacific Rebalance 2025 Presence and Partnerships*, CSIS.

16 *its new carrier program*: *The PLA Navy: New Capabilities and Missions for the 21st Century*, Office of Naval Intelligence.

16 *Senior Captain Zhang Zheng*: private interviews; *China Defense Blog*, http://china-defense.blogspot.com/2012/09/meet-sr-col-zhang-zheng-captain-for.html, September 2012.

17 *forty-five-kilometer "safety zone"*: private interviews; "US 'Plays Innocent' After Near Collision at Sea," Qiu Yongzheng and Yang He, *Global Times*, December 2013.

18 *behind the scenes*: private interviews.

CHAPTER 2—AMERICA'S OCEAN

21 *Antonio Pigafetta*: "Magellan's Voyage," *American Heritage*, October 1969, http://www.americanheritage.com/content/magellan%E2%80%99s-voyage.

22 *twenty-five thousand islands*: Geographic Guide Oceania, www.geographic guide.com/oceania-maps.htm.

22 *In an average year*: Hong Kong Observatory, *Annual Tropical Cyclone Report*, U.S. Joint Typhoon Warning Center (JTWC); the (US) National Hurricane Center; Navy News Desk.

23 *In 1944*: Naval History and Heritage Command.

23 *Typhoon Orchid*: Merseyside Maritime Museum; Hong Kong Observatory.

23 *Typhoon Utor*: Shipwrecklog.com.

23 *research ship* Melville: "A Rare Peek Inside Floating Lab," Greg Moran, *San Diego Tribune*, February 2015.

23 *USS* San Francisco: U.S. Navy investigation, Navy News Desk.

24 *"Ghost Ship"*: "U.S. Coast Guard Sinks Japanese Boat Washed Away by Tsunami," Chelsea J. Carter, CNN, April 2012, edition.cnn.com/2012/04/06 /us/japan-tsunami-ship/?hpt=us_c1; "Japanese 'Ghost Ship' Sunk off Alaska," Associated Press, April 2012, http://www.cbc.ca/news/canada /british-columbia/japanese-ghost-ship-sunk-off-alaska-1.1207936.

24 *Nearly three dozen nations*: South China Sea, Hayton; United Nations Economic and Social Commission, http://www.unescap.org/stat/data; *Inter Press Service*, http://www.ipsnews.net/news/economy-trade/trade-investment/.

24 *Malacca Strait*: "Malacca Strait Transits Grow 2% to Record in 2015, Boxships See Dip in H2," *Seatrade Maritime News*, January 2016; Marine Vessel Traffic Malacca Strait Ship Traffic Tracker, http://www.marineves seltraffic.com/2013/07/marine-traffic-malacca-strait-dual.html.

24 *modern frigate*: AMI International email to author; private interviews.

25 *Start with Russia*: The Naval Institute Guide to Combat Fleets of the World: *Their Ships, Aircraft, and Systems*, 16th Edition, Eric Wertheim (Naval Institute Press, 2013).

25 *head south along the coast*: private interviews; AMI; *Asia's Cauldron*,

Kaplan; *South China Sea*, Hayton; *Asia-Pacific Rebalance 2025 Presence and Partnerships*, CSIS.

32 *USS* Freedom: embarkation on *Freedom*; private interviews.

32 *2,471 Americans killed*: speech, December 2005, Texas congressman Ted Poe.

33 *Pacific Squadron*: U.S. Pacific Fleet Command History.

33 *USS* Potomac: *America's Naval Heritage: A Catalog of Early Imprints from the Navy Department Library,* Naval Historical Center (Government Printing Office).

33 *was another massacre*: The Dawlish Chronicles, www.dawlishchronicles.com.

34 *Commodore Matthew Perry*: *Brief Summary of the Perry Expedition to Japan, 1853*, Naval History and Heritage Command.

34 *Commodore George Dewey*: "Dewey at Manila Bay: Lessons in Operational Art and Operational Leadership from America's First Fleet Admiral," Commander Derek B. Granger, U.S. Navy, *Naval War College Review* 64, no.4 (Autumn 2011).

34 *Yangtze River Patrol*: *Yangtze River Patrol and Other US Navy Asiatic Fleet Activities in China, 1920–1942, as Described in the Annual Reports of the Navy Department*, Naval History and Heritage Command; *The Sand Pebbles*, Richard McKenna (Harper & Row, 1962); *The Sand Pebbles* (movie), Twentieth Century Fox, 1966.

35 *September 1945 Japan's navy*: Naval History and Heritage Command; History.com.

35 *The British Royal Navy*: World War II Database, http://ww2db.com; *Pacific Crucible: War at Sea in the Pacific, 1941–1942*, Ian W. Toll (W. W. Norton, 2012).

36 *navy could still muster*: www.navy.mil.

36 *The Cold War*: private interviews; *A Century of Spies: Intelligence in the Twentieth Century*, Jeffrey T. Richelson (Oxford University Press, 1995).

37 *USS* Gudgeon . . . *USS* Tautog: "A Cold War Fought in the Deep," Christopher Drew, Michael L. Millenson, and Robert Becker, *Chicago Tribune, Newport News Daily Press*, January 1991; *Blind Man's Bluff: The Untold Story of American Submarine Espionage*, Sherry Sontag, Christopher Drew, and Annette Lawrence Drew (Public Affairs, 1998).

37 *USS* Scorpion: Submarine Force Museum; private interviews.

37 *U.S. Navy officers and sailors look back*: private interviews.

39 *In 1990*: navy.mil; private interviews.

39 *base budget*: U.S. Navy, Defense Department budgets.

39 *Camp H.M. Smith*: personal visit; *Almanac of American Military History*, Spencer C. Tucker (ABC-CLIO, 2012).

40 *regional combatant commands*: U.S. Defense Department, defense.gov.

40 *biggest combatant command*: Pacific Command, www.pacom.mil/.

41 *For every ship*: private interviews; *Restoring American Seapower*, CSBA.

42 *USS* Ronald Reagan: personal embarkation; private interviews; *Carrier*, Clancy and Gresham; Navy Fact File.

43 *biggest civilian container ships*: personal experience.

44 *"carrier strike group"*: private interviews; personal embarkations.

44 *navy spends*: navy budget documents.

45 *Every sailor*: private interviews.

47 *EA-6B Prowler*: Navy Investigation (report); "Congressman Says Most Killed in *Nimitz* Crash Showed Traces of Drugs," Robert Reinhold, *New York Times*, June 1981.

47 *accident waiting to happen*: Naval Safety Center, http://www.public.navy .mil/NAVSAFECEN/Pages/index.aspx.

47 *crewman being sucked headfirst*: https://www.youtube.com/watch?v =v2v1Pgpzp88.

47 *2010 a chief electrician's mate aboard the* Reagan *was electrocuted*: "Local Sailor Killed on Carrier IDd," NBC San Diego, December 2010.

47 *machinist's mate*: "Navy Punishes 4 in USS *Reagan* Carrier Death, Generator Mishap," Seth Hettena, *San Diego Union-Tribune*, May 2005.

48 *landing on the USS* Eisenhower: "Navy Human Error to Blame for Incident Injuring 8 Sailors on Carrier Ike," *Navy Times*, July 2016.

48 *$4 billion in damages*: "U.S. Navy Mishap Costs Soar with Recent Incidents," Michael Fabey, *Aerospace Daily & Defense Report*, June 2016.

48 *USS* William P. Lawrence: "Sailors Killed in Red Sea Helicopter Crash Identified," Lea Sutton and Christina London, NBC San Diego, September 2013.

48 *USS* Frank Cable: "Report Calls for Review of USS *Frank Cable* officers' Actions," Allison Batdorff, *Stars & Stripes*, May 2007; "USS Frank Cable— Officials: Sailor killed by helicopter rotor," Chris Plante, CNN, March 2001.

48 *USS* Carter Hall: "Missing Sailor Prompts Navy Search-and-Rescue Operation Off North Carolina Coast," Sarah Begley, *Time*, April 2016.

49 *USS* Shiloh: http://www.public.navy.mil/surfor/cg67/Pages/Missing CrewmemberIdentified.aspx#.WPFWD6KIvIU.

49   *amphibious assault ship*: "After the War: The Homecoming; A Return to
     North Carolina, Marred by Loss of 2 Sailors," Robert D. McFadden, *New
     York Times*, May 2003.

49   *small boys*: private interviews.

49   *USS* Guardian: U.S. Pacific Fleet, www.cpf.navy.mil/.

49   *the cruiser* Port Royal: "Navy Wraps Up $40 Million in Repairs to *Port
     Royal*," William Cole, *Honolulu Advertiser*, September 2009.

50   *USS* San Francisco *in 2005*: http://www.navy.mil/submit/display.asp?story
     _id=18257.

50   *USS* Montpelier: "'Sub, dead ahead!' How a Warfare Exercise Committed
     the Navy's Cardinal Sin," Corinne Reilly, *Virginian-Pilot*, June 2014, navy.mil.

50   *USS* Hartford: "S.D.-Based Navy Ship, Sub Collide in Strait of Hormuz,"
     Steve Liewer, *San Diego Union-Tribune*, March 2009, navy.mil.

50   *USS* Greeneville: "U.S. Sub and Japanese Boat Collide," Thomas E.
     Ricks and Paul Arnett, *Washington Post*, February 2001; U.S. Navy Court
     of Inquiry, Pacific Fleet; "Navy Sub, Transport Ship Collide in Oman,"
     Andrea Stone, *USA Today*, January 2002.

50   *what do all those navy ships actually do*: Navy News Desk, navy.mil.

53   *Typhoon Haiyan*: UNICEF USA, https://www.unicefusa.org/mission
     /emergencies/hurricanes/2013-philippines-typhoon-haiyan, Navy News
     Desk; private interviews.

53   *one command master chief*: private interview.

CHAPTER 3—LIEUTENANT WU'S NEW NAVY

55   *Lieutenant Wu Chao Huang*: private interviews; personal embarkation;
     "Chinese Checkers in the Pacific," Michael Fabey, *Aviation Week*, Au-
     gust 2014; "Inside China's First Rimpac Naval Exercise," Michael Fabey,
     Aviation Week, July 2014; "Aboard a Chinese Destroyer," Jeanette Steele,
     San Diego Union-Tribune, July 2014.

57   *Luyang II–class*: *Congressional Research Service*; *Defense Department
     Annual Report to Congress, Military and Security Developments, People's
     Republic of China*, DOD; *People's Liberation Army Navy: Combat Systems
     Technology: 1949–2010, James C. Bussert and Bruce A. Elleman, (Naval
     Institute Press, 2011)*.

57   *No longer*: *The PLA Navy: New Capabilities and Missions for the 21st Century*,
     Office of Naval Intelligence.

58 *Like most young*: private interviews; personal embarkation; "Chinese Checkers in the Pacific," Fabey; "Inside China's First Rimpac Naval Exercise," Fabey; "Aboard a Chinese Destroyer," Steele.

59 *the "Little Emperors"*: *China Underground*, Zachary Mexico (Soft Skull Press, 2009).

60 *invoked in public speeches*: *The Governance of China*, Xi Jinping (Foreign Languages Press, 2014).

60 *the new Chinese navy*: CRS; *The PLA Navy: New Capabilities and Missions for the 21st Century*, Office of Naval Intelligence; private interviews.

61 *attitude that informs*: private interviews; personal embarkation.

62 *For centuries . . . during the RimPac*: ibid.

63 *"Chinese laundrymen"*: "The Legacy of the Korean War: Cold War Thinking Framed by Conflict," Merrill Goozner, *Chicago Tribune*, July 1993.

64 *Taicang in Jiangsu Province*: "The Fantastic Voyage," Raymond Zhou, *China Daily*, October 2008.

64 *Zheng He was a member*: *When China Ruled the Seas: The Treasure Fleet of the Dragon Throne, 1405–1433*, Louise Levathes (Simon & Schuster, 1994); Hong Kong Maritime Museum.

66 *dramatic miniseries*: *Zheng He Xia Xiyang*, CCTV-8, 2009.

66 *"During the overall course"*: *When China Ruled the Seas*, Levathes; Hong Kong Maritime Museum.

66 *a single piece of land*: *Harmony and War: Confucian Culture and Chinese Power Politics*, Yuan-kang Wang (Columbia University Press, 2010).

67 *periodic battles*: *Pirates of the South China Coast: 1790–1810*, Dian H. Murray (Stanford University Press, 1987).

67 *The Opium Wars*: *On China*, Kissinger.

68 *China's sailors*: private interviews; *The PLA Navy: New Capabilities and Missions for the 21st Century*, Office of Naval Intelligence.

68 *the People's Liberation Army Navy*: ibid; *Naval War College Review* 68 (Summer 2015).

70 *Taiwan Strait Crisis*: private interviews; *On China*, Kissinger; *Mayday*, Cropsey.

70 *William Perry*: "Christopher to Meet his Chinese Counterpart," Steven Erlanger, *New York Times*, March 1996.

71 *Liu Huaqing*: *Naval War College Review* 68 (Summer 2015).

72 *Zhao Xiaogang*: private interview; "PLAN Commander Is a RimPac First," Michael Fabey, *Aviation Week*, September 2014.

73 *The Chinese navy now . . . Annual Chinese military spending*: private inter-
views; *The PLA Navy: New Capabilities and Missions for the 21st Century*,
Office of Naval Intelligence; *China Naval Modernization: Implications for
U.S. Navy Capabilities—Background and Issues for Congress*, Congressional
Research Service (CRS), June 2016; *Defense Department Annual Report
to Congress, Military and Security Developments, People's Republic of China*,
DOD; World Bank.

74 *China's merchant fleet*: "China's Merchant Marine," a paper for the China
as "Maritime Power" Conference, Dennis J. Blasko, CNA Conference,
July 2015; "China-Owned Ships: Fleet Expansion Accelerates," *Hellenic
Shipping News*, March 2016; *China's Quest for Great Power: Ships, Oil, and
Foreign Policy*, Bernard D. Cole (Naval Institute Press, November 2016).

74 *two-ship Chinese task force*: private interviews; *The PLA Navy: New Capabilities and Missions for the 21st Century*, Office of Naval Intelligence; *China
Naval Modernization: Implications for U.S. Navy Capabilities—Background
and Issues for Congress*, CRS; *Defense Department Annual Report to Congress,
Military and Security Developments, People's Republic of China*, DOD.

75 *"Chinese participation"*: private interview; "PLAN Commander Is a RimPac
First," Fabey.

76 *"barbarian handlers"*: private interviews.

CHAPTER 4—ACTS OF (WARM) WAR

77 *April Fool's Day 2001: Born to Fly*, Osborn; CRS; private interviews.

84 *Tom Cruise flies his inverted F-14A*: private interviews; moviemistakes.com.

87 *Hainan Island hangs*: personal visit; *Pirates of the South China Coast*, Murray;
Mayday, Cropsey.

88 *F-104 that had strayed*: *Journey into Darkness: The Gripping Story of an
American POW's Seven Years Trapped Inside Red China During the Vietnam
War*, Philip E. Smith (Pocket, 1992).

88 *KA-3B Skywarrior*: pownetwork.org.

88 *Osborn wrestles: Born to Fly*, Osborn; *China–U.S. Aircraft Collision Incident
of April 2001: Assessments and Policy Implications*, CRS.

90 *Zhao Yu*: "2nd Pilot Blames U.S. Crew For Mishap," CBS News, April 2001.

91 *Wang's widow*: "Chinese Pilot's Wife Sends Bush Emotional Letter,"
Wang Wei, CNN, April 2001, http://www.cnn.com/2001/WORLD/
asiapcf/east/04/06/letter.to.bush/.

91 *Whidbey Island*: "US Spy Plane Crew Comes Home to A Hero's Welcome," Agence France-Presse, April 2001.

92 *crisis comes*: private interviews; *China–U.S. Aircraft Collision Incident of April 2001: Assessments and Policy Implications*, CRS.

93 *Osborn and his crew*: *Born to Fly*, Osborn.

93 *"Guardian of Territorial Airspace and Waters"*: "Missing Pilot Awarded Title of 'Guardian of Territorial Airspace and Waters,'" http://www.china.org .cn/english/2001/Apr/11188.htm.

93 *crippled EP-3E*: private interviews; *China–U.S. Aircraft Collision Incident of April 2001: Assessments and Policy Implications*, CRS.

95 *Hainan Island today*: personal visit; private interviews; chinatravelguide.com.

95 *Yulin*: personal visit; private interviews; *Mayday*, Cropsey; *The PLA Navy: New Capabilities and Missions for the 21st Century*, Office of Naval Intelligence; *China Naval Modernization: Implications for U.S. Navy Capabilities—Background and Issues for Congress*, CRS.

98 *USNS* Impeccable: private interviews; CRS; *Fire on the Water*, Haddick; www.msc.navy.mil/inventory/ships.asp?ship=106; https://www.youtube .com/watch?v=hQvQjwAE4w4; "Close Encounters at Sea: The USNS *Impeccable* Incident," Captain Raul Pedrozo, *Naval War College Review* 62 (Summer 2009).

100 *cannon shot*: *South China Sea*, Hayton.

100 *U.S. started it in 1945*: *History of the Maritime Zones Under International Law*, National Oceanic and Atmospheric Administration.

101 *China takes the position*: private interviews; CRS; *South China Sea*, Hayton.

102 *Impeccable's crew*: private interviews; *China–U.S. Aircraft Collision Incident of April 2001: Assessments and Policy Implications*, CRS.

102 *commercial fishing fleet*: "China's Merchant Marine," Blasko; "China-Owned Ships: Fleet Expansion Accelerates"; *China's Quest for Great Power*, Cole; https://www.youtube.com/watch?v=hQvQjwAE4w4; "The Time the U.S. Nearly Nuked North Korea Over a Highjacked Spy Ship," Colin Schultz, Smithsonian.com, January 2014, http://www.smithsonianmag.com/smart-news /time-us-nearly-nuked-north-korea-over-highjacked-spy-ship-180949514/

105 *the USNS* Bowditch: "Close Encounters at Sea," Pedrozo; "2001-2009 - South China Sea Developments," GlobalSecurity.org, http://www.globalsecurity .org/military/world/war/south-china-sea-2009.htm.

105 Kitty Hawk: private interviews; "A Chinese Submarine Stalked an American Aircraft Carrier," Kyle Mizokami, *Popular Mechanics*, November 2015.

105 *Chinese antisatellite*: private interviews; *The PLA Navy: New Capabilities and Missions for the 21st Century*, Office of Naval Intelligence; *China's Anti-Satellite Weapon Test*, CRS, April 2007; *Defense Department Annual Report to Congress, Military and Security Developments, People's Republic of China*, DOD.

106 *USS* Lake Erie: private interviews; "Navy Succeeds in Intercepting Non-Functioning Satellite," navy.mil; https://www.youtube.com/watch?v=pDqNjnUNUl8.

106 *USNS* Victorious: private interviews; CRS; "Chinese Vessels Approach Sealift Command Ship in Yellow Sea," www.navy.mil/Submit/display.asp?story_id=45048; "Chinese Boats Harassed U.S. Ship, Officials Say," Barbara Starr, CNN, May 2009.

107 *USS* John S. McCain: private interviews; "China Sub Collides with Array Towed by U.S. Ship," Richard Cowan, Reuters, June 2009; "Sub Collides with Sonar Array Towed by U.S. Navy Ship," Barbara Starr, CNN, June 2009.

107 *"broke international law and Chinese laws and regulations"*: "China hits out at US on Navy Row," BBC, March 2009.

108 *USS* Chung-Hoon: "Navy Sends Destroyer to Protect Surveillance Ship After Incident in South China Sea," Ann Scott Tyson, *Washington Post*, March 2009.

108 *At the highest echelons*: private interviews.

CHAPTER 5—PANDA HUGGERS

109 *an air of tense anticipation*: private interviews.

110 *Admiral Jonathan Greenert*: U.S. Navy Biographies; private interviews.

114 *Admiral Samuel Locklear*: "Admiral Locklear: Climate Change the Biggest Long-Term Security Threat in the Pacific Region," Center for Climate and Security, March 2009, https://climateandsecurity.org/2013/03/12/admiral-locklear-climate-change-the-biggest-long-term-security-threat-in-the-pacific-region/.

114 *"little too roughly"*: "Chief of US Pacific Forces Calls Climate Biggest Worry," Bryan Bender, *Boston Globe*, March 2013.

114 *one navy admiral*: private interviews.

114 *pure Bull Halsey stuff*: "Dear Admiral Halsey," John Wukovits, *Naval History Magazine*, April 2016, US Naval Institute.

115 *training exercises*: private interviews.

116 *To accomplish*: private interviews.

116 *a thousand ships*: www.navy.mil/navydata/our_ships.asp.

117 *Japan has more to answer*: *The Rape of Nanking: The Forgotten Holocaust of World War II*, Iris Chang (Basic Books, 1997); *Intimate Rivals: Japanese Domestic Politics and a Rising China*, Sheila A. Smith (Columbia University Press, 2015).

118 *one recent poll:* "Hostile Neighbors: China vs. Japan," Bruce Stokes, pewglobal.org, September 2016.

118 *the Obama administration*: private interviews.

119 *"the importance of raising the level"*: "Navy Sends Destroyer to Protect Surveillance Ship After Incident in South China Sea," Tyson.

119 *Navy ships to China*: Navy News Desk, navy.mil; "Remarks at the Center for Strategic and International Studies," Admiral Jonathan Greenert, May 2014, http://www.navy.mil/navydata/people/cno/Greenert/Speech/140519%20CSIS.pdf.

119 *U.S.-China mil-to-mil contacts*: *Issues for Congress*, CRS, October 2014.

119 *Soviet general staff*: "The Washington Summit: For First Time, a High Soviet Officer Gets Inside Pentagon," John M. Broder, *Los Angeles Times*, December 1987; "Ranking Soviet to Visit Pentagon Inner Sanctum," December 1987, UPI Archives, http://www.upi.com/Archives/1987/12/08/Ranking-Soviet-to-visit-Pentagon-inner-sanctum/6483565938000/.

119 *U.S. military officers were ordered*: private interviews.

120 *Here's Greenert*: "U.S.-China Relationship Part of Greenert's Legacy," Michael Fabey, *Aerospace Daily & Defense Report*, September 2015.

120 *host of incidents*: *Intimate Rivals*, Smith; *South China Sea*, Hayton; *U.S.-China Military Contacts: Issues for Congress*, Congressional Research Service, March 2012; private interviews.

121 *Yellow Sea*: "South Korea Cracks Down on Illegal Chinese Fishing, with Violent Results," Lyle J. Morris, *Diplomat*, November 2012; *U.S.-China Military Contacts: Issues for Congress*, CRS; private interviews.

121 *2011 a Chinese navy frigate*: "The China-Philippines Dispute in the East Sea," Vietnamnet Bridge, http://english.vietnamnet.vn/fms/special-reports/106862/the-china-philippines-dispute-in-the-east-sea.html.

121 *cut the sonar cables*: "Chinese Patrol Boats Confront Vietnamese Oil Exploration Ship in South China Sea," Joseph Santolan, World Socialist Web Site, www.wsws.org.

121 *Scarborough Shoal*: *South China Sea*, Hayton.

121 *East China Sea*: *Intimate Rivals*, Smith; CRS; private interviews.

121 *chummy with the Chinese navy*: private interviews.

121 *September morning in 2013*: private interviews.

122 *Zhang Zheng*: private interviews; "Focus on Zhang Zheng, Captain of Liaoning," Sina English, http://bbs.english.sina.com/archiver/?tid-105448 .html; "Chinese Aircraft Carrier *Liaoning* Takes Up Role in South China Sea," Chan.

122 *Captain Dai Ming Meng*: private interviews; "China Trains More Carrier-Borne Fighter Pilots," Xinhua; "Operational Aircraft Carrier a Few Years Away: Admiral," *South China Morning Post*.

122 *Admiral Wu Shengli*: private interviews; "The Next Generation of China's Navy," *Diplomat*; *Biographies of Key Chinese Military Officers*, CNA China Studies, April 2013; "China's Military Modernization: The Legacy of Admiral Wu Shengli," Jeffrey Becker, Jamestown Foundation, *China Brief*, August 2015.

125 *USS* Harry S. Truman: http://ipv6.navy.mil/view_image.asp?id=44898.

125 *pilots have been killed*: "Fatal Crash of Chinese J-15 Carrier Jet Puts Question Mark over Troubled Programme," Choi Chi-yuk, *South China Morning Post*, July 2016.

126 *Speaking through an interpreter*: private interviews.

126 *heart-racing experience*: personal embarkations and associated interviews.

126 *F/A-18E Super Hornet*: Navy Fact File.

128 *senior and master chiefs*: private interviews; embarkations and personal observations.

130 *Chinese navy doesn't have anything*: private interviews; *The PLA Navy: New Capabilities and Missions for the 21st Century*, Office of Naval Intelligence.

130 *USS* Jefferson City: ipv6.navy.mil/view_image_list.asp?id=153&page=148.

131 *USS* Fort Worth: private interviews; "Chinese Navy Leader to Visit San Diego," navy.mil, September 2013.

131 *navy's littoral combat ships*: Navy Fact File; private interviews.

132 *some top navy leaders*: private interviews.

132 *dumbest things*: private interviews.

132 *All of the Independence-class LCSs*: "USN Seeks to Improve Crew Training, Readiness to Support LCS Overseas Maintenance," Michael Fabey, *IHS Jane's Navy International*, November 2016.

132 *twenty-five-foot-high*: "Need for Speed Still Drives LCS," Michael Fabey, Aviation Week Intelligence Network, December 2012.

133 *plagued with cost overruns*: "What Price Freedom? LCS-1 Leaves Dry Dock Amid Questions About Worthiness," Fabey, Aviation Week Intelligence Network; "What Price Freedom? Cost Concerns Continue to Bedevil LCS," Michael Fabey, Aviation Week Intelligence Network, May 2012.

133 *middle of the ocean*: private interviews; "USS *Freedom* Reports Seawater Cooling System Faults," Michael Fabey, Aviation Week Intelligence Network, April 2013.

133 Freedom *was a big hit*: direct observation; ship tours; private interviews; "USS Freedom Takes Spotlight at IMDEX," Michael Fabey, Aviation Week Intelligence Network, May 2013; "What Price Freedom?," Fabey.

133 *LCSs aren't multipurpose ships*: ship tours; private interviews; *Littoral Combat Ship Concept of Operations*, U.S. Navy.

134 *Admiral Wu notices*: private interviews.

134 USS Fort Worth *isn't a powerful ship*: Navy Fact File; *The Naval Institute Guide to the Ships and Aircraft of the U.S. Fleet*, internal navy strategy documents.

135 *Jiangdao-class*: CRS; *The PLA Navy: New Capabilities and Missions for the 21st Century*, Office of Naval Intelligence.

135 *Washington, D.C.*: Navy News Desk.

136 *Over the coming few years*: private interviews; Navy News Desk.

136 *different operational concept*: private interviews.

CHAPTER 6—CRASHBACK

139 *Gombert issues another order*: *Cowpens* deck log; private interviews.

139 *emissions control*: "Enterprise's EW Module Stays Below the Radar," navy .mil, January 2004; Navy News Desk.

140 *Built in the Ukraine*: *China Naval Modernization: Implications for U.S. Navy Capabilities—Background and Issues for Congress*, Congressional Research Service (CRS), June 2016; "How Does China's First Aircraft Carrier Stack Up?," *ChinaPower*, Center for Strategic and International Studies (CSIS), April 2016; "Exposed: How China Purchased Its First Aircraft Carrier," Zachary Keck, *National Interest*, January 2015.

141 *its hangar*: "Chinese Aircraft Carrier *Liaoning* Takes Up Role in South China Sea," Chan.

141 *From the* Cowpens's *bridge*: private interviews.

141 *The amphibs*: *China Naval Modernization*, CRS; *The Naval Institute Guide to the Combat Fleets of the World*, Wertheim.

141 *If the* Cowpens: private interviews.

142 *The Chinese escort ships'*: private interviews; *China Naval Modernization*, CRS; *The Naval Institute Guide to the Combat Fleets of the World*, Wertheim.

145 *Gombert's orders*: private interviews.

150 *the young navy surface warfare officer*: private interview.

151 *"while lawfully operating"*: U.S. Pacific Fleet statement, December 2013; "U.S., Chinese Warships Narrowly Avoid Collision in South China Sea," David Alexander and Pete Sweeney, Reuters, December 2013; "China Confirms Near Miss with U.S. Ship in South China Sea," Sui-Lee Wee, Reuters, December 2013.

153 *"claim innocence"*: "US 'Plays Innocent' After Near Collision at Sea," Qiu and Yang.

153 *"we will block you"*: Liz Carter, *Foreign Policy*, December 2013.

153 *Not long after*: private interviews; *Agreement Between the Government of the United States of America and the Government of the Union of Soviet Socialist Republics on the Prevention of Incidents On and Over the High Seas*, U.S. Department of State, 1972, https://www.state.gov/t/isn/4791.htm.

155 *Unplanned Encounters*: private interviews; "Pacific Navies Agree on Code of Conduct for Unplanned Encounters; Agreement Comes After Rise in Territorial Tensions," Jeremy Page, *Wall Street Journal*, April 2014; "Navy Leaders Agree to CUES at 14th WPNS," April 2014; Navy News Desk.

155 *precise signals*: private interviews.

157 *As for Admiral Wu*: private interviews; "Pact to Reduce Sea Conflicts," Zhao Shengnan, *China Daily*, April 2014.

157 *"something strange"*: *Command Investigation into Ship's Readiness and Leadership ICO USS* Cowpens *(CG-63)*, Commander, U.S. Naval Surface Force, July 2014.

162 "Cowpens' *Bizarre Cruise*": "CO Seldom Left In-Port Cabin During Second Half of Ship's Deployment, Report Found," *Military Times*, August 2014.

163 *To this day*: private interviews.

CHAPTER 7—DRAGON SLAYER

165 *oh-dark-thirty*: private interviews; personal initiation flight; "Pacific Fleet Commander Gets Close Look at P-8 Advanced Capabilities," Navy News Desk, January 2014; U.S. Navy Biographies; Navy Fact File.

167 *first Asian-American*: private interviews; U.S. Navy Biographies.

170 *"act of asymmetrical warfare"*: *Death in Camp Delta*, Seton Hall University School of Law Center for Policy and Research, December 2009.

171 *"air defense identification zone"*: *Intimate Rivals*, Smith; *China's ADIZ over the East China Sea: A "Great Wall in the Sky"?*, Jun Osawa, Brookings Institute, December 2013.

171 *U.S. promptly*: "China Enforcing Quasi-ADIZ in South China Sea: Philippine Justice," Prashanth Parameswaran, *Diplomat*, October 2015.

171 *the Obama administration*: private interviews.

172 *"alarmist warnings"*: "Air Defense ID Zone to Deter Those with Designs on China's Territory," Zhang He, *People's Daily*, November 2013.

172 *since 1950*: "What's an ADIZ?," David A. Welch, *Foreign Affairs*, December 2013.

172 *Harris's heart*: private interviews.

172 *old Orions*: U.S. Navy Budget Submissions; Navy Fact File.

172 *as he settles*: private interviews; Navy Fact File.

173 *Chengdu J-10s*: *China Naval Modernization*, CRS; *The PLA Navy: New Capabilities and Missions for the 21st Century*, Office of Naval Intelligence.

174 *take up position*: private interviews.

175 *carrier USS* Ronald Reagan: direct observation; personal embarkation; private interviews.

176 *Rim of the Pacific*: "U.S. Navy Says China Spy Ship Proves International Waters Recognition," Michael Fabey, Aviation Week Intelligence Network, July 2014; "Inside China's First Rimpac Naval Exercise," Fabey; Navy News Desk.

178 *J. Randy Forbes*: *U.S.-China Military Contacts: Issues for Congress*, CRS.

179 *During many trips*: private interviews.

179 *Dana Rohrabacher*: "Spying Concerns, Regional Belligerence Cloud Chinese Role in Pacific Naval Exercises," Bill Gertz, *Washington Free Beacon*, June 2014.

179 *U.S. law prohibits*: "China to Attend Major U.S.-Hosted Naval Exercises, but Role Limited," Phil Stewart, Reuters, March 2013.

180 *China also withdrew*: private interviews; "Chinese RIMPAC Delegation Snubs Japanese Sailors," Sam LaGrone, *US Naval Institute News*, July 2016.

180 *the four Chinese ships*: private interviews; direct observation; "In Pacific Drills, Navies Adjust to New Arrival: China; Political Challenges Arise with China's Participation in U.S.-led Rimpac Exercises," Jeremy Page, *Wall Street Journal*, July 2014; "Inside China's First Rimpac Naval Exercise," Fabey; "Aboard a Chinese Destroyer," Steele.

180 *Chinese navy spy*: direct observation; personal embarkation; private interviews.

181 *"chosen to disrespect"*: "US Official Chides China over Spy Ship," William Lowther, *Taipei Times*, August 2014.

181 *defund any future*: *Terrorism: Commentary on Security Documents Volume 136. Assessing the Reorientation of U.S. National Security Strategy Toward the Asia-Pacific*, Douglas Lovelace, Jr., ed. (Oxford University Press, 2014).

182 *senior U.S. Navy commanders*: private interviews.

182 *"outside the territorial seas"*: "China Defends RIMPAC Spy Ship," Sam LaGrone, *US Naval Institute News*, July 2014.

183 *"acceptance by the Chinese"*: "PACOM Chief: U.S. Not Worried About Chinese Intel Ship at RIMPAC," *Navy Times*, July 2014.

184 *Back in Washington*: private interviews.

184 *about 135 miles east of Hainan*: "China Continues International Harassment of U.S. Forces," Michael Fabey, Aviation Week Intelligence Network, August 2014; "Pentagon Undeterred by Chinese Interception of P-8," Michael Fabey, Aviation Week Intelligence Network, August 2014; private interviews.

186 *unpublicized close encounters*: private interviews.

186 *"knife at the throat"*: "Chinese Interceptions of U.S. Military Planes Could Intensify Due to Submarine Base," Greg Torode and Megha Rajagopalan, Reuters, August 2014.

186 *"Our pilot's operation"*: "Chinese MOD Calls for a Stop of U.S. 'Close-In' Surveillance Flights," Sam LaGrone, *US Naval Institute Press News*, August 2014.

187 *Greenert and Admiral Wu*: private interviews.

188 *USS Blue Ridge*: "China, US Navies Planning Joint Exercise," Erik Slavin, *Stars and Stripes*, August 2014.

188 *"Behavior for the Safety"*: U.S.-China Air Encounters Annex Sept. 2015, Department of Defense.

188 *antipiracy exercise*: "US, China Conduct Anti-Piracy Exercise," navy.mil, December 2014.

CHAPTER 8—MISSILE MEN

189 *desperately needs*: private interviews.

190 *ten or twenty years ago*: "NavWeek: LCS Got Game," Michael Fabey, Aviation Week *Ares* blog, March 2014; private interviews.

191 *basic choreography*: Research & Gaming, U.S. Naval War College, https://www.usnwc.edu/Research---Gaming.aspx; private interviews.

191 *in a position*: U.S. Navy Biographies; private interviews.

192 *"Defense is absolutely vital"*: "Navy Admiral Seeks to Add Power to Force," Michael Fabey, *Aerospace Daily & Defense Report*, December 2015.

192 *since World War II*: private interviews.

192 *Soviets had developed*: *Mayday*, Cropsey; private interviews.

193 *navy's primary mission*: private interviews.

193 *1970s-era Harpoon*: "Admiral Highlights Missile, Sub Needs in Asia-Pacific," Michael Fabey, *Aerospace Daily & Defense Report*, March 2016; private interviews.

193 *land-based military*: *Fire on the Water*, Haddick; *Winning the Salvo Competition: Rebalancing America's Air and Missile Defenses*, Center for Strategic and Budgetary Assessment (CSBA), May 2016; private interviews.

193 *a key figure*: *Thread of the Silkworm*, Iris Chang (Basic Books, 1995); private interviews.

194 *Chinese arsenal*: *Fire on the Water*, Haddick; *Winning the Salvo Competition*, CSBA; private interviews; *China Naval Modernization: Implications for U.S. Navy Capabilities—Background and Issues for Congress*, CRS; *The PLA Navy: New Capabilities and Missions for the 21st Century*, Office of Naval Intelligence.

195 *"The East is Red"*: *Thread of the Silkworm*, Chang.

195 *a ballistic missile*: private interviews.

196 *finned warhead*: *Fire on the Water*, Haddick; *Winning the Salvo Competition*, CSBA; private interviews; CRS; *The PLA Navy: New Capabilities and Missions for the 21st Century*, Office of Naval Intelligence.

196 *gamechanger weapon*: "CNO: U.S. Asia-Pacific Operations Unaffected by Chinese Anti-Ship Ballistic Missiles," Michael Fabey, Aviation Week Intelligence Network, May 2013.

197 *widespread belief*: private interviews.

197 *"anti-access/area denial"*: "NavWeek: Keeping Asian Waters Pacific," Michael Fabey, Aviation Week *Ares* blog, March 2013; "NavWeek: Singapore Fling," Michael Fabey, Aviation Week *Ares* blog, May 2013; *China Naval Modernization: Implications for U.S. Navy Capabilities—Background and Issues for Congress*, CRS; private interviews; *Fire on the Water*, Haddick; *Winning the Salvo Competition*, CSBA.

198 *"Air-Sea Battle"*: "Asia-Pacific Defense Partners Discuss Air-Sea Battle Concept," Michael Fabey, Aviation Week Intelligence Network, May 2013; private interviews.

199 *the navy's attitude*: "Asia-Pacific Defense Partners Discuss Air-Sea Battle Concept," Fabey; "CNO: U.S. Asia-Pacific Operations Unaffected by Chinese Anti-Ship Ballistic Missiles," Fabey; private interviews.

199 *use 3-D printers*: private interviews.

199 *serve as a decoy*: Navy Fact File; private interview.

200 *a Chinese bluff*: private interviews.

200 *a highly sophisticated*: private interviews; "CNO: U.S. Asia-Pacific Operations Unaffected by Chinese Anti-Ship Ballistic Missiles," Fabey.

200 *proudly shown off*: "Pentagon Unconcerned by DF-21 Parade Appearance," Michael Fabey, *Aerospace Daily & Defense Report*, September 2015; "Showtime: China Reveals Two 'Carrier-Killer' Missiles," Andrew S. Erickson, *National Interest*, September 2015.

201 *navy routinely sends*: Navy News Desk; private interviews; Pacific Fleet Command, Pacific Command.

201 *"into harm's way"*: private interview.

202 *so desperately needs*: "NavWeek: LCS Got Game," Fabey, Aviation Week *Ares* blog; private interviews.

202 *"distributed lethality"*: "'Distributed Lethality' Good Fit for Asia-Pacific, Navy Commander Says," Michael Fabey, *Aerospace Daily & Defense Report*, January 2015; *Surface Force Strategy: Return to Sea Control*, Commander, Naval Surface Forces, January 2017.

203 *"You want destroyers"*: private interviews.

205 *"offense wins"*: "Navy Admiral Seeks to Add Power to Force," Fabey, *Aerospace Daily & Defense Report*; private interviews.

205 *Harris agrees*: Admiral Harry Harris, speaking at Center for Strategic and International Studies (CSIS), January 2016.

206 *of Norway*: "Norwegian Ship Proves Tropical Use of Strike Missile," Michael Fabey, *Aerospace Daily & Defense Report*, July 2014.

206 *Naval Strike Missile*: Kongsberg company site, https://www.kongsberg.com/en/kds/products/missilesystems/navalstrikemissile; Raytheon, private interviews.

207 *USS* Ogden: https://www.youtube.com/watch?v=AaSPvWiqgeM; U.S. Pacific Fleet release, July 2014.

207 *Rowden and others*: private interviews.

208 *Long Range Anti-Ship Missile (LRASM)*: "Lockheed Hones LRASM Surface Launch," Michael Fabey, *Aerospace Daily & Defense Report*, July 2016; "Lockheed Touts LRASM Missile for LCS/Frigate," Graham Warwick and Michael Fabey, Aviation Week Network, January 2016.

208 *submarine-launched Tomahawk*: Navy Fact File; Boeing company material, private interviews.

209 *"Nasty" Manazir*: private interview; personal observation.

209 USS Enterprise: *Carrier*, Clancy and Gresham; personal embarkations.

210 *F-14 Tomcats*: personal interview; U.S. Navy Biographies.

210 *"centerpiece of naval aviation"*: "NavWeek: *Ford* Tour," Michael Fabey, Aviation Week *Ares* blog, April 2014.

210 *son of a marine*: personal interview; U.S. Navy Biographies.

210 *flying a Tomcat*: private interview.

211 *aboard the* Ford: personal interview; direct observation.

211 *$13.2 billion*: personal interviews; "Ford Carrier Delayed Again Due to 'First-of-Class Issues,'" Megan Eckstein, *US Naval Institute News*, July 2016.

211 *Manazir insists*: personal interviews.

212 Ford *looks different*: direct observation; personal interviews; Navy Fact File.

213 *the F-35*: Navy Fact File; personal interviews; direct observation; Lockheed Martin company information.

214 *MQ-25 Stingray*: Navy Fact File; personal interviews; navy budget documents; "Unmanned Carrier Aircraft Good Idea, Analysts Say," Michael Fabey, *Aerospace Daily & Defense Report*, February 2016.

215 *seemed like fantasy*: "CSBA: Shorter-Range Missile Defense Equals Bigger Savings," Michael Fabey, *Aerospace Daily & Defense Report*, May 2016; *Navy Lasers, Railgun, and Hypervelocity Projectile: Background and Issues for Congress*, CRS, March 2017; private interviews.

215 *navy is thinking bigger*: private interviews; "Industry Seeks Power Boost for Navy Lasers," Michael Fabey, *IHS Jane's Navy International*, January 2017.

216 *railgun is a cannon*: "CSBA: Shorter-Range Missile Defense Equals Bigger Savings," Fabey, *Navy Lasers, Railgun, and Hypervelocity Projectile: Background and Issues for Congress*, CRS; private interviews.

216 *enormous electrical power*: CRS; private interviews; "Navy to Fire 150 kW Ship Laser Weapon from Destroyers, Carriers," Michael Fabey and Kris Osborn, *Scout Warrior*, January 2017.

216 *joint high speed vessels*: private interviews; "Railgun Remains Priority for U.S. Navy," Michael Fabey, Aviation Week Intelligence Network, April 2014.

217 *Hypervelocity projectiles*: "CSBA: Shorter-Range Missile Defense Equals Bigger Savings," Fabey; *Navy Lasers, Railgun, and Hypervelocity Projectile: Background and Issues for Congress*, CRS; private interviews.

217 *the Zumwalt-class destroyer*: "NavWeek: Ballad of the Traveling Gun," Michael Fabey, Aviation Week *Ares* blog, June 2014; "New Stealthy Navy Destroyer Starts Combat System Activation," Michael Fabey, *Scout Warrior*, January 2017; "USN Considers Alternatives to LRLAP for Zumwalt Gun System," Michael Fabey, *IHS Jane's Navy International*, December 2016; "Navy Updates Radar Software on Stealthy Zumwalt," Michael Fabey, *Defense Systems*, November 2016; "In Transit: Zumwalt Class Tackles Challenges as It Readies for Service," Michael Fabey, *IHS Jane's Navy International*, December 2016.

219 *"Batman had a ship"*: "Zumwalt Stokes Pacific Command Interest," Michael Fabey, *Aerospace Daily & Defense Report*, January 2016.

219 *unmanned underwater*: private interviews; Lockheed Martin company information.

CHAPTER 9—A GREAT WALL OF SAND

221 *Poseidon flies westbound*: "Exclusive: China Warns U.S. Surveillance Plane," Jim Sciutto, CNN, September 2015; private interviews.

222 *The Spratlys*: *South China Sea*, Hayton; *Before and After: The South China Sea Transformed*, Asia Maritime Transparency Initiative, Center for Strategic and International Studies (CSIS), February 2015; *Asia's Cauldron*, Kaplan; private interviews.

224 *Johnson South Reef*: https://www.youtube.com/watch?v=uq3oCY9nWE8; https://www.youtube.com/watch?v=Uy2ZrFphSm; *South China Sea*, Hayton; private interviews.

224 *Mischief Reef*: *Incident at Mischief Reef: Implications for the Philippines, China, and the United States*, Stanley E. Meyer (US Army War College, 1996); *South China Sea*, Hayton; *Before and After: The South China Sea Transformed*, Asia Maritime Transparency Initiative, CSIS; private interviews; *China Occupies Mischief Reef in Latest Spratly Gambit*, Daniel J. Dzurek (Durham University, 2013).

225 *Paracel Islands*: "The 1974 Paracels Sea Battle, A Campaign Appraisal," Toshi Yoshihara, *Naval War College Review* (Spring 2016); *Asia's Cauldron*, Kaplan; private interviews.

225 *Second Thomas Shoal*: *South China Sea*, Hayton; *Before and After*, Asia Maritime Transparency Initiative, CSIS; private interviews.

226 *"exclusive economic zone"*: *South China Sea*, Hayton; *Before and After*, Asia Maritime Transparency Initiative, CSIS; private interviews; CRS; *Asia's Cauldron*, Kaplan; UN Convention on the Law of the Sea, 1982.

226 *"Nine-Dash Line"*: *Before and After*, Asia Maritime Transparency Initiative, CSIS; CRS; private interviews.

227 *Chinese plan all along*: private interviews; "Seeing the Forest Through the SAMs on Woody Island," Center for Strategic and International Studies (CSIS), February 2016; *Countering China's Adventurism in the South China Sea: Strategy Options for the Trump Administration*, CSBA; *South China Sea*, Hayton; "Joint Declaration of ASEAN and China On Cooperation in the Field of Non-traditional Security Issues" (Phnom Penh4, November 2002) http://wcm.fmprc.gov.cn/pub/eng/topics/zgcydyhz/dlczgdm/t26290.htm.

227 *China was rapidly expanding*: private interviews; *The PLA Navy: New Capabilities and Missions for the 21st Century*, Office of Naval Intelligence.

228 *tons of sand*: *Military and Security Developments Involving the People's Republic of China 2016*, DOD Annual Report to Congress; *Countering China's Adventurism in the South China Sea*, CSBA; *Before and After*, Asia Maritime Transparency Initiative, CSIS; private interviews.

228 *Fiery Cross soon bristled*: *Countering China's Adventurism in the South China Sea: Strategy Options for the Trump Administration*, CSBA; *Before and After*, Asia Maritime Transparency Initiative, CSIS; private interviews.

230 *The Chinese foreign minister*: "China's Will to Safeguard Sovereignty 'Unshakable' Foreign Minister," Xinhuanet, May 2015, http://news.xinhuanet.com/english/2015-05/16/c_134244810.htm.

230 *Even President Barack Obama*: "Obama Says Concerned China Uses Size to Bully Others in Region," Emily Stephenson, Reuters, April 2015.

231 *Admiral Harris is giving a speech*: Admiral Harry Harris speech, Australian Strategic Policy Institute, Canberra, March 2015.

232 *Harris's staff get a call*: private interviews.

233 *leaders in Aspen*: Aspen Security Forum Remarks by Adm. Harris, Pacific Command, July 2015.

233 *gets blunter still*: Harris's statement before Senate Armed Services Committee, February 2016.

233 *Harris an archvillain*: "China Slams US Admiral's South China Sea Remarks," *China Daily Europe*, February 2016.

234 *the "Japanese admiral"*: private interviews.

234 *"impossible to ignore"*: "US Admiral Harry Harris Has the Measure of China," David Feith, *Australian*, August 2016.

234 *Harris generally ignores*: private interviews.

234 *The term FONOP*: Department of Defense Freedom of Navigation Program Fact Sheet.

234 *at two Navy F-14 Tomcats*: "U.S. Shoots Down 2 Libya Jets; Kadafi Vows to Seek Revenge: F-14s Fired in Self-Defense, Carlucci Says," John M. Broder, *Los Angeles Times*, January 1989.

235 *Harris wants to send*: private interviews.

235 *"a core tenet"*: Admiral Harry Harris, Defense One Leadership Briefing, November 2016.

235 *ever cautious*: private interviews.

235 *a "routine patrol"*: private interviews; "*Fort Worth* Patrols South China Sea, Practices Cues with PLAN Ships," Michael Fabey, *Aerospace Daily & Defense Report*, May 2015.

235 *is rigged out*: "Possible Smaller LCS Fleet Seen with Bigger Aviation Punch," Michael Fabey, Aviation Week Intelligence Network, January 2014.

235 *just in case*: private interviews.

236 *"name and shame"*: ibid.

236 *Mount Everest*: "China to 'Name and Shame' Tourists Who Leave Graffiti on Mt. Everest," Neil Connor, *Telegraph*, May 2016.

236 *at all unusual*: private interviews.

236 *he knows the Chinese*: ibid.

236 *satellite images*: Before and After, Asia Maritime Transparency Initiative, CSIS.

237 *reach out to CNN*: private interviews.

237 *Poseidon flies near*: "Exclusive: China Warns U.S. Surveillance Plane," CNN.

237 *under their skin*: "U.S. Threatens Peace in South China Sea, Beijing Says," Brad Lendon, CNN, May 2015.

238 *"United States will fly"*: "Carter Warns China U.S. Will Go Wherever Global Law Permits," David J. Lynch, Bloomberg, May 2015.

238 *"tougher stand against China"*: private interviews.

238 *An official state*: ibid.

238 *it takes months*: ibid.

238 USS Lassen: "'Hope to see you again': China Warship to U.S. Destroyer After South China Sea Patrol," Yeganeh Torbati, Reuters, November 2015.

239 *It's an ambiguity*: private interviews.

239 *who is summoned*: private interviews; "U.S.-China Naval Relations Grow More Tense," Michael Fabey, *Aerospace Daily & Defense Report*, October 2015.

240 *Out at PACOM headquarters*: private interviews.

240 USS William P. Lawrence: "U.S. Warship Challenges China's Claims in South China Sea," David Tweed, Bloomberg, May 2016; "China Scrambles Fighters as U.S. Sails Warship Near Chinese-Claimed Reef," Michael Martina, Greg Torode, and Ben Blanchard, Reuters, May 2016; private interviews.

241 *"decade upon decade"*: "U.S. Carrier Strike Group's South China Sea Operations Sending Message," Michael Fabey, *Aerospace Daily & Defense Report*, March 2016; remarks by Secretary Carter in a Media Availability aboard USS *John C. Stennis* in the South China Sea, U.S. Defense Department, Apri 2016, https://www.defense.gov/News/Transcripts/.

242 *in The Hague*: "Tribunal Rules Against China in Territorial Dispute," Michael Fabey, *Aerospace Daily & Defense Report*, July 2016; private interviews.

242 *Shengli tells his counterpart*: "Wu to CNO: Beijing Won't Stop South China Sea Island Building," Sam LaGrone, *USNI News*, July 2016; private interviews.

242 *a packed hall*: direct observation.

243 *That summer and fall*: Navy News Desk; private interviews.

244 *"time to say goodbye, my friend"*: "Philippines President Duterte Says 'Time to Say Goodbye' to America," *Guardian*, October 2016; "Philippines President Duterte Says 'Time to Say Goodbye' to America," Lindsay Murdoch, *Sydney Morning Herald*, October 2016.

CHAPTER 10—COURSE CHANGE

247 *two sets of budgetary books*: private interviews.

249 *Trump and his team*: "What Would Trump's 350-Ship Navy Look Like?," Kyle Mizokami, *Popular Mechanics*, December 2016; "Naval Think Tank

Study Calls for More Submarines, Smaller Carriers," Michael Fabey, *Scout Warrior*, February 2017; private interviews.

249   *it's fair to say*: private interviews.

249   *Philip Bilden*: "President Announces Navy Secretary Nominee," White House release, January 2017; "Trump Names Businessman as Navy Secretary," Tom Vanden Brook, *USA Today*, January 2017; "Philip Bilden Withdraws from Navy Secretary Consideration," David B. Larter, *Navy Times*, February 2017.

250   *In Obama's view*: private interviews.

250   *One China policy*: "Beijing Concerned by Trump Questioning 'One China' Policy on Taiwan," Josh Chin, *Wall Street Journal*, December 2016; *On China*, Kissinger; "China Approves 38 New Trump Trademarks for His Businesses," NBC News, March 2017; private interviews.

251   *USNS* Bowditch: "Statement by Pentagon Press Secretary Peter Cook on Incident in South China Sea," December 2016; "Chinese Seize U.S. Navy Underwater Drone in South China Sea," *DOD News*, December 2016; "Pentagon Demands China Return US Underwater Drone," Barbara Starr and Ryan Browne, CNN, December 2016; "China Said It Would Return a Seized U.S. Naval Drone. Trump Told Them to 'Keep It,'" Missy Ryan and Emily Rauhala, *Washington Post*, December 2016.

251   *Trump's new secretary*: "Did Trump's Team Just Threaten War with China?," Michael H. Fuchs, *Defense One*, January 2017.

251   *The Chinese reaction*: "Chinese State Tabloid Warns Trump, End One China policy and China Will Take Revenge," Brenda Goh and J. R. Wu, Reuters, January 2017; "Beijing Pushes Back on Trump Admin Over Disputed Islands in South China Sea," Richard Engel, Marc Smith, and Eric Baculinao, NBC News, January 2017; private interviews.

251   *through the Taiwan Strait*: "Taiwan Scrambles Jets, Navy as China Aircraft Carrier Enters Taiwan Strait," Wu, Hung, and Martina; private interviews.

252   *Trump is playing*: ibid.

254   *the next time*: private interviews.

Index